D1174415

Bridges of Faith Across the Seas

William J. Harvey III

Published by The Foreign Mission Board
National Baptist Convention, U.S.A., Inc.
701 S. 19th Street, Philadelphia, PA 19146

Library of Congress Cataloging in Publication Data
Harvey, William J., III
Bridges of Faith Across the Seas
Bibliography: p. 356
Includes Index
89-081799
ISBN: 0-9624649-0-2

Printed in the United States of America by Neibauer Press,
Warminster, PA 18974
First Edition

9 8 7 6 5 4 3 2

DEDICATION

"Knowledge must come through action; you can have no test which is not fanciful save by trial." Sophocles, 455-406 B.C.

This book is dedicated to the hundreds of missionaries and the thousands of supporting churches and individuals who, over the years, matched their knowledge of the Gospel with their action to spread the "Good News" to those in the lands of our roots. While their sacrifices in the cause of missions are too numerous to count, too private to be self-revealed, their love for God and His people is too deep to go unrecognized. Through this volume may they receive in some part the recognition they deserve and be rewarded by having their stories motivate future generations to follow in their footsteps.

CONTENTS

ILLUSTRATIONS

FOREWORD

Today we, as a people and as a race, are standing on the brink of a whole new future. Before us lies a shining array of possibilities and challenges, of obstacles, yes, but also of unbounded opportunity.

Today we have Black men and women serving in government office, heading corporations, owning businesses, practicing professions hitherto closed to those of our race. Today, more than at any other time in our history, the doors of success are open to all who are brave enough — and prepared enough — to walk through.

What has brought us to this point in time? What has led us to overcome — time and time again — seemingly insurmountable odds? What will prepare us to walk, with steady steps and heads high, through the shining doorway of the future?

Thomas Jefferson, writing during the early years of our great nation, said, "History, by apprising people of the past, will enable them to judge of the future." And Jefferson was not alone in proclaiming the importance of knowing one's history. Centuries ago, Cicero, that famous Roman statesman and orator, declared, "To be ignorant of what happened before you were born is to be ever a child."

These, and hundreds more of the world's greatest leaders — past and present — declare that knowing our history is the key to shaping our future. I, too, would like to humbly add my "amen" to that belief. It is only through understanding our past, by taking to heart the lessons of our failures so that they will not be repeated, and by knowing and building upon our own past successes and the successes of those who have gone before us, that we will get the preparation we need to conquer the future.

We, as a denomination and as a race, must be able to judge the future in light of the past. We must not ignorantly remain "ever a child." We must boldly unroll the scroll of prophecy which is our road map for the coming years.

Our spiritual growth as Black Mission-Oriented Christians, must also be based on this same road map.

Yet where are we to get this historical information we so desperately need? "From whence cometh our help" in studying the lives and work of those who preceded us?

Although recently more books on Black history have begun to appear on library shelves, they still occupy scant space when compared to other texts. While Black history has become part of the curriculum in many schools, Black *religious* history is seldom a part of these courses. More specifically, the history of our great denomination, encompassing over 30,000 churches and 7,000,000 members, has never been completely told.

Motivated by the warning voices of the past and the firm belief that our people *need* and *want* to know our shared history, I give you this book.

Bridges of Faith Across the Seas is a complete historical text on the founding and growth of the Black Baptist movement in general and on Black missionary endeavors in particular. While so many of our churches include the word "Missionary" in their name, this is the first comprehensive text that tells the "Why?" and "How" of our mission history. Although our outreach to the lands of our foreparents began over 108 years ago, this is the first time the saga of our mission journey has been set down in a detailed historical account for all to read.

"Bridges" is a work of love and faith, of agony and ecstasy. Only those who write know the agony and loneliness of sitting, hour after hour, researching, compiling and finally facing those blank pages waiting to be filled with words of truth that others will share. Only those who live with writers know the sound of the typewriter clicking late into the night during times of inspiration, or the silent tears of frustration when the words refuse to flow. Yet at each step,

God was at my elbow — inspiring, directing, encouraging me to "go on," filling me with the belief that we truly have "A Story To Tell To The Nations."

This book is my labor of love — my tribute to the past — my legacy to the future. Yet it is so much more than even this. It is a story written by the blood, sweat and tears of countless thousands who went before us and, until now, have often been hidden in obscurity. It is YOUR story, to read and study, to use as a modern-day revelation of what is yet to be. It is a road map to your children and your children's children, a guide to light their way as they carry on the work when all of us have passed.

In light of the vast materials omitted, this book might well serve the purpose of inspiring others to continue the story in depth, giving more time to the individual contributions made by so many religious leaders and personalities of this organization.

It is my prayer that you will welcome "Bridges" into your hearts and into your homes, churches, schools and libraries. May you use it as it is meant to be used; as a stirring not stuffy history, as an exciting educational tool, as a "light unto your path." May you find in its pages the thread of your own faith. For all who have done so much for missions, may it be a mirror of your sacrifices. For those who have not yet answered the Macedonian call, may it be a summons that cannot be denied, a call to follow in the great tradition set for you.

With prayers and love I give you this legacy — *Bridges of Faith Across the Seas.*

> *William J. Harvey, III*
> *Executive Secretary*
> *Foreign Mission Board*
> *National Baptist Convention, U.S.A., Inc.*
> *December 1988*

ix

"Oh Love that Will Not Let Us Go"

Within the heart of all Black American Christians pulses a love for the people and places of their homelands — Africa, Central America and the Caribbean. Throughout history this love has manifested itself as the action-oriented goal of saving the souls and improving the physical life of those on foreign shores.

While Blacks in this country were still living — and dying — under the yoke of slavery, they were reaching out across the seas with the freeing message of the Gospel. Thus, even before there was a National Baptist Convention, U.S.A., Inc., there was a Black foreign mission movement. The history of this movement and the formation of our denomination are interwoven; indeed they are so inseparable that it is impossible to study one without knowing the other.

Now, for the first time, we have a complete text which traces the Black foreign mission movement and the development of the NBC in exactly the way history has written them — as one epoch journey of faith. And who better to write this saga, to record the itinerary of our journey than perhaps the greatest mission leader of modern times, our own Dr. William J. Harvey, III, executive secretary of our Foreign Mission Board for the past 28 years?

Here, in this thoroughly researched volume, we can study and pass down to our children to study, the mission heritage of our people. Thanks to years of painstaking work by William Harvey, we now have the keys to our past, the doorway to our future.

It is with great pride and deep thankfulness to God and to our predecessors, as well as to those who even now are fighting the good fight to spread the Gospel, that we salute our Foreign Mission Board and especially its leader, Dr. William Harvey. May his most enlightening history recorded here be a continuing saga of National Baptists' dedication to making "disciples of all people, baptizing them in the name of the Father, Son and Holy Spirit."

Dr. T. J. Jemison, President
National Baptist Convention, U.S.A., Inc.

"Study to Show Thyself Approved unto God"

"Study to show thyself approved unto God, a workman that needeth not to be ashamed, rightly dividing the word of truth." *(2 Timothy 2:15)*

How familiar are these words to all of us who have been raised in a Christian atmosphere. Yet how often have we who are charged with the education of others felt the vacuum in which we have been forced to teach. What is it that our students are to study? Where, besides the Bible, are we to find the way to rightly divide the word of truth?

Are we to look to the traditional history books, those limitless tomes relating the achievements of mainly white Christians? To study only these imparts the impression that men and women of our own race have done little or nothing in the way of evangelism. Our more than 100 year history of carrying the Gospel to the homelands of our foreparents is barely mentioned if at all.

Bridges of Faith Across the Seas is the long awaited answer to this dearth of Black missionary history. Here we find the true stories of those who went before. Here we see the long line of sainted men and women who, fearing nothing, not even the loss of their own lives, bravely traversed mountains, seas and political barriers to reach out in Christ's name.

Bridges is a text, but it is also a testimony. It is a well researched teaching tool that presents the facts without ignoring the emotions these facts evoke.

Who can help but swell with pride at the story of Emma Delaney, single-handedly clawing out the ground to form the foundation for today's thriving Suehn Mission? Who can hold back the tears while reading the heart-rending letter from Mrs. Stewart upon the suspicious death of her husband in the bush country? Who even realizes today that while still bound in slavery in this country, our foreparents were sending out missionaries to liberate the spirits of their African brothers and sisters?

Bridges brings us who teach the most complete vehicle for accomplishing our task. *Bridges* brings those who study a true source for learning. *Bridges* brings all — black or white, student or teacher, pastor or lay Christian — a link with the past, a bridge to the future.

Dr. T. Oscar Chappelle, Sr., President
National Baptist Sunday School and B.T.U. Convention

"Learning the Lessons"

Today Black Americans are embroiled in a controversy over what we prefer to be called. The terms "colored" and "Negro" seem anachronistic, relics from a past too many of us have chosen to forget. Among the middle-aged, "Black", while not offensive, leaves this age group divided.

Today a new title is emerging — African American! And it is stirring debate among all ages, all economic groups. Yet, if I may borrow a few words from Shakespeare, "What's in a name?"

The time has come for us, as Negroes, as Blacks, as African Americans, to care more about *who we are* than *what we're called!*

How can we find the pride in ourselves as individuals and in our race as a whole that will make us forget the debate over how we should be addressed? The answer, I believe, lies in rediscovering our roots and valuing our historical achievements.

Bridges of Faith Across the Seas is the most important tool that has come along in generations to lead us to this discovery and knowledge. Through its pages we can all learn the lessons of our ancestors — lessons that will fill us with pride in our shared past — lessons that will challenge us to continue our forward march of progress for the future in the name of Christ.

Dr. E.V. Hill, Pastor
Mount Zion Baptist Church, Los Angeles

INTRODUCTION

The first major organized endeavor of Black Baptists in America was directed toward sending the Gospel to Africa. Even the first convention of Blacks, organized in New York in 1840, was missionary in character. It took the name, "The American Baptist Missionary Convention." In 1880, the parent body of the National Baptist Convention was organized in Montgomery, Alabama. The name chosen was the Baptist Foreign Mission Convention. The stated objective of the Convention was:

> Whereas it becomes necessary and is our duty to extend our Christian influence to advance the kingdom of Christ, and, as African missions claims our most profound attention, and feeling that we are most sacredly called to do work in this field and elsewhere abroad, therefore, we the representatives from the various churches, Sunday schools and societies of the Baptist denomination in the United States, do solemnly organize ourselves in a convention for the above named objects.[1]

The freedmen felt a close relationship to the land of their fathers and immediately after emancipation began to work toward raising the quality of life in the lands from which they came. Their great desire was to make a difference in that land and they felt that it was their responsibility, more than that of any other people,

1

to undertake this task. As the late Dr. L. K. Williams put it, "The work of saving Africa is largely the task of American Negroes. Others have gone there with gunpowder, rum, firearms and propaganda to exploit the Africans, but we must go there carrying the open Bible and the uplifted Christ."[2]

It is very clear that the missionary enterprises in Africa have had remarkable results. Anyone who travels to that continent can see the contrast between those communities where Christian missionaries have set up stations and raised the spiritual, moral and social quality of life of the people, and those areas and people the missionaries have not been able to reach. Clearly the missionaries have made a difference wherever they have been privileged to serve. They have broken the bonds of ignorance and superstition among thousands. They have created a new sense of self respect and a new sense of inner freedom and of salvation from many of the difficulties which enslaved the minds and spirits of the people they served. Indeed they have inculcated in many an understanding of their potential and have stimulated and nurtured the basic human desire for freedom. The rise of the independence movement among the African nations owes much to the enlightenment and inspiration received by African leaders who were influenced by missionaries.

Many of these political leaders had their horizons extended and their determination strengthened by having the opportunity to study in the United States. Here they saw Black people enjoying freedom from colonialism and benefiting from other aspects of a more advanced society than that from which they came. Many who came to this country journeyed here as a result of having been inspired by a missionary sent under the auspices of the Foreign Mission Board of the National Baptist Convention as well as boards representing other groups. It has been well stated that the outstanding West African leaders who were pioneers in the effort to secure national independence were all products of the labors and teachings of missionaries. Included among these were Namdi Azikiwe who was the first premier of Nigeria when it gained independence in 1960; Kwame Nkrumah, the first premier of

Ghana; Sekou Toure, premier of Guinea, and Houpouet-Boigny, leader of the Ivory Coast.

Above all, the Foreign Mission Board of the National Baptist Convention, U.S.A., Inc., has emphasized that its primary mission and contribution has been evangelism — telling the story of the redemptive message of Jesus of Nazareth and the resulting abundant life which accrues to those who accept him as Lord and Master. The social and economic uplift as well as the ministry of healing which the missionaries brought, have played a great part in making Christianity real to the people they served.

To understand the missionary enterprise in general, and particularly the story of the Foreign Mission Board of the National Baptist Convention of the United States of America, Incorporated, it is necessary to take account of the nature of the Christian faith. This is a religion which grew out of the teachings of a historical person, Jesus of Nazareth, a man who walked the roads of ancient Palestine and, while bearing in himself the marks of deity, showed the men and women of his time how to understand the meaning of God in human experience.

The heart of the message of Jesus was that God is to be understood as Father — one always ready to give the gifts of the spirit to those who trust in him. This was a God who required his worshippers to practice justice and love toward their neighbors as well as complete commitment to him. This God also demanded that his people inculcate in their lives the standards of righteousness as set forth in the Sermon on the Mount.

No longer need men and women feel bound by the yoke of sin. The Father God is always ready to forgive those who repent and from that time forward they may walk in newness of life. This God neither slumbers nor sleeps. No matter where his servants may be or what may befall them, they may rest assured that they are always ultimately in his care. Moreover, the Christian faith includes the assurance that this life is not the be-all nor the end-all of existence. "I go to prepare a place for you,"[3] said the Master. This world has only temporary significance for those who love God and walk in his ways. While we must continually work to

3

make it a better place — alleviating human suffering, meeting human need and promoting the rule of God in the hearts of men — in the divine scheme of things there is inevitable justice, if not in this life, certainly in the next. There is no sorrow nor pain, but everlasting joy in the land in which there is no darkness and no night.

All of this is the Gospel, the "Good News," and the people to whom Jesus gave this message experienced a new sense of meaning and significance which they had never felt before. Life was lived on new dimensions. The ultimate authority in their lives was not Caesar in far off Rome, but the Father God in whose presence they could live daily. It was from the God of justice, mercy and love, from whom they came, in whose spirit they lived, and to whom they returned.

One of the attractive features of the new religion was the fact that those who professed it were saved from the bondage of sin and death. This salvation was available to all men, of whatever race, nationality or social status. In Christ there was "neither Jew nor Greek, male nor female, East nor West," but, "one great fellowship of love throughout the whole wide earth." Here was a spiritual democracy that transcended all earthly powers or kingdoms, and out of and within it was established the Church, properly defined as a "fellowship of believers."

The early Christians were prepared not only to *live,* but to *die* for their faith. An astonishing number of people were drawn to it and became converts. They rejoiced in the "Good News." They were inspired by the "fellowship of kindred minds." But most of all for our study, they were not content to be a closed circle of believers. Instead, they had the compulsion to share this liberating faith with others.

From the viewpoint of history, the most important early convert to Christianity was Saul (later Paul) of Tarsus. Annoyed by this band of deviators from the established norms of Judaism, Saul became actively hostile. But one day on the Damascus road, he was forced by the power of God to make a complete turnaround, a radical change of mind and heart. He discovered who

4

Christ really was and what his significance was for human history. In loyalty to his new commitment, and especially in recognition of that impelling command, the Great Commission, "Go ye into all the world and preach the Gospel," Paul devoted the rest of his life to carrying and spreading the Gospel through many parts of the Mediterranean world. He made four missionary journeys, including one to Macedonia, from whence he had heard the insistent call, "Come over into Macedonia and help us."

Paul's missionary journeys were a reflection of the attitude generally engendered among those who come into possession of news that is especially good — too good to keep to oneself. They want to share it. It is this spirit which underlies the missionary enterprise. From the time of the earliest Christian missionaries to the present, these men and women have taken their religion and with it built bridges of faith between their own and other lands, between themselves and other people.

The story of the Foreign Mission Board of the National Baptist Convention of the United States of America, Incorporated, recorded here, shows that Black people in this country, whether slave or free, never totally forgot the land of their fathers. Before Emancipation their opportunities to do much about this were very limited. As we shall see, however, two men, George Lisle and Lott Carey, Black Baptist preachers who came to enjoy freedom long before the Emancipation Proclamation, pioneered as missionaries. Each built bridges of faith across the seas, one in the Caribbean and the other in West Africa. Imbued by the power of the Gospel in their own lives and the desire to share it with those in spiritual need, they set the stage and served as role models for others to emulate.

The ways in which representatives of the foreign mission enterprise and the Foreign Mission Board of the National Baptist Convention of the U.S.A., Inc., labored abroad, constitute the basic theme of the chapters of this volume.

William J. Harvey, III

Notes

1. *Mission Herald,* (September-October 1935) p. 8.
2. NBC *Minutes,* 1924, p. 37.
3. John 14:3.

CHAPTER ONE
BEGINNINGS OF THE BLACK BAPTIST MOVEMENT IN AMERICA

The first Blacks to arrive on American shores, according to one historian, were members of a party led by Panfilio de Navarez whose expedition landed near Tampa, Florida, in 1528. In addition, some Black slaves were with Hernando DeSoto on his expedition to Florida in 1539, and in 1559, some slaves were with Tristan DeLuna who tried to establish a settlement on Pensacola Bay in northwest Florida.[1] No permanent settlement was made by any of these groups.

It is generally believed that the first group which heralded the beginning of the slave trade and the growing number of Blacks in this country was landed at Jamestown, Virginia, in 1619. In the nearly 250 years between that date and the end of the Civil War in 1865, the total number of Blacks in America increased to approximately 4 million.[2]

In the meantime, the men and women who were captured in Africa and survived the infamous "Middle Passage"[3] across the Atlantic to this country, brought with them the religious traditions of the communities from which they came. Each tribe had its own religious heritage and practices; each its own holy places. Finding themselves in a strange land, and deliberately intermingled according to tribal and linguistic backgrounds, it is not surprising that in course of time much of the religious heritage they brought with them was lost. How much of this was retained has been a matter of controversy for some time.[4] In any case, instruction in the Christian religion was given to the slaves fairly early, first by the Catholic missionaries on the eastern seaboard, particularly in Maryland, and later by missionaries under the auspices of the Society for the Propagation of the Gospel in Foreign Parts. This society, organized in 1701 to evangelize primarily Blacks and Indians, was the principal agency whose representatives gave religious instruction to the slaves.[5]

Several denominations became active in the endeavor to make converts of the slaves. Notable among these were the Catholics, the Church of England, the Presbyterians, the Quakers and the Moravians. The work of these groups generally met with success.

One of the principal issues in connection with the religious instruction of slaves was whether, upon being converted, they should be given their freedom. It is understandable that the planters who had so much invested in the slaves would hardly be amenable to setting them free upon their conversion. Perhaps the best example of a denomination manumitting their slaves is that of the Quakers who, because of the humanitarian preaching of men like George Fox and John Woolman, were gradually persuaded to cease the slaveholding practice. Some slaveholders justified the system by maintaining that Blacks were on a level of morality different from that of other human beings, or that they were sub-human and therefore not entitled to the ethical considerations given to ordinary persons. Certain others held that the bringing of Blacks from Africa to civilization in America was a divine blessing to the race as a whole. This opinion was not confined to slaveholders and their sympathizers, however. After the missionaries employed in South Africa by the Foreign Mission Board of the National Baptist Convention, U.S.A., Inc., had brought such enlightenment to his community, the head chief of the Makkaukkua tribe in Basutoland urged one of the missionaries to give the following message to the Board: (dated July 4, 1930)

> Dear Sir:
> ...Convey my best wishes to our fellow people over there and inform them that, through them shall we only be

enlightened...It's a full belief in me that it was all through the love of God that Americans were made slaves and from thence they merged into a feared civilized nation and the world through, in industry, education, development and general progress towards the betterment of the Negro. So let our fellow Negroes share the little they have with us so as to enable us to get nearer their mark than ever...Oh, rescue us, for we have high hopes that some day you will save us immediately in God's name.[7]

Even the sainted Dr. J. E. East, Corresponding Secretary of the Foreign Mission Board of the National Baptist Convention, U.S.A., Inc., expressed this opinion in an editorial published in the *Mission Herald.* In writing on "The Sacred and Solemn Obligation of the Negro Church of America to Africa," he stated:

Years ago a few of the Black people were miraculously taken from Africa and planted in America. Evidently the purpose of God in bringing them here was that they might get the torchlight of Christianity and civilization and carry it back to their own people...How long will the Black people of Africa look for us with tearful eyes in vain?[8]

However difficult it may be to allege Black slavery in America as God's way of dealing with the African people, there were a number of persons who shared the views expressed above.

Certainly one of the anomalies of religious history is that Black people, while in bondage, generally adopted the religion of their oppressors. One of the basic emphases of Christianity is respect for human personality. Jesus taught that persons are children of God and that the Kingdom of God is within each person. This obliges all to treat their fellowmen not as objects, but as subjects — centers of high value and worth. There can be no justification in the economy of God for one man to hold another in chattel slavery. In what was called the "peculiar institution," however, men, women and children were considered as mere chattel having hardly any more ultimate significance than did the animals in the fields. Indeed, the slaves were bred, bought and sold much the same way as were cattle.

Nevertheless, the slaves found in the religion of Jesus an interpretation of the relation of man to God which inspired their imagination and gave hope for a future in which the justice of God would ultimately prevail. So they adapted the Christianity they were taught and shaped it to their unique spiritual needs. They believed in the eternal goodness of God, but concluded that "everybody talkin' 'bout heaven ain't going there."

If the basic thrust of their faith was otherworldly, this is quite understandable. From generation to generation of bondage, theirs had been a life of degradation. While they expressed the hope for deliverance in this life, for a Moses who would come down and set God's people free, they realized in their darkness that their ultimate hope lay in that Great Beyond, by and by, "When the morning comes."

The texts of sermons preached to the slaves often consisted of those passages in the New Testament in which servants are admonished to obey their masters and which state that the "powers that be" or the local authorities, are "ordained of God." The slaves, however, did not accept sermons from these texts uncritically. Indeed, one preacher to slaves reported that when he read these passages, most of the slaves present arose and walked out of the room.

In a number of instances, Blacks were members of predominantly white churches, although they were required to sit in the balcony or to worship at a time different from that of the whites.

Meanwhile, in many communities, certain slaves developed their spiritual gifts to the point where they were allowed to preach as "exhorters." These men were of much influence, and some were allowed to go from plantation to plantation to expound upon the Gospel as they understood it. As a preparation for this activity, they were taught to read. But as increasing numbers of slaves learned to read and write, they were considered a threat to the establishment.

It is to be remembered that some Christians were appalled at and opposed to slavery. A considerable number did their best to find a solution to the problem. Accordingly, anti-slavery societies eventually were organized in several cities of the North. These were effective in marshalling, reinforcing and directing the sentiments of the opposition to the "peculiar institution."[9]

The nation became increasingly divided over the slavery issue, while some of the slaves themselves from time to time rose up in violent revolt against their condition. The historian of slave revolts, Herbert Aptheker, reports finding "records of approximately 250 slave revolts and conspiracies in the history of American Negro slavery."[10] The most notable of these were one led by Denmark Vesey, a free Black who had purchased his freedom in Charleston, South Carolina in 1822, and Nat Turner's rebellion in 1831 in Southampton, Virginia. Turner was an influential religious leader, able to read and write, who felt that his insurrection was ordained of God. He gathered an inspired following, and in the uprising he led, more than fifty-seven whites were killed before Turner was captured and he and his followers executed.[11]

Nat Turner planning the 1831 slave uprising.

Turner's insurrection instilled fear in the hearts of the slaveholders. As a result, in several states which had no such regulation, legislatures passed laws making it a criminal offense for anyone to teach Blacks to read and write. In addition, it was made a criminal offense for Blacks to hold meetings of any kind without the presence of some trusted white person to monitor the proceedings. An example of these laws was the one passed by the General Assembly of Virginia in 1832. In part it read:

> ...it is enacted that no slave, free Negro or mulatto shall preach, or hold any meeting for religious purposes either day or night; any slave or free Negro so offending shall be punished at not exceeding thirty-nine lashes. Slaves and free Negroes who attend any religious meeting conducted by any slave or free Negro preacher, ordained or otherwise, and slaves who attend any preaching at night, although conducted by a white minister, without the permission of the master, shall be punished by stripes...Masters may, however, permit their slaves, employed or bound, and free Negroes to go with them to religious worship conducted by a white minister. Also, religious instruction may be given in the day time by a licensed white minister to slaves and free Negroes.[12]

After the legislature of Virginia passed this law, one of the members said, "We have as far as possible closed every avenue by which light may enter the slave minds. If only we could extinguish their capacity to see the light, our work would be about completed, and they would be on the level of the beast of the field and we would be safe.[13]

In the meantime, tensions over the issue greatly increased. These were marked by the divisions of the Baptists, Methodists and Presbyterians over the question, plus the publication of *Uncle Tom's Cabin* by Harriett Beecher Stowe, and the daring raid on Harpers Ferry, West Virginia, by John Brown in 1859. After

Beginnings of the Black Baptist Movement in America

Abraham Lincoln abolished slavery by proclamation in 1863 and the subsequent Civil War ended with the surrender of Robert E. Lee at Appomattox in 1865, the way was cleared for the education of Blacks. These were the events establishing the conditions by which the ex-slaves would be prepared to take their place in America as free men.

Long before slavery ended, as we have seen, certain Black preachers had laid the foundation for the engagement by their people in the missionary enterprise. George Lisle, a Baptist, has the distinction of having been the first ordained Black preacher in America. He was born a slave in Virginia in 1750, and was the body servant of one Henry Sharp, a Baptist deacon. Sharp moved to South Carolina, taking Lisle with him and ultimately giving him his freedom. After his ordination, Lisle became the pastor of what is recognized as the first Black Baptist church in America.

George Lisle

This rare woodcut was discovered by Reverend Lewis G. Jordan and is preserved in the archives of the Sunday School Publishing Board.

This was the Silver Bluff Baptist Church in Silver Bluff, Aiken County, South Carolina, just across the river from Augusta, Georgia. The exact date of the organization of this church is

13

somewhat in question. The tradition kept by the church as well as the date on the cornerstone indicates 1750 as the year of its founding. On the other hand, however, the exhaustive and scholarly research of Dr. W. H. Brooks led to his conclusion that the church was founded "not earlier than 1773 nor later than 1775.[14] These dates are accepted by most scholars. Two men, David George and Jesse Peters, were converted under George Lisle. They, along with Lisle, became well-known for their preaching. In 1775 Lisle journeyed to Savannah, Georgia, and later became the pastor of the First African Baptist Church there.[15]

Of great significance is the fact that George Lisle is credited with being not only the first ordained Black preacher in America, but also the first foreign missionary in modern times. This occurred because, upon the death of Henry Sharp, Lisle's master, efforts were made by some of Sharp's relatives to re-enslave Lisle. Through the help of some white friends, Lisle was able to leave the country. In 1783 he went to Jamaica, British West Indies, where he began to preach and later organized a Baptist church. Thereupon he was the first person to build a bridge of faith across the seas in modern times. A monument to George Lisle has been erected on the grounds of the church where he served in Savannah, Georgia.

> Long before William Carey left England for India or David Livingston went to Africa, long before the American Baptist Foreign Mission Society was organized in Tremont Temple in Boston, before Adoniram Judson went to Burma — this Black Baptist preacher launched out as a trailblazer in modern missions.[16]
>
> Seven years after George Lisle went to Jamaica, the Reverends David George, Hector Peters and Sampson Calvert went to Africa and began a preaching mission on the West Coast.[17]

Meanwhile, many Blacks were attracted to the Baptist faith. The non-liturgical nature of the Baptist church and the organizational freedom characteristic of Baptists doubtless were important factors in this development. It is estimated that by 1800, there were 40,000 Black Baptists in this country.[18]

Lott Carey

The Black preacher who was the missionary pioneer in West Africa was Lott Carey. Carey was born about thirty miles south of Richmond, Virginia, around 1790. In 1800 he was moved to Richmond where he was employed in a tobacco plant.

Lott Carey

It is said that shortly after moving to Richmond, he fell victim to the vices of the city for about three years. Despite this fact, however, Carey eventually was converted by the preaching of the Reverend John Courtney, pastor of the First Baptist Church. Upon his baptism, Carey became a member of that church. By carefully saving his earnings and with contributions from whites who enjoyed his preaching, Carey was able to buy his freedom and that of his family for the price of $850.[19]

Lott Carey learned to read and write by attending a night school during 1815-1817. This project was conducted by William Crane and other white persons who held the class in the white church

15

building. In 1814 this building was sold to the Black members and the new congregation became known as the First African Baptist Church of Richmond. Carey became a powerful preacher, not only to Blacks, but to whites as well.[20]

Lott Carey organized the African Baptist Foreign Missionary Society in 1815. This was the first organization for foreign missions founded by Blacks in this country.

He was secretary of that society from the time of its organization until he sailed for Africa in 1821. His commission was received from the Foreign Mission Board of the Baptist Triennial Convention and he was supported for this office by the First Baptist Church of Richmond, Virginia.

During this period, there was growing concern among some whites over the ultimate disposition of the free Blacks whose new status caused many whites to fear that these people posed a threat to such peace and tranquility as was found among the slaves. One of the proposed solutions was that the free Blacks be transported to Africa. The organization advocating this view was the American Colonization Society, founded in 1816. Most of the free Blacks and some whites were opposed to this idea. Some conceived of the Colonization as "a sort of unholy alliance" between its organizers and southern slaveholders, and as a scheme to get rid of free Blacks and to make slavery more secure.

The leading Blacks inveighed against it in no uncertain terms. William Lloyd Garrison waged a spirited campaign in opposition to the idea. It represented not only a forced removal to an unfamiliar land, but also an effort to strengthen the institution of slavery. Many free Blacks did not like the prospect of being forcibly removed to an unfamiliar land. Yet the Colonization Society moved ahead with its plans and sent representatives to West Africa to explore the area for a suitable site for the settlement of the expatriated Blacks. After some negotiations with the leading chief of the area, King Peter, for a portion of land between Sierra Leone and the Gold Coast, a deal was consummated by which what was to become Liberia was traded for some supplies desired by the chief.

16

The name of the new settlement was derived from the Latin word for freedom and the capital, Monrovia, was named in honor of President Monroe of the United States under whose administration the final arrangements were concluded.[21]

Whatever may have been the attitudes with respect to American Blacks settling in Africa, Lott Carey worked persistently toward his objective of taking the message of the Gospel to the land of his forefathers. He was assisted in his efforts by Colin Teague, also a free Black preacher, who shared Carey's ambition to convert the Africans to Christianity. In addition, the Richmond Baptist Missionary Society petitioned the largest organization of Baptists in the country, the General Baptist Convention, which met every three years, to support Carey and Teague as missionaries to Africa.[22] Using money from his own savings, the sale of his farm for $1,500, a contribution of $700 from the African Baptist Missionary Society which he organized in Richmond, and contributions from some whites including $200 in cash and $100 in books from the Triennial Convention of the General Baptist, plus the support of the American Colonization Society, Carey and Teague sailed to Liberia on January 16, 1821. They spent their first months in Sierra Leone.

Upon finally settling in Liberia, Lott Carey began the process of establishing himself as a bulwark of Christian inspiration there, especially among the Vai people of Grand Cape Mount County. Carey established the Providence Baptist Church in Monrovia and at the same time became a leading figure in defending his settlement against hostile tribes. In a strange turn of circumstances, while he was engaged in preparations for defense against an attack by hostile tribes, Carey was killed by an accidental explosion of gunpowder in November 1828. In brief, Lott Carey laid the foundations for Christian missions in West Africa. His impact on the Christian missonary enterprise is enduring.

Despite the controversy over the colonization idea, a number of shiploads of Blacks emigrated to Liberia and became the nucleus of a group that was to become the ruling and privileged class in the new republic. These Americo-Liberians dominated the political, economic and social life of the country from the time of its founding until they were overthrown by a coup in the early 1980s.

American Baptist interests in sending missionaries to Africa continued through the years. The Richmond African Baptist Missionary Society regularly sent contributions to the Baptist Missionary Union until 1845.[23] In 1846, the Reverend John Day, "a Negro of piety and eminent scholarship," and A. A. Jones were sent out by the Southern Baptist Convention, and from that year forward this Convention maintained missionary interest in Africa. The Richmond African Missionary Society was inactive during the Civil War, but was reorganized in 1871. The new birth of freedom had doubtless rekindled the determination to do something, in the spirit of Lott Carey, for the redemption of Africa. Accordingly, this organization cooperated with the Southern Baptist Convention in supporting the Reverend Solomon Cosby, a Black preacher from Virginia, as a missionary in Nigeria. In addition, the Southern Baptist Convention sent the Reverend W. W. Colley first to Liberia and then to Nigeria. Colley remained

Reverend Solomon Cosby   *Reverend W. W. Colley*

two years before returning, leaving the missionary station in the hands of Cosby who continued his work there until his death near Lagos, the capital.[24] As we shall see, the Reverend Colley was to become the moving spirit in the organization of the Foreign Misson Convention in 1880, the founding body of the National Baptist Convention, U.S.A., Inc. Colley was among one of the first groups of missionaries sent out by the Foreign Misson Convention.

It is interesting to observe the evidence of the deep sense of relationship American Blacks felt toward Africa. Sometimes the word "African" was made a part of the name of organizations. The church founded by Richard Allen was called the African Methodist Episcopal Church. Later the African Methodist Episcopal Zion Church was founded. Several individual churches used the word in the names they adopted, such as the African Baptist Church. It is clear that such usages reflected a sense of pride on the part of many Blacks in the continent of their heritage. There was, at the same time, a deep concern for the people in Africa who were being shamelessly exploited by some of the European power structures.

We have seen that even before Emancipation, Blacks had organized churches in the free states as well as in such slave states as South Carolina and Georgia. The contributions of men like George Lisle, David George and Lott Carey reflect a concern for the spreading of the Gospel not only at home, but across the seas. From the appearance of the first Blacks in this country to Lott Carey's mission to Africa, the majority of Blacks in America, bond and free, demonstrated a keen interest in the Baptist faith. They accepted the religion of those who enslaved them, but adapted it to their peculiar situation. Deep within them was a sense of affinity with the land of their ancestors. This was a primary factor in directing their concerns and activities toward spreading the Gospel to the land of their forebears.

Bridges of Faith Across the Seas

Notes

1. Edwin L. Williams, "Negro Slavery in Florida." *Florida Historical Quarterly,* Vol. XXVIII, No. 2. (October 1949) p. 93.

2. Philip D. Curtain, *The African Slave Trade: A Census,* Madison, 1969.

3. Herbert S. Klein, *The Middle Passage: Comparative Studies in the African Slave Trade,* Princeton, 1978. Eric Williams, *Journal of Negro History* Vol. XXV, The Golden Age of the Slave System in Britain, (January 1940).

4. Cf. E. Franklin Frazier, *The Negro in the United States.* New York: Macmillan Company, 1949, and Melville J. Herskovitz, *The Myth of the Negro Past.* Boston: Beacon Press, 1958.

5. Cf. Carter G. Woodson, *History of the Negro Church,* Washington: Associated Publishers, 1921, pp. 6-7.

6. Cf. Woodson, *op. cit.,* pp. 12-19 and C. C. Jones, *The Religious Instruction of Negroes in the United States.* Savannah: T. Purse, 1842, *passim.*

7. *Mission Herald,* (September 1930) p. 30.

8. *Mission Herald,* (October 1927) p. 6.

9. John Hope Franklin, *From Slavery to Freedom,* Knopf, New York, p. 506.

10. Herbert Aptheker, *American Negro Slave Revolts.* New York: International Publishers, 1969. p. 164.

11. John B. Duff, and Peter M. Mitchell, eds. *The Nat Turner Rebellion: The Historical Event and the Modern Controversy,*
(a pamphlet) New York, 1971.

12. June Purcell Guild, *Black Laws of Virginia.* Richmond: Whittet and Shepperson, 1936. p. 107.

13. Ibid.

14. W. H. Brooks, "The Priority of the Silver Bluff Church." *Journal of Negro History,* Vol. 7., No. 2 (April 1922) p. 180.

15. Ibid., p. 191.

16. Adapted from a tract by S. S. Hodges and published by the Home Mission Board of the Southern Baptist Convention, 1974, p. 5.

17. L. G. Jordan, *Up the Ladder in Foreign Missions.* National Baptist Publishing Board, 1901, p. 15.

18. Ibid., p. 6.

19. *Mission Herald,* (July 1928) p. 33.

20. *Mission Herald,* (April 1923) p. 9.

21. John Hope Franklin, *From Slavery to Freedom,* Knopf, New York, p. 155.

22. J. E. East, "Lott Carey, The Pioneer Missionary," *Mission Herald,* (July 1928) pp. 11, 33.

23. L. G. Jordan, *Afro-American Mission Herald,* (March 1896) p. 1.

24. L. G. Jordan, NBC *Minutes,* 1936, p. 97, and in the *Afro-American Mission Herald,* (March 1896).

CHAPTER TWO
THE FOREIGN MISSION BOARD AND THE CONVENTION MOVEMENT

The desire to form associations for self-expression and mutual benefits was strong among Black people for decades before the Civil War. The development of the convention movement among Black Baptists parallels a similar activity among groups with no denominational alignment, and continued to the end of the 19th century. In 1850 free Blacks held their first national convention, and for the remaining years before the Civil War a number of national and state conventions were held to promote a variety of causes. "Temperance, education, and moral reform stood high on the agenda of many Negro conventions throughout the era — and the influence of such deliberations was carried home by the participants and used to make their communities better places in which to live."[1] The primary goal of the conventions of the Black Baptists was spreading the Gospel in Africa because it was the land of their forebears and therefore excited a special interest among those of the Diaspora.

Among the Baptists the movement to organize associations began as early as 1836. Churches comprised of free Blacks or those who were refugees from slavery who were living in cities from Buffalo to as far west as Chicago and south as far as Cincinnati, organized the Providence Baptist Association in Ohio. Shortly afterward the Wood River Baptist Association was organized in Illinois. The most significant of the early organizations and the first convention so named was the American Baptist Missionary

Convention organized in 1840 at the Abyssinian Baptist Church in New York. The organizing group was comprised of Blacks from New England and the Middle West. This was the beginning of a national organization of Black Baptists.[2]

In 1853 the Colored Baptist Convention was organized. This group was comprised of churches in what was called the Western States and Territory.

Continuing on a wider scale the Northwestern and Southern Baptist Convention was organized in 1864. The purpose of this convention was to serve areas not in the jurisdiction of the American Baptist Missionary Convention.[3] In the effort to unify the Baptist convention movement, the Consolidated Baptist Missionary Convention was formed in 1866. This organization represented the merger of the Northwestern and Southern Convention and the American Baptist Missionary Convention and thus was closer to a national movement than had been the earlier groups.

The movement destined finally to become national and lasting in scope was begun by the Reverend W. W. Colley of Virginia and culminated in 1880. He received his education at the Richmond Theological Institute, one of the units which later became Virginia Union University. After serving as a missionary in Africa under the auspices of the Southern Baptist Convention, he returned in November 1879, and shortly afterwards, with the encouragement of other Baptist leaders in the State, launched a vigorous effort among the Baptist ministers of the country for the purpose of forming a national convention devoted to the promotion of foreign missions. His efforts were eminently successful. On Saturday, November 24, 1880, 151 delegates from eleven states met at the Baptist church in Montgomery, Alabama.[4] This meeting was characterized by deep emotions and high expectations. The organization chose the name, Baptist Foreign Mission Convention of the United States of America. Officers elected included the Reverend W. H. McAlpine of Alabama, president, and the Reverend W. W. Colley, corresponding secretary. Eleven vice presidents, one from each of the states represented, were elected.

Reverend and Mrs. W. W. Colley , Reverend and Mrs. J. H. Presley

The headquarters of this convention was established in Richmond, Virginia. This organization evolved into what is now the National Baptist Convention of the U. S. A., Inc.

Meanwhile, the organization of state conventions had begun immediately after the close of the Civil War in 1865. In that year Black Baptists in Louisiana formed a convention . They were followed by North Carolina in 1866, Alabama and Virginia in 1867, Arkansas in 1868, Kentucky and Mississippi in 1869, Georgia in 1870 and Florida in 1874.[5]

The Foreign Mission Convention of America attracted increasing interest and support, although the net receipts for foreign missions were far from what were desired. In 1883 the Reverend Colley and his wife, and the Reverend and Mrs. J. H. Presley, were appointed missionaries to Africa. Two unmarried young men, the Reverends J. J. Coles and Hence McKinney, were also appointed to sail with them to study for missionary work on the field.

The Reverend Joseph E. Jones, a professor at Richmond Theological Institute, (now Virginia Union University) was elected corresponding secretary to succeed the Reverend Colley; the Reverend Holland Powell was named Travelling Agent. Professor Jones held the office for ten years.[6] He was a highly regarded instructor whose memory is still kept alive at Virginia Union.

The third corresponding secretary was the Reverend John J. Coles who was elected at the convention in Washington, D.C. He had returned from his tour of duty in Africa somewhat impaired in health. In fact, his health was so seriously impaired by the fevers in Africa that he died a few months after being elected. His widow was elected to complete his term.[7]

Reverend John J. Coles

The urge for the establishment of a strong national Baptist Convention was not abated by the formation in 1880 of the Foreign Mission Convention, the central focus of which was African missions. Another convention organizational effort was initiated by the Reverend W. J. Simmons of Louisville, Kentucky. In his open letter to Baptist clergymen and laymen he stated that he was urged to make the call by "many whose names and endorsements are hereunto affixed," and "by their advice and solicitations." The stated purposes of the convention which met on August 28, 1886, at the First Baptist Church in St. Louis, Missouri, were as follows:

CALL FOR A NATIONAL CONVENTION OF COLORED BAPTISTS: 1886

Dear Brethren:
August 5, 1886, an open letter to the Baptist clergy and laymen was issued by Rev. William J. Simmons, an American Baptist, asking if we should have a National Convention to discuss questions of interest to our beloved denomination. At that time the following reasons were given:

1. To promote personal piety, sociability, and a better knowledge of each other.

2. To be able to have an understanding as to the great ends of the denomination.

3. To encourage our literary men and women, and promote the interests of Baptist literature.

4. To discuss questions pertaining especially to the religious, educational, industrial, and social interests of our people.

5. To give an opportunity for the best thinkers and writers to be heard.

6. That united, we may be more powerful for good and strengthen our pride in the denomination.

Having been solicited to write the call by many whose names and endorsements are hereunto affixed, the Call is hereby made by their advice and solicitations for said convention to meet in St. Louis, Mo., August 25, 1886, 10 o'clock A.M. in the First Baptist Church, and the pastor thereof is hereby requested to serve as a Committee on Arrangements, with power to select his associates.

W. H. Steward, Louisville, KY and Rev. R. H. Cole, 2609 Goode Avenue, St. Louis, are hereby requested to serve as a Committee on Transportation.[8]

In response to this call, some 600 delegates from seventeen states attended. According to one account, included in this group were:

> Graduates in law, medicine, and theology; professors of philosophy, German, French, Latin, Greek, and Hebrew; a number of ex-state senators, two ex-lieutenant governors; editors and teachers, not a few; a Baptist senator from Mississippi, and a Baptist missionary from London, England.[9]

The academic and professional achievements found among this group were indeed remarkable for persons only twenty-one years from slavery. The Reverend W. J. Simmons was elected president of the new convention.

Reverend W. J. Simmons

The Baptist Foreign Missionary Convention carried forward the missionary program of the new organization.

In 1893 another convention of Black Baptists was organized primarily for the purpose of determining the educational policies of the denomination. This movement grew out of the desire on the part of some Black leaders to have a greater role in the operation of schools for Blacks than was then the case with respect to the institutions controlled by the white Northern Baptist Convention. This natural desire led to the founding of a number of schools independent of control by whites. Among such institutions were Virginia Seminary and College, Lynchburg, Virginia; Arkansas Baptist College, Little Rock; Selma University, Selma, Alabama, and numerous others. While the motives of self-help and independence leading to the establishment of these schools may have been admirable, the principal problems faced by these institutions were the limited financial resources for developing and operating as viable centers of quality education. That they succeeded as well as they did was remarkable; nevertheless the comparatively low income of Blacks in American society made it difficult for these schools, without organized white support, to obtain funds sufficient to enable them to attain and maintain full accreditation by the appropriate accrediting agencies. The name of the new organization was the National Baptist Educational Convention.

By the time this organization was formed, the Foreign Mission Convention had suffered some losses. Mr. Hence McKinney, one of the early missionaries to Africa, had passed away while there. Also, Mrs. Hattie Presley had died in Africa. The Reverend J. J. Coles and family had returned from Africa. The work in Africa was seriously impeded by tribal wars which resulted in the almost complete annihilation of the Vai tribe. The house built by the Foreign Mission Convention at Bendoo had been abandoned and the lumber disposed of to individuals in Cape Mount. The formation of this new convention was the occasion for once again strengthening the work of missions in the foreign field.[10]

By the 1893 session of the Foreign Mission Convention, a total of twelve missionaries had been sent out by this organization. As reported by the Reverend J. J. Coles at the 1893 session, these missionaries were as follows:

Rev. E. B. Topp and wife, in 1887, served two months and on account of sickness returned home.

Rev. George H. Bailey, a Liberian, in 1889, served six months and returned home.

Mrs. J. H. Presley, in 1884, served seven months and died on the field.

Rev. J. H. Presley, in 1884-85, served seventeen months and on account of sickness, returned to America.

Rev. J. J. Diggs, and not having the means to continue his work, returned to America.

Rev. W. W. Colley and wife, after two and a half years service, on account of ill health, in 1886 returned to America.

Rev. H. McKinney, after three years and three months service, died on the field.

Your humble servant (J. J. Coles) after serving about seven and a half, and my wife five and two thirds years in Africa, being several times ousted by tribal wars and our mission field devastated by savage tribes, have returned to you.

Thus eleven missionaries have been employed under your auspices; and Rev. J.O. Hayes, who is now in Africa, makes the twelfth.[11]

It is clear that dedication to the missionary enterprise required tremendous courage to face the risks and hazards involved. Among some whites there was the belief that because of their African heritage, American Blacks could fare better in Africa than whites. Throughout this history, however, it is apparent that in general American Blacks were hardly more immune to the ravages of climate and disease than were any other people with the exception of the native Africans themselves.

The Organization of the National Baptist Convention of the U.S.A.

The 1894 session of the Baptist Foreign Mission Board met in Montgomery, Alabama. At the 1893 session it had been planned that the Foreign Mission Convention and the New England Baptist Convention meet jointly in 1894, but the latter two did not show up. According to one account, each of these bodies was living at a "poor dying rate. The Foreign Mission Convention was without a missionary and the whole field deserted; the Educational Convention was without a school or student, and the American National Baptist Convention had cast the Nashville or 'Tennessee fuss' overboard."[12]

At this meeting the resolution to form a merger was offered by Reverend A. W. Pegues. It read as follows:

Whereas the interests and purposes of the three national bodies, namely, the Foreign Mission, National, and Educational Conventions, can be conserved and fostered under the auspices of one body; and

Whereas the consolidation of the above named bodies will economize both time and money, therefore,

Resolved, that the Foreign Mission Convention appoint a committee of nine, who shall enter immediately into consultation with the Executive Boards of the National and Educational Conventions, for the purpose of effecting a consolidation of the three bodies upon the following plan:

1. That there shall be one national organization of American Baptists.

2. Under this, there shall be a Foreign Mission Board, with authority to plan and execute the Foreign Mission work, according to the spirit and purpose set forth by the Foreign Mission Convention of the United States.

3. There shall be a Board of Education, and also, a Board of Missions to carry into effect the spirit and purpose of the National and the Educational Conventions, respectively.[13]

Separate committees were appointed to work jointly in planning and preparing a constitution and plan of merger to be presented at the meeting in Atlanta, Georgia in 1895. A merger was consummated, despite the fact that the Foreign Mission Convention of Richmond, Virginia did not report.

Thus, what was destined to become among Black Baptists the major unifying organization was formed — the National Baptist Convention of the United States of America — at the Friendship Baptist Church in Atlanta, Georgia. The first president was the Reverend E. C. Morris of Little Rock, Arkansas. A Foreign Mission Board was appointed comprised of the Reverends John H. Frank, chairman; L. M. Luke, of Louisville, KY, corresponding

Reverend L. M. Luke

secretary; David A. Caddie, treasurer; William H. Steward, recording secretary. Other Boards formed were the Home Mission Board and the Education Board.[14]

Reverend L. M. Luke, the first corresponding secretary of the Foreign Mission Board of the newly organized convention, was a native of Cado Parish, Louisiana. Prior to his election to this position he had served two years as the Field Secretary of the Foreign Mission Convention based in Richmond, Virginia. It is said his earnestness was demonstrated in the delivery of his noted sermon, "Give Me the Crumbs."[15] Elected in September, 1895, he died in December of that year.

The Reverend Lewis G. Jordan Elected Corresponding Secretary

In February 1896 the Reverend L. G. Jordan, pastor of the Union Baptist Church, Philadelphia, Pennsylvania, was elected to succeed the Reverend Mr. Luke. A man of scholarly insights, profound learning and deep dedication to foreign missions, Dr. Jordan, as we shall see, made a significant impact upon the foreign mission work of the Convention, as well as upon other concerns of the denomination as a whole.

We have observed that at the very beginning of the national movement the emphasis was upon sending the Christian message of spiritual, social and physical uplift to Africa. The concern for the land of their ancestors was the primary motivating force in Black Baptist organizational endeavors, although home missions and education were included in their program. It is evident that the formation of the associations and conventions recorded here, and the sending of missionaries to far-off Africa involved a considerable amount of sacrifice on the part of those in sympathy with the goals. The income of most Blacks was relatively meager and yet many gave of their substance and time to further the cause of building bridges of faith across the sea.

31

Reverend L.G. Jordan

With the exception of Prof. J. E. Jones who served ten years, the first corresponding secretaries of the Foreign Mission Convention in 1880 served relatively short terms. Rev. W. W. Colley served three years and Rev. J.J. Coles only a few months. Despite these unsettling factors, however, the vision *of* and dedication *to* a strong commitment to answer the Macedonian Call from Africa was never lost. With the election of Rev. L. G. Jordan as Corresponding Secretary of the Foreign Mission Board, a new day dawned for Black Baptists and the missionary enterprise.

Basic Responsibility of the Foreign Mission Board

Since its organization, the Foreign Mission Board of the National Baptist Convention, U.S.A., Inc. has undertaken several basic responsibilities. First of all, its basic responsibility is to serve as the clearing house for all the hopes and dreams of the thousands of Baptist churches which comprise the National Baptist Convention and seek to carry out the Great Commission of our Lord and Savior Jesus Christ on foreign fields. It is that arm of the parent body whose major function is to interview prospective candidates for missionary service; set qualification standards; employ them under contractual agreements; pay their salaries; pay for transportation to and from the fields of service; provide fields of service; build and maintain living accommodations; purchase equipment and material for the mission stations and negotiate with governments, kings, paramount, tribal and clan chiefs regarding property and specific services. This is part of the function of the Foreign Mission Board as it relates to implementing the missionary program on the foreign field.

On the domestic scene the Foreign Mission Board must formulate an overall plan for the continued promotion of these missionary objectives. It must promote fund raising drives in the various cities and states, through conventions, associations and conferences. It must provide information concerning the work being accomplished on the field through the media of the *Mission Herald,* tracts, booklets, catechisms and correspondence. It must keep and publish a strict account of all funds received and how they are disbursed. To do this it must have a trained secretarial and bookkeeping staff and all the necessary business equipment for conducting such a responsibility.[16]

Notes

1. Howard H. Bell, *A Survey of the Negro Convention Movement 1830-1861,* New York: The Arno Press and the *New York Times,* 1969. p. 3.

2. *Mission Herald,* (September-October 1935) p. 8.

3. Moses, *op. cit.,* p. 12.

4. L. G. Jordon, *Up the Ladder in Foreign Missions.* Nashville: National Baptist Publishing Board, 1901, pp. 88-90

5. N. H. Pius, *An Outline of Baptist History.* Nashville: National Baptist Publishing Board, 1911, p. 67; George P. and Richard I. McKinney, *History of the Black Baptists of Florida, 1850-1985.* Miami: Florida Memorial College Press, 1987, p. 58.

6. Jordon, *op. cit.,* p. 95.

7. C. C. Adams and Marshall A. Talley, *Negro Baptists and Foreign Missions.* Philadelphia: The Foreign Mission Board of the National Baptist Convention, U.S.A., Inc., 1944, pp. 35-36.

8. National Baptist Convention, U.S.A., Inc., *Minutes,* 1950, p. 10.

9. Richard B. Cook, *The Story of the Baptists in all Ages and Countries.* Baltimore: R. H., Woodward and Co., 1889, p. 427.

10. Jordon, *op. cit.,*pp. 98-100.

11. *The Mission Herald* (February 1929) 32nd Anniversary Issue.

12. L. G. Jordan, *Minutes,* National Baptist Convention, 1929, p. 224.

13. National Baptist Convention, *Minutes,* 1929. pp. 219-220.

14. Ibid., p. 225.

15. *Mission Herald,* (September-October 1935) p. 7.

16. *Mission Herald,* (November-December 1962) p. 1.

CHAPTER THREE
TWENTY-FIVE YEARS
OF EXPANSION — 1896-1921
The Tenure of Dr. Lewis G. Jordan

The commitment of Black Baptists to building bridges of faith across the seas remained intact during the decade preceding the turn of the century, even though by 1895 there was hardly any foreign missionary activity by the Convention in progress. The missionaries who had been sent out by the Black Baptists earlier had ended their mission. The financial resources for foreign mission work were depleted. A new beginning was required. A dedicated leader in missions was needed.

In 1896, the Foreign Mission Board looked to the self-educated and dynamic pastor of the Union Baptist Church in Philadelphia, the Reverend Lewis G. Jordan, to revitalize and carry forward its commitment to foreign missions. The Reverend Mr. Jordan brought to the position a background of successful pastoral experience and proven leadership ability.

Born on a farm near Meridian, Mississippi, Dr. Jordan said of his early life that he came "up from slavery without the love of a mother or the protection of a father," and that he was "robbed of a chance to get an education." He did, however, manage to get an elementary education and to attend the Roger Williams University in Nashville, Tennessee. Prior to coming to Philadelphia, he served as pastor of churches in his home state of Mississippi and later in Texas. It was because of his background and his distinguished leadership at the Union Baptist Church in Philadelphia that he was chosen to fill the position of Corresponding

Secretary of the Foreign Mission Board. He resigned from his church in October 1896 to give full time to the work of the Board.

From a study of the records, it is clear that Reverend Jordan had both the strong intellectual and deep spiritual qualifications needed for the demands of his new position. A dynamic personality is reflected in all the accounts of his work with the National Baptist Convention, U.S.A., Inc.

Writing about assuming the position of corresponding secretary forty years later, Dr. Jordan said:

> In the winter of 1896, I was peacefully pastoring the Union Baptist Church, Philadelphia. The holidays passed and the rubbish from decorations of the holiday season were being cleared away, and my church, like other organizations, was settling down to the year's work. It was on the 13th of February that the Foreign Mission Board, then located in Louisville, Kentucky, selected me as corresponding secretary. The Board was new, having been reorganized in Atlanta, Georgia, in November 1895, and moved from Richmond, Virginia, to Kentucky. This entailed a complete change of my work and life plans, but there was a force compelling me to follow on, and till now I feel it was God. I faced it and amid the sobs and tears of a great congregation and a good people, I gave my resignation to take effect in October of that same year.

> When the time came, I pulled up root and branch and moved from Philadelphia to Louisville to take charge of a disorganized work, about which I knew little and many of the good men of the denomination knew less.[1]

A great challenge confronted the new corresponding secretary. It was necessary to re-educate the Baptist constituency to the importance and significance of the missionary enterprise. Moreover, since the Black community by that time was only thirty-one years removed from slavery, the growth and development of churches on the home front occupied much of their attention

36

and energies. In addition, "Jim Crow" laws were being enacted increasingly throughout the South, creating even heavier psychological burdens upon the Black community in their struggle for survival.

Dr. Jordan recognized that new ground had to be broken. A firm foundation for the support of foreign missions had to be established. His immediate predecessors had neither the resources nor the time to do this. Professor J. E. Jones, who held the office for ten years, was unable to build wide foreign mission support while carrying forward a regular teaching load at Virginia Union University. The Reverends J. J. Coles and L. M. Luke were cut down before they could get a good start at laying the foundations. Besides these limitations, Dr. Jordan noted that since the organization of the Black Baptists in 1880, the foreign mission work "had been left to a handful of men who seemed to feel they owned it and in 1894, because of some offense, real or imagined, they did not meet the Convention at all in Montgomery, Alabama, nor in Atlanta, Georgia, in 1895, hence a new Board and a new location."[2] All of this meant that the work of the foreign missions was not moving forward. Dr. Jordan stated that when he took office "there was not a missionary on the field and not a dollar in the treasury." A centralized and concerted effort was needed to galvanize support for the task ahead.

One of Dr. Jordan's first moves after taking office was to establish a journal for disseminating information to the Baptist constituency regarding the work of the Foreign Mission Board. He stated that he was "always a believer in printer's ink." A month after he took office, he arranged with the editor of *The Christian Banner* to publish *The Mission Herald*. The very first issue appeared in mid-March 1896 under the title, *Afro-American Mission Herald,* and consisted of only four pages 6 x 9 inches each. The first editorial comment in the initial issue was, "The needs of the cause of Foreign Missions demand the consideration of every member of our churches and the AFRO-AMERICAN MISSION HERALD enters the field as its advocate." In this issue was printed the announcement of what was called "African

Vol. 1. No. 1.   Philadelphia, Pa., March, 1896.   Price 25 cents per year.
Single Copy; 1 cent.

"HOW SHALL THEY HEAR WITHOUT A PREACHER ?"

SALUTATORY.

THE needs of the cause of Foreign Missions demand the consideration of every member of our churches and THE AFRO AMERICAN MISSION HERALD enters the field as its advocate. Whether or not it will be continued as a monthly, depends entirely upon how much value our pastors place on it as a medium to reach the people. Write your views concerning its usefulness in assisting the noble cause in which we are engaged to the editor.

DR. GORDON'S LETTER.

The following are the closing paragraphs of Dr. Gordon's last pastoral letter to the Clarendon Street Church, sent to all the members on the completion of twenty-five years of labor with them. In a large degree these words summarize his teaching and training of the church in the line of Christian activity :—

" Forget not that your first and principal business as a disciple of Christ is to give the gospel to those who have it not. He who is not a missionary Christian will be a missing Christian when the great day comes for bestowing the rewards of service. Therefore :—

"Ask yourself daily what the Lord would have you do in connection with the work of carrying the news of salvation to the perishing millions. Search carefully whether He would have you go yourself to the heathen if you have the youth and fitness required for the work. Or, if you cannot go in person :—

" Inquire diligently what blood mortgage there is upon your property in the interest of foreign missions—how much you owe to the heathen, because of what you owe to Christ, for redeeming you with his precious blood. I warn you that it will go hard with you when your Lord comes to reckon with you if He finds your wealth invested in superfluous luxuries or hoarded up in needless accumulations instead of being sacredly devoted to giving the gospel to the lost.

"But remember that consecrated giving will be impossible unless there be first a consecrated giver. Therefore I counsel you to seek the special grace and anointing of the Holy Spirit, that He may work in you that consecration of heart and life on which so much depends.

"Yours in Christ,
"A. J. GORDON."

The reputation of our great denomination is at stake in our African work.

We used every effort possible to get a picture and sketch of our late Dr. Luke but failed. Let us speak of his worth on our "African Mission Day."

We are greatly indebted to Rev. W. H. Brooks, D. D., of the 19th Street Church, Washington, D. C., for most of the answers to questions in the African Mission Day Exercises. Much of this very important information as to the early missionary efforts of Negro Baptists was unknown to us heretofore.

For a good cut of yourself send photo to the Philadelphia Heliograph Company. They make the best.

Mission Day" to be observed by "all the Colored Baptist Churches in America" on March 29, 1896, by order of the National Baptist Convention of U.S.A. A significant feature of this issue was the model program to be used for the observance of "African Mission Day." This consisted of an extensive question and answer section highlighting the history of Black Baptists in foreign mission work.[3]

The subscription price of the *Herald* was twenty-five cents per year; single copies were priced at one cent. After three months, the publication was made larger. Some time later the term "Afro-American" was dropped.

In time the format of the *Mission Herald* consisted largely of editorial comments, news items relative to missions, letters from missionaries on the field and detailed reports of financial contributions from churches and individuals. By 1901 the circulation had reached 8,000 and the *Herald* was described as an "indispensable mouthpiece" of the Foreign Mission Board. Dr. Jordan declared that the journal found its way "in nearly every city, hamlet or town. From Miami to California, people whom we could never reach through this agency have become our vocal supporters." The publication of this journal significantly decreased the travel expenses of the corresponding secretary in spreading the Gospel of foreign missions and provided a tangible reference source of information about this important work of the Convention.[4]

In 1900, the Foreign Mission Board took the opportunity to enter into a plan of cooperation with the Missionary Union of Boston, Massachusetts. This was for the purpose of raising the consciousness of the constituency with respect to their obligations to support foreign missions. Such a plan was doubtless a stimulus to both parties. The president of the convention, Dr. E. C. Morris, was the cooperative agent for the two organizations. It was his feeling that the cooperative plan was a great success and the spirit of amity between the two organizations would be kept alive.

The Convention and the Foreign Mission Board, cognizant of all that is implied in the beginning of a new century, established in 1900 a project designated as "The Twentieth Century Offering" for foreign missions. Pledges were solicited and paid amounting to more than $3,842 during the Convention year. The proceeds of these contributions were designated for the construction of mission stations in Africa and for the development of the work there so as "to command the respect of the entire world."[5]

In 1901, Dr. Jordan reported to the Convention that there had been a considerable increase in the support of foreign missions by individuals, churches, associations and conventions. These, he felt, were signs of a deeper growth. "Men and women," he said, "have made great sacrifices to respond to our appeals...For many years, we have struggled hard to interest our churches as a whole in this work...This year marks an epoch unknown in the history of the work — a year when more churches have done their duties in supporting the missionaries who represent them in heathen lands than heretofore."[6]

Since Dr. Jordan, as he said, started his assignment without a missionary on the field or a dollar in the treasury, it obviously was a result of the kind of support indicated above that the Foreign Mission Board was able to send out as many missionaries as were commissioned during the new corresponding secretary's first five years in office. Certainly, the distribution of the *Mission Herald,* along with personal visitations to as many associations and conventions as possible, contributed to the success indicated here.

Women's Connection Established

It was in the year 1900 during a meeting of the National Baptist Convention in Richmond, Virginia, that Dr. L. G. Jordan, Secretary of the Foreign Mission Board, called Fifth Street Baptist Church to discuss the organization of a women's convention auxiliary. This group of women was made up primarily of the wives of the pastors in attendance at the national convention. After much discussion, it was decided that a formal call would be sent out to all interested churches in the Convention asking them to send women messengers to the next session of the Convention which was to be held in Cincinnati, Ohio, to formally organize the auxiliary.

And so in 1901, the National Baptist Convention, U.S.A., Inc., *Women's Convention Auxiliary* was formally organized. Notice what they said:

> We the Women of the Churches connected with the National Baptist Convention, desirous of stimulating and transmitting a missionary spirit and grace of giving among the women and children of the Churches and aiding in collecting funds for missions to be disbursed as ordered by the Convention, organize and adopt the following Constitution. The object of the Convention is to organize the women and children for the purpose of collecting and raising money for education and missions at home and abroad.[27]

This was the original wording of the preamble to the Women's Convention's constitution and though it was refined in later years, this was their original purpose.

And so this organization came into being with Mrs. S. Willie Layten elected as the first president and Miss Nannie Helen Burroughs, the first secretary. Interestingly enough, their first big objective was the building of a mission house at the Providence Industrial Mission at Chiradzulu, Nyasaland, for Miss Emma Delaney of Florida, who was the Foreign Mission Board's first outstanding woman missionary to Africa.

In 1904 Miss Delaney wrote to the Women's Convention:

> I want to thank God for you the Women of the Women's Convention for sending me, through the Foreign Mission Board, the funds to erect a Mission House. It is now completed, and it serves as a place for me and five children to live in. It is here we hold services to worship God and exalt Christ. It is here we minister to the sick and feed the hungry. For every penny given we say thank you, thank you...

In 1912 that same intrepid woman journeyed to West Africa and, defying the natives who did not want Christ, established the Suehn Mission.

One of the annoying problems confronting the Foreign Mission Board in this and later periods was that of certain individuals claiming to be representatives of the Board and collecting contributions under false pretenses. This practice tended to undermine confidence in the fund-raising efforts of the Board, and at all times the Board had to be alert to these dishonest individuals and warn its constituency to be on guard against them.[7]

Combining research and writing during his first four years in office, Dr. Jordan published a significant volume entitled, *Up The Ladder In Foreign Missions.*[8] This volume shows the careful, extensive, and broad research done by Dr. Jordan who gave attention to the entire missionary enterprise of which the work of the Foreign Mission Board was a part. The book was commended as "a useful handbook in foreign missions...which should be in every Baptist family and in every preacher's library. The book fills a long felt need as we had nothing of its kind on the market."

In 1897, the Board commissioned the Reverend R. A. Jackson of Holly Springs, Mississippi, to open a mission station in South

Reverend R. A. Jackson   *Reverend J. I. Buchanan*

Africa. He was followed in that same year by the Reverend J. I. Buchanan of West Mississippi. Reverend Jackson began preaching in the Cape Town area among those people referred to as Coloreds by the British Colonists and the Africaaners who dominated the political structure. Coloreds were those persons who represented a racial mixture of whites, Blacks and bushmen; the latter were an indigenous tribe who inhabited that area in South Africa.

Reverend Buchanan chose to work in the Middledrift area where he not only established churches but also schools. Under his leadership, a convention was organized and the South African preachers whom he ordained assumed leadership of the churches which Reverend Buchanan was instrumental in organizing.

Missionary activity in South Africa was hampered by the English-Boer War around the turn of the century. Sending of supplies and ease of transportation and travel were adversely affected. Despite these difficulties, missionaries such as the Reverend E. B. Koti were able to make progress in their work. Reverend Koti, from Queenstown, organized the first African Baptist Association and made plans for developing a federation of mission stations.[9] A significant contribution to Reverend Koti's work was made by Dr. E. W. D. Isaac, secretary of the BYPU Board, who pledged $750 from his organization to aid in the construction of a $1,500 chapel at the station in Queenstown.

The Reverend J. I. Buchanan demonstrated the kind of missionary activity of which the Foreign Mission Board was proud. He held the first baptismal service in Queenstown in 1897, at which twenty-six candidates were immersed. During the next three years, he held two baptismal services leading to a total of 478 new members received into the church by this ordinance, in addition to twenty members received by letters.

Among the difficulties encountered in this mission were the terrible drought, locust, rindpest, "and the most cruel war which is between our Magistrate Government and the Boers.[10] Nevertheless, Mr. Buchanan stated that he could only exclaim" in a humble tone, 'God be praised for his wonderful kindness shown to his children of men.' "

The Providence Industrial Mission and John B. Chilembwe

One of the outstanding mission stations established by the Foreign Mission Board was Providence Industrial Mission in Chiradzulu, Nyasaland, British Central Africa. The first missionary at this station was the Reverend John Chilembwe. He was recommended to the Foreign Mission Board by Mr. Booth, an Englishman who brought him to this country in 1897. The Foreign Mission Board sent Reverend Chilembwe to the Virginia Seminary and College where he spent nearly three years. He was then ordained and returned to British Central Africa in 1900 where he established the work which, in time, became one of the leading missionary enterprises sponsored by the Foreign Mission Board. In 1901, the Foreign Mission Board sent the Reverend L. N. Cheek of Jackson, Mississippi to work with Mr. Chilembwe at the mission.

Reverend John Chilembwe and family

Reverend L. N. Cheek

Miss Emma B. Delaney

Another missionary sent to the Providence Industrial Mission was Miss Emma B. Delaney. Indeed, she was one of the truly

44

outstanding missionaries to be sent to the foreign field. Born in Fernandina, Florida, in 1871, Miss Delaney received her high school education at a Catholic convent, but later enrolled at Spelman Seminary (now Spelman College) where she took the academic course and special courses in nursing and seminary work. Miss Delaney came to the attention of a Baptist Women's Missionary Group in Boston in 1897, where she was well received

Miss Emma B. Delaney

and encouraged to continue her interest in missionary work. As early as 1900, the Women's Auxiliary of the Baptist General State Convention of Florida passed a resolution that Miss Delaney be sent as a missionary to Africa. Two years later this resolution was approved by the Foreign Mission Board of the National Baptist Convention, U.S.A., and shortly thereafter Miss Delaney was sent to the Providence Industrial Mission at Chiradzulu. There she labored with the Reverends Chilembwe and Cheek for three years before returning for an extended furlough in 1905.[11]

Shortly before she left, Miss Delaney sent a letter "to the Baptist Sisterhood of America," in which she gave in detail some of her experiences in British Central Africa. Among these were the following:

> The attendance of girls this year has increased and I have been pleasantly surprised. When some of them came the early part of the term asking for work saying they wanted cloth to wear to school and church, while I gave them the work, I had my doubts about attending regularly. But, they have been as faithful to every call of the bell as you could find anywhere. Their improvement in sewing class has surpassed anything I could hope for in so short a time and their deportment is good: these are the village girls to whom I refer. Certainly we expect all this from the girls on the station. These village girls have many drawbacks that our people at home would give as good reasons why they could not answer every call. Think of them hoeing all morning until time for sewing class and then sewing for an hour and a half, sometimes going to hoe again until a certain task is accomplished, stop an hour before school to go to the stream and bathe, and then remain in school until 4:00 o'clock, go home, pound their meal, or go to the garden to get what is wanted for the next day (and this was during the rainy season).[12]

Some Land Problems at Providence Industrial Mission

In one of his letters to the Foreign Mission Board, Reverend Chilembwe indicated that everything was not going well at the mission in Chiradzulu. He wrote:

> I thank you very much for the order of $25 just received. It came in a most needy time. Our work in East Africa is doing well. Elephant hunting in this part of Africa is profitable, but we must pay the government $125 a year for license. Will the Board give me this amount? I am sorry Dr. Jordan did not come this way, as we are having

some little tangle about our land. The Lord bless you and grant you a splendid session in your forthcoming national convention.

Yours in Africa,
John Chilembwe[13]

It is clear that the land problem was serious for around the same time Miss Delaney, who was also a missionary at the same station, sent this letter to Dr. Jordan on the subject:

My Dear Brother,
We are having some trouble with reference to our land, but if it is lost, I truly hope you will make an effort to save the buildings. It would be too bad after all the years of toil, suffering, and sacrifice, to have the work destroyed at this point. Mr. Cheek has been to the government office trying to get the matter straightened out, but as yet has not succeeded.

Yours in his service,
E. B. Delaney[14]

In time it was realized that the question of legal ownership of the property occupied by this mission was not settled. It was not until 1897 that this problem was finally resolved.

Early Achievements of Dr. Jordan

In the five year period from the time of Dr. Jordan's election as corresponding secretary including 1901, a number of developments in foreign mission work occurred. At the 1901 session of the National Baptist Convention, U.S.A., Inc., President E. C. Morris declared that, "Each year's experience in mission work has added to the zeal and efficiency of the officers and members of the Foreign Mission Board, and the Convention may justly congratulate itself on having such an aggressive and wide awake set of brethren to conduct the work on the foreign field...To me, the outlook is very hopeful and promises an abundant harvest."[15] "The wonderful advancement" of which Dr. Morris spoke included the sending out of several missionaries of the Foreign Mission Board. Among these were the Reverend Majola Agbegi to Nigeria; E. B. Koti, the Reverend and Mrs. G. F. A. Johns, the Reverend George Thomas, the Reverend R. A. Jackson, and the Reverend J. I. Buchanan, all to South Africa; the Reverends John Chilembwe, L. N. Cheek and Miss Emma B. Delaney to East Central Africa; and the Reverend H. N. Bouey and Reverend and Mrs. R. L. Stewart to Liberia (where Stewart unfortunately came to an untimely death not long after he began service).

Reverend H. N. Bouey

One of the serious problems with which the missionaries had to deal was that of children being sold into slavery by parents who were unable to care for them. It was believed that Reverend Stewart was killed by someone opposed to his efforts to secure some slave children for the purpose of educating them. He left a wife and two children.

Writing to Secretary Jordan on March 2, 1901, Mrs. Stewart tells of her husband's death in words that express the anguish of a young widow and mother, left fearful and alone on the strange and sometimes hostile shores of Africa:

Dear Brother Jordan:

This comes bearing the sad intelligence of the death of my dear husband and your brother, R. L. Stewart. He left here in August in pursuit of children for his school, but had to return after four months because of my illness from an attack of paralysis. He remained only eight days and on Christmas day went again to bring the boys he had secured, but alas, he fell sick, so the natives say, but of what cause I am unable to say. My poor husband breathed his last far, far, in the darkest part of Africa, and was buried by the native custom. He had been dead nine days when the sad news reached me. Oh, how painful to me to be deprived of health and strength and my husband.

His little boy Charlie, in London, has just sent a letter stating his needs. Brother Stewart is no more, his body and all he had is in the interior. Do see if the Christians will help us and for the love of Jesus send Charlie to me.

I am penniless, two children here, and what must I do. Read Charlie's letter which I enclose and ask the Christians and friends and see what they will do. Poor little Richie, an orphan, what will the friends do, for her father spent his life for the work and left her and little Charlie orphans. Pray for me, I am sick, and write soon concerning the children.

Yours bereft,
(Mrs.) A. L. Stewart

Secretary Jordan commented that Reverend Stewart's "example of faithfulness unto death will stimulate us to the extent that we will redouble our efforts. All the stories of murdered missionaries only lead more men to consecrate their lives to the winning of Africa to her rightful King."[16]

The Reverend Mr. Stewart's death, as well as the difficulties we have indicated other missionaries encountered, are indications of what the men and women who answered the Macedonian Call in Africa were prepared to face because of the depth of their commitment and consecration.

Reverend R. L. Stewart

The foreign mission work of the Convention continued to prosper under the leadership of Secretary Jordan. In 1904, he reported seven principal mission stations in Africa sponsored by the Convention. The progress of the work was such that in his annual address in 1904, President E. C. Morris stated: "The foreign mission work occupies the first place among Negro Baptists on the principle 'freely ye have received, freely give.' " Later he remarked that, "the foreign mission spirit has never had such a hold on the Baptists of the country as at present. The handsome amounts coming in from almost every state and territory in the Union indicate that there is a great missionary wave sweeping over the country.[17] By this time, Black Baptists had been invited to participate in missionary councils and to be representatives at national and international missionary conferences.

After having been in office seven years, Dr. Jordan heeded the insistent call of South African Christians to pay an official visit to them and to assist in improving the organization of the work and to give it character and standing before authorities in that country.[18]

The main purpose of his visit to South Africa was to examine a situation existing between the European Baptists and the native Baptist churches. He found no dealings between these two groups. The white Baptists had begun work in South Africa as early as 1820, whereas the Black Baptists did not begin work there until 1897.

The white Baptists were disturbed by some of the practices and certain irregularities carried on by their Black brethren. These practices included men entering the ministry without being ordained and deacons doing the work of ministers such as baptizing and administering the Lord's Supper. In reaction to such practices, the white Baptists passed resolutions disassociating themselves from the work carried on by missionaries of the native Baptist conventions sponsored by the Foreign Mission Board.[19]

Dr. Jordan was able to correct these irregularities which were being practiced in spite of instructions given by the Foreign Mission Board. In his report, he stated that, "In every direction I went, I began overcoming the irregularities, knowing no set of Baptists in all the world are greater sticklers for Bible Baptist principles than the Colored Baptists of America. Had to go eighty miles over land to reach the community where deacons had decided they did not need any pastors. Enroute, I ordained three pastors who had not been properly set apart."

As a result of Dr. Jordan's visit, the following agreement was reached:

> That there may be proper denominational fellowship and cooperation among Baptists of the S. A. Baptist Union, composed of Europeans with some native followers, and Baptists of the South African Baptist

51

Association, composed of colored Baptists, and the Foreign Mission Board of the National Baptist Convention, we, the representatives of these bodies, do submit for their consideration, the following:

1. That we are all anxious to see the truth — Bible regeneration, "One Lord, one faith and one baptism," taught among the natives.

2. All persons going from the churches of one organization to those of the other must take letters which will be duly accredited.

3. That all the territory possible must be covered and more of the vast army of the lost will be reached in this country, both organizations will not attempt to work where one can meet the needs in a given locality.

4. That we may have proper leaders for the people, we will encourage those feeling called of God to preach the Gospel, to attend school until they attain to the 6th standard before ordination.

5. One in hope, one in doctrine, we will do what we can under God to aid each other in every effort to lift up the millions who now plod on in darkness more dense than night.[20]

Dr. Jordan's visit to Africa in 1904 was hailed as a great success. President Morris stated that Dr. Jordan went out with very little material resources and came back "with such tidings as cannot fail to move every loyal Baptist to action in support of the work begun by Brother Jackson ten years ago in South Africa."

Certainly Secretary Jordan's trip to the mission field created a new interest in the work of the Foreign Mission Board. In his report to the Convention in 1904, he pointed out that the Convention year had been one of great rejoicing in the several fields. An increasing number of baptisms had been recorded and a deepening of the Christian faith had been noted. In fact, according to Dr. Jordan, "All that has been done is due to larger faith, more earnest wrestling in prayer and larger giving by members of our churches at home — the results of intelligent information scattered by tracts, personal appeal, and the aid of the denominational press. More and more we are learning that we *are* our brother's keepers."

Through the years, the Women's Convention Auxiliary of the National Baptist Convention worked cooperatively with the parent body in the support of missions. Secretary Jordan, following his inspection of Africa, wrote to the secretary of the Women's Convention, Miss Nannie Burroughs, conveying a special request from the officials at the Academy founded by the National Baptist Convention at Queenstown, South Africa, "that the Baptist women of the country contribute $800 for a female dormitory." Dr. Jordan added:

> There is but one way by which we can hold our own in South Africa and that is by erecting a denominational school, sending five or six of our best men to do missionary and educational work and by laying the foundation for a great industrial training school. The women of South Africa are looking to your organization to come to their rescue.[21]

In time, as we shall see, the Women's Auxiliary made significant contributions to the work of the Foreign Mission Board, the latest being the financing of the construction of a hospital named in honor of Mrs. S. W. Layton who, for many years, was national president of the Auxiliary.

Move of Headquarters

Doubtless because of the central location it afforded, in 1897 Dr. Jordan persuaded the Board to move the headquarters of the Foreign Mission Board from Richmond, Virginia to Louisville, Kentucky. This move was the source of dissatisfaction on the part of some of the brethren in the Convention.

Particularly displeased were some pastors in Virginia, North and South Carolina, the District of Columbia, and Maryland. So unhappy were these men with this move that they threatened to discontinue their support of foreign missions. Nevertheless, the headquarters remained in Louisville for fifteen years. In 1915, the headquarters was moved from Louisville to Philadelphia, Pennsylvania, where it has remained ever since.[22]

The Formation of the Lott Carey
Foreign Mission Convention

In the meantime, another controversy was brewing which came to a head in 1898. Up until that time in its history, the Black Baptist churches had been using Sunday school and other religious educational materials published by the Northern Baptist Convention. Some of the agents for marketing this literature were clergy of the National Baptist Convention. There were, however, some of the brethren who felt strongly that the National Baptist Convention was capable of and morally obligated to prepare its own religious educational materials. It was a matter of racial pride that prompted this point of view. Perhaps the most eloquent expression of this attitude was made by the Reverend Harvey Johnson, the leading Baptist minister in Baltimore, Maryland. Dr. Johnson, at that time, was pastor of the Union Baptist Church in Baltimore and a staunch advocate of Black independence and the progress of Black Americans. At the convention in 1897, he had urged the Black Baptists to establish their own institutions in order to better achieve the kind of experience and enjoy the positions that would result in the development of leaders. It was his feeling that in any cooperative relationship with white religious organizations, Blacks were certain to experience adverse discrimination.[23]

In 1898, the Reverend E. K. Love of Georgia recommended to the Convention that it create its own publishing house and produce its own literature. This recommendation threatened the financial benefits which those brethren who were agents of the American Baptist Publications Society of the Northern Baptist

Convention were receiving. The National Baptist Convention, however, voted overwhelmingly to adopt Dr. Love's recommendation. Following this, the men whose finances were adversely affected by the move were instrumental in forming the Lott Carey Baptist Foreign Mission Convention which has continued since that time to carry on an active missionary enterprise.[24]

Establishment of the Suehn Mission

After spending seven years on furlough during which she raised a considerable amount of money for foreign missions, Miss Emma B. Delaney returned to Africa in 1912 under the auspices of the Foreign Mission Board. Upon reaching Monrovia, she traveled up the St. Paul River and stepped ashore at Arthington where a man named Saul Hall gave her 325 acres of land near the town of Suehn for the purpose of establishing a mission station. The acreage which was given was the site where the last battle between the Americo-Liberians and the natives had been fought. This battle was won by the Americo-Liberians, thus the site had historical significance. Miss Delaney established a mission and named it after the nearby town. She labored there for eight years with distinction before returning to the United States and to her native home in Fernandina, Florida.[25] This mission, as will be seen later, developed into one of the most important missionary outposts sponsored by the Foreign Mission Board.

Formation of the National Baptist Convention of America, Unincorporated

One of the most important developments in the history of the National Baptist Convention which was to affect the future of the Black Baptists in America for years to come, was the controversy which resulted in a division or split of the organization. This unfortunate incident had its beginning in September 1896 when the National Baptist Convention, in its annual session in St. Louis, Missouri, approved a resolution to issue a series of Sunday school literature and elected a publishing committee. The Reverend R.

H. Boyd was made corresponding secretary and was charged with the responsibility of carrying out the mandate to organize and implement the publishing enterprise in the name of the National Baptist Convention. The publishing committee adopted as their name the National Baptist Publishing Board of the National Baptist Convention. As reported in the minutes of the Convention in 1916, the activities of the Board were set forth:

> In pursuance of the order, R. H. Boyd came to Nashville, Tennessee, in the early part of November 1896 and proceeded to make arrangements to carry out the Convention's plans. There was no question raised as to the authority of the National Baptist Convention. Boyd acknowledged the authority of the Convention, went to work, and with the aid of this Committee and other prominent Baptist leaders throughout the country, succeeded in putting on foot plans which afterwards developed into a mammoth publishing concern...The Negro Baptists believed all the time that they were building and supporting an institution owned and controlled by them through their organized bodies, namely, the Publishing Board and the National Baptist Convention. At the convention in Chicago in 1915, Boyd flatly refused to report the affairs of his board...Notwithstanding, he was asked to do so. Of the seven boards belonging to the Convention, the Publishing Board alone refused to make its report.[26]

Prior to 1915, E. C. Morris, President of the Convention, had praised R. H. Boyd a number of times for the way in which he was carrying forward the business of publications at the Chicago Convention. However the Boyd committee based their refusal to make a report on the ground that they were separate and distinct from the National Baptist Convention. Indeed, they had taken the step to be chartered under the laws of the State of Tennessee. Dr. Boyd and his group was able to get the parent body to ratify this action in spite of protest on the part of some of the members.

Later, however, as already indicated, the Convention was to regret this action. The Reverend R. H. Boyd and his group attempted to take over the Convention in 1915 and took out an injunction against President Morris and other officers to achieve this end. The injunction, however, was not upheld and, as a result, the attempt of the Boyd group to take over the Convention failed. Later this group established a new organization known as the National Baptist Convention of America, Unincorporated. The parent body took the name National Baptist Convention, U.S.A., Inc. This unfortunate division meant that a new set of Convention boards was established by the dissenting group and the unity of the organization formed in 1895 was no more.

Dr. L. G. Jordan continued as corresponding secretary of the parent body. During the remaining six years of his tenure, a number of missionaries were sent out, and he continued to inspire increased support for foreign missions on the part of churches across the country.

One of the significant movements in 1916 was the erection of a monument to honor George Lisle. This was done "in gratitude to our Father for the life and work of that old Baptist hero, George Lisle, and as a mark of our deep sense of appreciation as sons so worthy a Baptist father, the Foreign Mission Board of the National Baptist Convention have erected and unveiled and dedicated a monument to his memory at Savannah, Georgia, September 9, 1916..."[27] This monument was conceived by Dr. L. G. Jordan. He and a Dr. Parrish of Kentucky went as commissioners to Jamaica in 1915 at the request of Baptist ministers there who traced their organization back to George Lisle. The monument was made in Virginia where Lisle was born and erected in Georgia from whence he sailed as a missionary to Jamaica in 1781.[28]

Dr. Jordan had a high regard for the history of Blacks in Africa. In 1916, as part of his annual report to the Convention, he stated that the early church in Africa had provided intellectual leadership of great strength. He wrote:

Of the twenty greatest names in the history of Christianity in the first four centuries after the Apostles, more

57

than one-half belonged to African origin. One of the greatest scholars and one of the brilliant intellects of the ancient world, Clement, the missionary, and head of the School of Alexandria; Tertullina, "the first great mind in Western Christendom;" Augustine, Cyprian and many others were among the foremost leaders of early Christianity for 250 years.[29]

In this same report, Dr. Jordan stated that during the history of the Foreign Mission Board, a total of fifty-six persons had been sent to foreign fields. In addition, more than 36,000 persons had been baptized and $307,000 had been raised for foreign missions.[30]

Moreover, a number of African youths were brought to this country to get an education. He, himself, brought back seven young Africans when he returned from his first trip there in 1904. These young people were sent to different schools including Morehouse College, Selma University, and West Virginia State College. In addition, a number of students were brought to this country from the West Indies, including Jamaica and Haiti. Some others were brought from South America to study in this country.

The Saga of the Reverend John Chilembwe

Earlier in this study we have made note of the contributions of the Reverend John Chilembwe who carried forward a significant ministry at the Providence Industrial Mission. One of the best accounts of the life and martyrdom of John Chilembwe was given in writing to the Reverend William M. Lamb of the Foreign Mission Board by the Reverend Wiley Pilgrim Chigamba in Blantyre, Malawi, during his visit there in February 1973. The Reverend Chigamba was born in 1890 in Nyasaland (now Malawi). He attended the Missionary School of the Church of Scotland from 1900-1909 and completed his primary education (standard six) in what was then Nyasaland. He taught for a while before going to the Providence Industrial Mission where he was closely associated with Pastor John Chilembwe until Chilembwe was assassinated in 1915. His description of the rebellion which resulted in the assassination and the closing of the Providence Industrial Mission is summarized as follows:

> As a result of slavery and color discrimination that existed at the time between Blacks and whites, the late Pastor John Chilembwe wrote a letter to Boma (government) requesting that the government look into the matter and bring the differences that existed between the Africans and the Europeans to a stop so that a mutual understanding between them could prevail.[31]

According to Reverend Chigamba, Chilembwe first complained to the government about African soldiers who were seriously wounded during the war in Somalia. There was an agreement between the African and European soldiers and the government that every soldier would be compensated for anything that might happen to him during the war. It was also agreed that the families or closest relatives of those who died in action would be compensated by being given farms to make it possible for them to survive. Reverend Chilembwe found that the government was compensating white soldiers according to this agreement, but was ignoring their obligation to Black soldiers and their relatives. "The African soldier was given very little money and relatives of those who died were given nearly nothing." Because of the attitudes of the British government and their refusal to give assistance to the Africans, as well as the very hard labor to which Africans were subjected, Chilembwe decided to cause an uprising against the government.

The government troops, better equipped, better armed, and better trained for warfare, prevailed. Before the conflict was over, the British government decided to take decisive action against the Providence Industrial Mission and also to kill Chilembwe. Fortunately the mission had been evacuated by the time the British troops arrived. The soldiers set fire to all the houses and destroyed the main center of worship at the mission. Eventually the troops found Chilembwe and he was killed along with one of his lieutenants, David Kaduya.

During his court trial, Benjamin Kaduya was asked why John Chilembwe desired to fight the whites. He answered, "Pastor Chilembwe did not desire to fight the whites, no. His wish was that there should be mutual understanding between the Africans and the Europeans and that the government policy on race and color discrimination be abolished in our country. Pastor John Chilembwe would have been more pleased to have the whites in this country to teach better methods of working to the land-owners of the country, to preach to the people about God, and to build churches and schools for the progress and development of the Africans."

But Pastor John Chilembwe discovered that the whites in his country brought divisionism, chains, and slavery, and robbed the Africans of their fertile land and gave them barren land to live on instead.

Pastor Chigamba was fortunate to survive an extended jail term imposed as a result of the uprising. He returned to the mission from where he was later sent to Southern Rhodesia to help establish new branches there.

This abbreviated account of Pastor Chigamba's narrative strikingly reveals the profound commitment of the Reverend John Chilembwe to the development of the people of his native land. His spirit lives on in the lives and activities, the hopes and dreams, of those who are carrying forward the ministry he began early in this century.[32]

Dr. L. G. Jordan Resigns

Because of ill health, Dr. Jordan resigned as corresponding secretary in September 1921. At that time he was named Corresponding Secretary emeritus. He had put the work of the Foreign Mission Board on a solid foundation. Moreover, he had been the inspiration for a number of young men and women to commit themselves to foreign mission work and had set a high standard of dedication and efficiency as well as total commitment to the cause of building bridges of faith across the seas.

In this chapter we have seen the development of the Foreign Mission Board under the leadership of one of the giants of the denomination. Certainly the Reverend Lewis Garnett Jordan put the work of foreign missions on a solid footing. He selected well qualified men and women who were prepared to make personal sacrifices to spread the good news of Christianity to people in great need of its saving grace. Recognizing the power of the printed word, he founded the *Mission Herald* and used it as an effective voice to herald the obligations and opportunities for work on the mission field.

The mission stations established during his tenure carried forward pioneering and creative work. Lost souls were saved. The quality of life of hundreds of people was enhanced. Instruction in better health habits and in effective methods of tilling the soil, as well as in the basic foundations of learning, produced inspiring results.

Dr. Jordan's book, *Up the Ladder in Foreign Missions,* opened the eyes of many to what the missionary enterprise was all about. Moreover, a number of promising African youth were brought to this country, received an education, and returned to Africa to carry forward an effective Christian ministry among their people.

In spite of decisions from the parent body resulting in the rival organizations of the Lott Carey Baptist Foreign Mission Convention and the National Baptist Convention of America, Unincorporated, the Foreign Mission Board of the National Baptist Convention, U.S.A., Inc., continued to grow and expand its impact on the continent of Africa. The success of the work of the Foreign Mission Board during the next twenty years would owe much to what had been accomplished during the previous twenty-five years of expansion.

President E. C. Morris Passes

On September 5th, 1922, the Reverend Elias Camp Morris, D.D., was called from labor to reward. Dr. Morris had served for twenty-eight years as the president of the National Baptist

Convention. His passing marked the end of an era of beginnings, for it was under his stalwart leadership that the Convention's permanent foundations were built by his incredible energy and steady hand.

Reverend E. C. Morris, D.D.

He was a principle figure in the establishment and early growth of the Foreign Mission Convention in the 1880's. In Arkansas, he established that state's first denominational newspaper, the *Arkansas Times.* In addition, he founded the Arkansas Baptist College, supported and controlled by the Negro Baptists of the state.

When chosen to lead the National Baptist Convention, it was his genius that enabled the Convention to weather the storms which arose for a group newly freed from the bonds of slavery.

Though born in Georgia in 1855, he was educated in the public schools of Alabama and at Roger Williams University in Tennessee. His funeral services were conducted at the Centennial Baptist Church of Helena, Arkansas. The mayor of the city issued a proclamation calling for all activities to cease for a half hour and the flags to be lowered to half-mast as a tribute to the esteem in which he was held by his fellow citizens.[33]

Notes

1. *Mission Herald,* (January-February 1936) p. 8.
2. Loc. Cit.
3. *The Afro-American Mission Herald,* March 1896, p.1.
4. NBC *Minutes,* 1901, pp. 40-41.
5. NBC *Minutes,* 1901, pp. 36-37.
6. NBC *Minutes,* 1901, p. 36.
7. NBC *Minutes,* 1901, pp. 39-40.
8. Nashville: Baptist Sunday School Publishing Board, 1901, 269 pp.
9. NBC *Minutes,* 1901, p. 42.
10. Ibid., pp. 42-43.
11. Biographical sketch of Miss Emma B. Delaney. Facts from unpublished records and oral history. Typescript 1978; authors unknown. Cf. The George McKinney Papers, Florida Memorial College; *Mission Herald,* (March-April 1974) p. 16, and, Ashley, Willie Mae, *Far From Home,* Florida 1987.
12. NBC *Minutes,* 1904, p. 360.
13. Ibid., p. 37.
14. Ibid.
15. NBC *Minutes,* 1901, p. 29.
16. NBC *Minutes,* 1901, p. 44.
17. NBC *Minutes,* 1904, p. 185.
18. Ibid.
19. Ibid.
20. Ibid.
21. Ibid.
22. *Mission Herald,* (November-December 1961) p. 4; *Mission Herald,* (November-December 1935) p. 3.
23. Leroy Fitts, *Lott Carey: First Missionary to Africa,* Judson Press, 1978, pp. 85-89.
24. *Mission Herald,* (November-December 1961) p. 4.
25. *Mission Herald,* (March-April 1956) p. 16.
26. NBC *Minutes,* 1916, p. 93.
27. Ibid., p. 151.
28. Ibid., p. 252.
29. Ibid., pp. 131-132.
30. Loc. Cit.
31. *Mission Herald,* (May-June 1974) p. 4.
32. Ibid., p. 4.
33. *Mission Herald,* (September 1922) p. 6.

CHAPTER FOUR
CONSOLIDATING THE GAINS, 1921-1941
The Tenures of Dr. James E. East and Dr. J. H. Jackson

With the resignation of Dr. L. G. Jordan as Corresponding Secretary of the Foreign Mission Board, the opportunity for carrying forward the work of the Board to new levels of achievement presented itself. During his twenty-five years of leadership, Dr. Jordan had dedicated himself wholeheartedly to achieving the objectives of the foreign mission thrust of the Convention. By traveling widely he had personally inspired countless numbers of individuals, churches, associations and conventions to recognize the responsibility of Christians to carry the message of the Gospel to the uninformed masses across the sea. In addition, he had used the columns of the *Mission Herald* to inform the thousands he could not reach in person and to galvanize their support. As we have seen, it is clear that his pen was a mighty instrument for raising the consciousness of the readers of the *Mission Herald* with respect to the significance of the missionary enterprise. While much progress was made during his administration, there were goals still to be achieved for foreign missions.

The standard of leadership in the missionary enterprise established by Dr. Jordan was one not easily matched under ordinary circumstances. Fortunately, however, at the time of his resignation a man of excellent preparation, broad experience and unexcelled dedication to missions was on the scene and available. The Foreign Mission Board saw in the Reverend James E. East, age forty, those qualities desirable for carrying forward the work which had such notable beginnings.

One of Dr. East's outstanding qualifications was that he had spent eleven years as a missionary in South Africa under the auspices of the Foreign Mission Board of the National Baptist Convention, U.S.A., Inc. He had been commissioned by Dr. L. G. Jordan, who had followed his career with much satisfaction. Dr. Jordan once remarked that he had "engineered" the Rev. Mr. East's election as corresponding secretary of the Foreign Mission Board. On the other hand, one member of the Board, the Rev. W. F. Graham, wrote that Reverend Mr. East did not at first come willingly to the office. "We begged him," says Reverend Mr. Graham, "and for a while he held out because of his desire to complete his work in South Africa. It was only when he saw that American missionaries would have a hard time landing in Africa that he decided to become corresponding secretary."[1]

Reverend Mr. East came from humble beginnings. He was born near Huntsville, Alabama, on January 27, 1881, sixteen years after the close of the Civil War. He was the third child and only son of James and Georgianna East who were farm people. When he was three years old his mother died. He began routine work on the farm as soon as he was old enough. As was common in those days, his early schooling was limited; only three months per year were normally allotted for public education of Blacks in his community, and he could not always take advantage of even these.

The young East had dreams of a much larger life than that of his early years. At the age of seventeen he left Alabama and moved to Tennessee to live in the home of his married sister. The jobs at which he labored were varied and included working in a brickyard and later driving a horse and wagon.

During this period he joined the church. Having heard some moving and challenging accounts of Africa, he vowed to become a missionary to that continent. To prepare himself for this, he attended the Missionary Training School in Nyack, New York. He enrolled at the Virginia Seminary and College in Lynchburg, Virginia. There he and a fellow student, Miss Lucinda Thomas,

Reverend James E. East   *Mrs. James E. East*

fell in love and married in 1904. He was licensed to preach that year, and three years later he was ordained.

In 1909 Reverend and Mrs. East sailed for South Africa as missionaries for the Foreign Mission Board of the National Baptist Convention. They went to the mission station founded by the Reverend J. I. Buchanan at Middledrift. Following the death of Reverend and Mrs. Buchanan, the work at Middledrift had gone unmonitored and the mission was not functioning at all. For eleven years Reverend and Mrs. East labored hard and diligently. They completely changed what was a totally inactive mission into one that was outstanding. In commenting on this, the Reverend Mr. W. F. Graham wrote:

> While in Africa he did a constructive missionary work — spiritual, teaching, building houses, farming and running blacksmith and carpenter shops. So high did he stand in Africa with the English government, his services were sought as an agricultural official demonstrator, and today an open door is ready for him at any time not only among the natives but among the whites as well.

67

During World War I, the English government made most rigid prohibition laws against American missionaries, especially Negroes entering her colonies in South Africa. Dr. East could go back but he could not take any missionaries with him.[2]

Also, while in South Africa, Dr. East's home church in Pittsburgh, the Ebenezer Baptist Church, was so impressed with his dedication and effectiveness that they gave him a stipend of $50 a month. This amount was later raised to $150 per month along with a supply of valuable books and other materials needed for the mission station.[3]

The Easts were parents of seven children, four of whom were born in Africa. Reverend East and his family were on furlough when he was elected corresponding secretary of the Foreign Mission Board.

One of Reverend East's first objectives was to strengthen the financial base of the Foreign Mission Board. When he took office he made a careful study of the financial procedures of the Board and endeavored to systematize the methods of making contributions to foreign missions. Finding only eight churches which gave monthly contributions to foreign missions, he made a strong appeal to all the churches to send contributions on a regular basis since the expenses and salaries of the missionaries had to be paid monthly. He started publishing in the *Mission Herald* a list of "Missionary Regulars," churches which gave all the way from $1.00 to $100.00 per month.[4]

These results underscore once again the effectiveness of the *Mission Herald* in financially undergirding the work of the Foreign Mission Board. In December 1924, Dr. East wrote that, "To the *Mission Herald* must be given credit for the achievements of our Board during the present administration. Exclusive of Pittsburgh, contributions have jumped from $2,000 in Pennsylvania, to more than $12,000 per year." The *Mission Herald* had been primarily responsible for the increase in contributions to foreign missions within three years from "less than $30,000 to more than $80,000 per year." In connection with this development was the increase in the circulation of that publication during 1924 to twice that of the previous year. This increase corresponded with the doubling of contributions to the Foreign Mission Board "from $43,000 the year before last (1923) to $85,000 the last year."[5]

As the number of churches contributing to foreign missions increased, so did the average amount given by certain churches. For example, in 1921 there were only two churches that gave more than $1,000 in a year to foreign missions. Five years later there were five such churches distributed as follows: Union Baptist Church of Philadelphia, $2,000; Metropolitan Baptist Church of New York, $1,400; Pilgrim Baptist Church of Chicago, $1,200 and the Ebenezer Baptist Church of Pittsburgh, $1,000 a year.[6] In addition, six churches were reported as giving yearly between $400 and $1,000, fifteen between $300 and $500, and fifty-six over $100! On a *per capita* basis, many contributions of the smaller churches were greater than those of the larger congregations.[7]

In addition to securing a more stable financial base, *and because of it,* four new missionaries had been sent to the British West Indies and five more had been installed or re-installed in South Africa.[8]

Much emphasis was placed upon churches sending their contributions for foreign missions directly to the Foreign Mission Board rather than to the associations or conventions. Moreover, this method of giving saved traveling expenses of an agent whose outreach and personal contact were necessarily limited. It also minimized the possible loss of funds.

One innovative fund-raising idea by a dedicated lady in a southern church was described in the *Mission Herald.* "One good woman...had saved $8.65 during the year by giving the eggs that her hens laid on Sundays for the spread of the Gospel. All of this she gave for foreign missions. A wonderful example of service!"[9]

In spite of these developments, the corresponding secretary was still concerned about the large number of pastors and churches who failed to show interest in foreign missions. Dr. East maintained that, "too large a majority of pastors and churches (demonstrate) an alarming indifference toward foreign mission work. The fact that millions are dying in heathen darkness who might be saved and whose lives might even be prolonged if they only had the Gospel, has not made an impression on the minds of these indifferent would-be Christians."[10]

Three years after he took office, the following assessment was made of the Reverend Mr. East's work:

> Since Dr. East took charge of the work in 1921, not-withstanding stumbling blocks and hindrances, the work has gone on and the people from all over the country are showing their faith by their deeds, by increased giving... We are keeping our missionaries paid up; we are improving our mission stations, and now we are getting ready in Liberia to establish a Bible, Industrial Academy, Collegiate Missionary Training Institution, that bids to create a center for Negro Baptists to operate through Liberia, and in time, all Africa.[11]

The economic, political and sociological conditions in Liberia were constant sources of interest and concern among Blacks in America and especially among members of the Foreign Mission Board. In an editorial, Dr. James East pointed out some contrasts between mission fields in the Orient and those in Africa. In Japan, India and China, for example, climatic conditions were more favorable for the maintenance of good health standards than were those in tropical Africa which make it difficult for persons from a different environment to survive there. It is shown throughout this history that in a strikingly large number of cases, American Blacks and Europeans alike did not keep their health long after residing in tropical Africa. According to Dr. East, tropical Africa was one of the most difficult parts of the world to which to become acclimated. It was hard for a foreigner to remain longer than three to five years at a time.[12]

Another contrast pertains to language problems. While India, China and Japan possessed written languages, there were no written tribal languages in the areas of missionary activity in Africa. On the other hand, there were thousands of different dialects, no written page, and thus a "confusion of tongues." There was a need to reduce the dialects to writing, a necessity for each of the tribal groups.[13]

Along with certain other organizations of Blacks in America as well as individual Black leaders, there was always concern on the part of Black Baptists for the financial well-being of Liberia. Unlike the African colonies under the aegis of some European powers where the financial health of the colony was tied in with that of each particular ruling power, Liberia did not enjoy an economic base supported by the long-stabilized governments. Because of its historical relation with the United States, however, this nation from time to time came to the aid of Liberia to help meet great needs. For example, in 1922 a loan of $5,000,000 was proposed for Liberia. An editorial in the *Mission Herald* strongly criticized the "demagoguery in the apparent attempt of House Democrats to block" that loan.[14]

Of great interest to all groups and individuals interested in Liberia was the agreement between the Liberian Government and the Firestone Rubber Company. There was fear on the part of some that this agreement would ultimately result in the end of Liberia's existence as an independent nation. On the other hand, there were those who saw in this contract a great opportunity for upgrading the economy of Liberia, including steady employment for thousands of Liberians as well as developing excellent roads and transportation facilities for commerce and regular travel. Roberts Field, a well equipped, spatially adequate airport for large planes, was built sixty miles from Monrovia, making international air travel convenient and thus facilitating the travel of missionaries as well as entrepreneurs in and out of Liberia. In commenting on this development, Dr. East said:

> One million acres of land that has been covered with dense forests almost since creation must be cleared of trees, root and branch, and in this place rubber trees will be planted. This will mean thousands of laborers

at work and millions of dollars spent in Liberia...It will also mean that this is the first time a great amount of American capital will be expended in Liberia. Heretofore Liberia's strong neighbors oppressed her and took her territory...Now a new day has dawned...New piers and roads will be built, rivers must be bridged. A great amount of machinery will be brought in. More money will be available for education.[15]

Among other things, this historic agreement, as revised in 1935, provided that the Firestone Company would pay the Liberian government "Four hundred thousand dollars ($400,000.00)...as rent in full upon the one hundred ten (110,000) acres, approximately, of land now held by it under the planting agreement and the lease dated March 1, 1935, for the 90-year period beginning October 2, 1935, and ending October 2, 2025." The further payment of the sum of two hundred and fifty thousand ($250,000.00) during the life of the agreement gave the Firestone Company the privilege of making imports and exports in general without the payment of the regular dues, taxes and import fees. In addition, the company's foreign employees would be permitted to travel in and out of the country without the payment of personal taxes. Moreover, the company was permitted to establish wire and radio communication systems. Also, the company agreed to pay the government "annually a revenue tax equivalent to one *per centum* of the value of all rubber and other commercial products of its plantations shipped from Liberia calculated on the price of such products prevailing in the New York market at the time of the arrival of each shipment of such products at its port of destination."[16]

Certainly this agreement between a major corporation and the Liberian government was destined to have a lasting effect upon the economic life of the country. In time missionaries traveling to Liberia no longer were limited to the sometimes awkward landings on the shores of Liberia.

These developments increased the interest on the part of Blacks regarding the progress of Liberia as a nation. Many Blacks associated the success of Liberia with the image and perceptions of Blacks in America. They felt that if Liberia failed, other people around the world would take that failure as an index of the inherent limitations of all Blacks in the ability to maintain a viable and effective government equal in integrity and dignity to any power in the world.

Both Dr. Jordan and Dr. East expressed this view and urged all Americans to support Liberia in whatever ways possible. These men were also greatly concerned with the ways in which Black mission boards would be judged in terms of the quality of the missionary endeavors established in Liberia. It was their conviction that the effectiveness of the missionary work in Liberia would be the determining factor in the Foreign Mission Board's plans for missions in other parts of Africa. Because Liberia was under the control of Blacks, Black mission boards were welcomed there. On the other hand, the European colonizers tended to be wary or suspicious of American Blacks in their colonies, fearing that the democratic ideals taught by Black Americans would undermine whatever complacency the natives might have. This was especially true in South Africa where regulations with respect to political and economic freedom of Blacks, as well as the social relations between the natives and whites, became increasingly stringent, especially around the turn of the century.

In general, however, Dr. East had positive feelings regarding the results of European colonization. His optimism was expressed in his 1926 report to the National Baptist Convention. There he stated:

> Since the great war, the evangelization and civilization of Africa are giving great concern to the civilized world. Africa is divided among six European nations who have followed in the very footsteps of pioneer missionaries of these respective nations and they have planted their national flag and annexed the territory. As the missionaries preach Christ and point the people to heaven, next come the governments and take the countries of these unfortunate people. But whatever may be the

attitude of these European inhabitants from these respective governments throughout Africa, the Black man is being developed, whether he be a servant or whether he be a neighbor of the white man. He is getting new ideals from his contact and throughout Africa there are signs of a great awakening of the sons of Ham.[17]

The Foreign Mission Board took a special interest in determining the nature of their mission thrust in Africa. While always emphasizing the evangelization of Africa as their primary mission, the Board, nevertheless, recognized the importance of upgrading the general economic and social well-being of those to whom they sent the Gospel message. In this connection, the Board expressed a strong feeling of need for an industrial institution in Liberia, noting that none of the other denominations doing work in that country gave much attention to industrial training. Accordingly, as Secretary East was getting ready for his first trip to Africa since taking office, he included making plans for selecting a fertile plot of land near a Liberian market and purchasing 2,000 acres of it for an industrial institution. Said Dr. East, "We want to introduce dairying and farming, two industries which are not practiced by the Liberians. It is our purpose to raise enough farm products to feed the students of the institution and supply a large quantity for the market...We have enough money to purchase the land, but funds are needed for fencing and stocking and constructing buildings."[18]

The emphasis upon combining evangelization with industrial training was a continuing concern of the Foreign Mission Board from that time forward. Besides saving the souls of the Africans, it was felt to be of great importance to upgrade their economic and physical well-being, and their living conditions as well.

Early in the tenure of Dr. East, the Foreign Mission Board set forth a catalogue of needs at home and abroad. These were summarized as follows:

1. The Need at Home
   To line up 12,000 churches to give systematically each month in every department for the spread of the

Gospel. Among the suggested ways of meeting this need were sending the *Mission Herald* to the pastor and key men of every church, to conduct the business of the Board with such efficiency as to inspire confidence and support, and to inspire more qualified young people to work for the Board.

2. Needs on the Foreign Field

To give the missionaries adequate housing and facilities for church and school for more effectively developing the native children of Liberia.

The need to relieve the people who are now beasts of burden, carrying loads on their backs for hundreds of miles, by improving transportation, etc.

The need to perpetuate our Baptist denomination to good advantage in numbers in Liberia, and to see that Baptists come into their own in the high walks of business and high government positions.

The need to educate thousands of American-Liberian children whose parents were from this country, who are now retrogressing into heathendom due to a heathen environment with no schools nor chance to rise.

The need to give an opportunity to many native children from the thousands of towns in Liberia where there is not a single *Mission Herald,* not one who knows of Jesus, no prayers made in his name, no Sunday schools, and no chance whatever of rising.[19]

Secretary East apparently felt these needs very deeply and throughout his tenure sought to meet them.

Mission Stations

As of January 1923, the Foreign Mission Board operated ten mission stations in Liberia and fourteen in South Africa. The mission stations in Liberia were:

1. Suehn Industrial Mission, forty miles from Monrovia; 325 acres

of land, three buildings, capacity for sixty students. Present workers: Mrs. E. T. Butler and Mr. Frank Goll.

2. Burroughs Industrial Mission, Mt. Carmel, Royesville, thirty miles from Monrovia; eighty acres of land, one building, about thirty boarding and thirty day students. Present workers: Miss Della E. Harris, Thomas I. Holman, Mr. and Mrs. Stevens.

3. Bible Industrial Academy, Fortsville, Grand Bassa County, seventy-five miles from Monrovia by sea, river and land; sixty miles through the country; about sixty-five students, 500 acres of land, two buildings, cattle and goats. Present workers: Miss Priscilla A. Bryant, Dr. K. M. Sissusa, Rev. and Mrs. D. R. Horton.

4. Mission of Harper, Cape Palmas, Maryland County, 250 miles from Monrovia by sea; no land, no property holdings, about forty children. Present workers: Rev. D. S. Nichols, Dr. W. J. Ezell, physician, and Mrs. Ezell, teacher.

5. Lloydsville Out-Station. The Bible Industrial Academy, fifteen miles from main station; about five acres of land, thirty day students and one building. Present worker: Miss Sarah Lloyd.

6. Hillsville Out-Station, ten miles from Suehn Industrial Mission; five acres of land, no buildings (just a bush arbor), but lumber on land for building — lumber paid for. Present worker: Reverend J. D. Conrad conducts services for the native people in their tongue.

7. South Africa Native Baptist Church, East London; ten members. The present pastor is Rev. Fred Vockerkodt.

8. Kliptown National Baptist Church, Johannesburg, was pastored for many years by Rev. William Lashiga, the founder. Present pastor: Rev. Joseph Mahlangu. The Ohio Baptists are now supporting this station.

9. Pretoria Native Baptist Church. This was once a flourishing church. A pastor is needed here.

10. Kimberly Baptist Church. Kimberly is a diamond mining center. A pastor is needed.

11. Herchel Baptist Church, founded by Rev. J. E. East, 200 miles from Middledrift. It has a membership of thirty and is without a pastor at present.

12. Cala Baptist Church has been without a pastor for twelve years. People are anxious for a shepherd.

13. Orange Free State Baptist Church. The pastor, Rev. Sondukwna, died recently. Rev. J. Mahlangu has oversight of these people. Rev. Joseph J. Lepala is also preaching there.

14. Basuto Land Baptist Church. Here we have a large congregation which was once connected with our Kliptown work at Johannesburg. Revs. Pietso and Ntla are now pastoring here.[20]

The Attitude of White Nations Toward American Blacks in Africa

In his annual report to the Convention in 1925, Secretary East reported that the European powers had held discussions on what should be done to prevent African Blacks from coming to America, securing an education and "getting ideas of freedom, and desires of freedom, and desires for equal opportunity for happiness and livelihood. Everything possible was done to discourage native Africans from coming to this country." Moreover, Secretary East pointed out that the next step was to prevent American Blacks from going to Africa, particularly representatives of religious institutions who were recognized leaders among their people. The only exception, however, was Liberia, to which Black missionaries were always welcome.

The situation in South Africa was described as particularly difficult where annoying hindrances were devised to make it hard for Blacks to enter the country. As Dr. East described it:

> After putting up large deposits and much pleading, we got them off on temporary permit. Now, however, the governments have notified their consuls representing them in this country not to vise (sic) passports, and have also notified steamship companies not to sell tickets to

77

any colored missionaries wishing to come to parts of Africa unless they produce a permit from such countries. Now when we go to get the permit, the next question that arises is, "Is there a white man at the head of the Society under which your missionaries wish to come out?" As soon as we say, "No," the permit is denied us. Of course, the reasons they give for this are that Negro missionaries are not practical, that they are agitators, and that they stir up the natives to rebellion against the respective Europeans in charge of them."[21]

In spite of such restrictions, however, the Foreign Mission Board has been able to carry forward a fruitful missionary enterprise in South Africa.

Attitudes of White Boards to Black Missionaries

It has been pointed out earlier in this study that the Southern Baptist Convention sent out a few Black missionaries to Africa shortly after the Civil War. It appears that the foreign mission boards of the various white Christian churches in America were hardly inclined to employ Black missionaries. In 1929, the late Dr. W. E. B. DuBois published in the *Crisis,* a report of a survey he made of attitudes of several white denominations towards sending out Black missionaries. He found that in 1929, "out of 158 African missionaries, the Protestant Episcopal Church had one American Negro; the Presbyterian, one out of eighty-eight; the Northern Baptist, one out of twenty; the Methodist Episcopal Church, five out of 91; the American Board, four out of ninety-seven. Of 973 other missionaries in Africa sent out by American missionary societies, there is not a single Negro!"[22]

Moreover, the Foreign Mission Board of the Southern Baptist Convention quite frankly stated: "Our policy is not to send American Negroes as missionaries." The Sudan Interior Mission wrote Dr. DuBois as follows: "Our brethren from the American Negro churches practically have to live on the same plane almost as their white brothers, and this creates a problem." The Woman's General Society of the United Presbyterian Church wrote to Dr. DuBois saying, "No action for or against the sending of Negroes to work as missionaries in Africa has been taken. I can see complications that might be unpleasant and hard to surmount."

> Dr. DuBois' comments on his survey are as follows: As a matter of fact, missionary societies of the United States started out, for the most part, with the obvious policy of sending Negroes to convert Africa. Then they found out that this involved social equality between Black and white missionaries, and their promotion and treatment as civilized beings. With few exceptions, American white Christianity could not stand this, and they constantly changed their policy. Several of them stopped sending Negroes altogether.[23]

These findings underscore the important role which the Foreign Mission Board of the National Baptist Convention, U.S.A., Inc. has played in sending the Gospel to those in great need of it in Africa. As we have already observed, many of the colonial powers had great reservations with regard to the kinds of democratic ideals which American Blacks were almost certain to inculcate among their African brothers.

In his report to the Convention in 1927, Secretary East pointed out that the number of Black missionaries working in Africa was quite small as compared with the missionaries of the various white boards. It was his feeling that:

> Africa is the neglected field. They send few missionaries there. Though they are doing little in Africa and much in other fields, yet they are doing practically all the missionary work that is done in all of Africa.

> There are about 7,000 white missionaries today on the continent of Africa, foreign born, while not fifty American born Negroes are there. Two thousand white missionaries are preaching the Gospel there, against less than three dozen American born, trained Negroes.

There are about 140 white medical missionaries (not counting nurses) against not one American born, trained Negro doctor.[24]

Dr. East said that if we wished the world to open its doors in other parts of Africa to American born Negro missionaries, it is necessary to demonstrate our ability by having well-built hospitals, schools and agricultural programs that are operated effectively.[25]

The Le Zoute Conference

In 1927, a large conference on African missions was held in Le Zoute, Belgium. To this conference missionary societies from various parts of Europe and the United States came. In addition, a number of missionaries were called from their stations to participate in this assembly. Moreover, some outstanding educators and others knowledgeable in the conditions of Africa were invited to attend as consultants. According to Dr. East, this was "one of the greatest conferences on Christian missions in Africa ever held." Following are some of the comments made by Dr. East on this significant gathering:

> The all important question of American Negroes entering the mission field in Africa had a very prominent place in this great conference. A very large committee was appointed, on which was placed several American Negroes...The attitude of some white African missionaries and of many government representatives was none too favorable to American Negroes going to Africa as missionaries. There seemed to have been a feeling that we are not practical enough in our missionary endeavors; we do not have enough practical accomplishments to our credit as a result of our past missionary endeavors in Africa. These, together with the failure of some colored missionaries who have been in Africa, and the Garvey movement seemed to have been the leading factors in the fight against Negroes entering Africa. One Belgian government official frankly said

that he thought the American Negro might advance the African too rapidly: That growth must be slow. Underlying all this was the fear that the American Negro might create within the mind of the African a love for liberty, a knowledge of his own power, a faith in his own possibilities to work out his salvation. Such a teaching is so contrary to the theory of racial inferiority and superiority that is being taught by white people in many parts of Africa. Such teaching does not inspire the natives to imitate and emulate his white brethren. Colored representatives fought to get the very best terms possible in the recommendation presented to the body for adoption. While it was not all we wanted, it went a long way in opening the doors of Africa to American Negro missionaries.[26]

From Ralph E. Diffendorfer's Report

The conference was called by the International Missionary Council, one of whose secretaries, Mr. J. H. Oldham, widely known as the author of Christianity and the Race Problem, was its chief executive..."Never has Africa had a light concentrated from so varied and represented an array of experts on its human, economic, and political, moral, intellectual and spiritual concerns."[27]

Findings of the Conference:

1. EVANGELISM — The spirit of evangelism is at the heart of all missionary work in Africa. In approaching the African mind with the Gospel message, the aim should be to conserve and develop all that is good in African life, remembering that the life of the African is essentially social and based on tribal conditions and customs. A Christian family life can only be reared on a monogamous marriage.

2. EDUCATION — The resolutions call for the creation in each territory of an Education Advisory Board, on which all the operating-parties shall be represented.

The resolutions propose a curriculum related to the total life of the community, with character development based on religion covering especially health, the building of a sound home life, an informed use of recreation, and concludes with a strong plea for a specifically religious education of the highest efficiency, including religious knowledge, ethics, practice and worship.

3. LAND AND LABOR — All lands to which the natives have prescriptive rights should be secured to the native community to afford it adequate opportunity for economic cultivation, etc.

4. HEALTH AND NATIVE WELFARE — Health education should be given in all schools including housing, food, personal hygiene, general sanitary habits and simple measures against disease.

5. AMERICAN NEGROES IN AFRICA — A special committee was appointed on this subject and after reviewing the facts as they now exist and after prolonged discussion, the conference recommended:

> (1) That the Negroes of America should be permitted by governments and encouraged by missionary societies to play an increasingly important part in the evangelization and education of Africa, and that the number of their missionaries should be increased as rapidly as qualified candidates are available.

> (2) That governments should be supported in requiring that American Negroes wishing to enter Africa for missionary purposes should go out under the auspices of responsible societies of recognized and well-established standing, and that owing to the difficult and delicate interracial situation in Africa, exceptional care should be used in the selection of men and women of character and a fine spirit of cooperation, who can meet the same tests as white missionaries.[28]

Mrs. Elizabeth Bouey was one of the missionaries in attendance at this conference and was greatly impressed by it for several reasons. She wrote of hearing many missionaries describe their stations, how every one had a nurse, a physician and an adequate supply of medical supplies, in addition to missionaries who were well prepared for their responsibilities. She remarked, "At some stations there were eighteen or more missionaries, good buildings for the work and nice homes for the missionaries to live in. Cannot we as a denomination have at least one such station?"[29]

Mrs. Bouey's appeal doubtless encouraged Dr. East, the Foreign Mission Board and other denominational leaders to redouble their efforts to provide a medical facility that would enhance the contributions which the missionaries were making in Liberia. Indeed, as early as 1924, as we shall see, Mrs. S. W. Layton, president of the Women's Auxiliary of the National Baptist Convention, U.S.A., Inc., advocated the need for modern medical facilities in that country. The need was to be fulfilled in the construction of the Carrie V. Dyer Hospital in Monrovia.

The Carrie V. Dyer Hospital

If the converts to the Christian missionary enterprise are to enjoy the full dimensions of the gospel promise of abundant life, it requires not only a spiritual rebirth but also the optimum conditions for physical well being. The salvation of souls should be accomplished along with structuring or restructuring the society so that the safety of the individual is secure. Such ideas were doubtless raised in the minds of most of the missionaries to the underdeveloped countries in Africa to which they went. Missionaries saw the need for the minimum basic conditions for healthful living: a well-balanced diet, adequate shelter, and especially those antiseptic and sanitary practices which lead to good health. In addition, missionaries saw people suffering needlessly because of certain misguided practices of medicine men and witch doctors. No sensitive person can observe various manifestations of human misery among a depressed people without wishing for some remedial measures to be applied.

Certainly, it was out of such information and reflections that the idea for a hospital on the mission field arose. The leadership of the Women's Convention of the National Baptist Convention

U.S.A. Inc. was greatly concerned over this issue and spearheaded the establishment of a hospital in Liberia. At the meeting of the National Baptist Convention in 1924, Mrs. Layton, President of the Women's Auxiliary, in talking about Africa said: "Think of its plight and our opportunity for service. There is not one hospital in all Liberia. We can do an inestimable service to future generations if we would undertake the establishment of such an institution. A well equipped hospital would not only prove a blessing in caring for the training of physicians and nurses, but could become a center for the scientific study of tropical and African diseases."[30]

Mrs. S. W. Layton Nannie H. Burroughs

A year later a recommendation by Mrs. Layton for her organization to collect funds for the erection of a hospital in Liberia was approved. The women from all over the country were called upon to do their part in making the hospital a reality. Under the leadership of Mrs. Layton and Dr. James E. East, Corresponding Secretary of the Foreign Mission Board, a "One Million Quarters" drive was initiated to be used primarily for constructing a hospital. In his report to the Convention in 1925, Dr. East stated:

We cannot overestimate the importance of a hospital in Liberia. Many of our missionaries who come home because of ill health might be relieved and their period of service prolonged if they had access to the hospital that we are trying to put up. Then it will mean much not only to our workers, but to the inhabitants of Liberia of all classes.[31]

Dr. East cited other less philanthropic, but realistic, justifications for the hospital. The projected attractive hospital building, he said, "will give us standing in Monrovia. Baptists must have something in the capital as well as the Methodists."[32]

These sentiments represent part of Dr. East's general appreciation for the work which the women of the Convention did. Some time later he said:

Too much praise cannot be given our women for their wonderful cooperation. They have given their praises, they have given their minds, they have given their lives unreservedly to the work of foreign missions. Some of the best stations we have were founded by our noble women missionaries, and the most money that is given to the cause of missions comes from women. The Women's Auxiliary Conventions in nearly every state give large donations to foreign missions unless their parent body interferes and prevents them. Too often that has been the case.[33]

All of the mission stations operated by the National Baptist Convention, U.S.A., Inc., were some distance removed from Monrovia, the only part of Liberia which most visitors to that nation saw. They, therefore, had no first-hand knowledge of what the Convention was actually doing in Liberia. The excellent mission stations at Suehn, Bendoo and other places were out of range for most visitors. An impressive hospital building rendering effective service would fill a two-fold purpose of providing much needed health care and, at the same time, a more adequate demonstration of the contributions being made by the Foreign

Mission Board of the National Baptist Convention that was visible to the routine visitor.

Choosing the Name of the Hospital

The hospital was named for one who gave her life to missionary work. Born in Michigan, Miss Carrie V. Dyer's dedication to missionary work was deeply rooted. The story is that prior to the Civil War, she and a young man friend of hers were very much concerned about slavery. They were in sympathy with the abolition of this institution and felt very keenly the evils of slavery. Each looked forward to making some contributions toward the emancipation of those who were held under such cruel, inhuman and degrading conditions.

When the Civil War erupted, this young man, whose name is not recorded, volunteered for the Union cause and went off to fight. Miss Dyer remained at home and continued her education. Unfortunately, the young man with whom she was in love was killed in battle. Miss Dyer then dedicated the rest of her life to the cause of educating the freedman. She never married.[34]

Even before the Civil War began, Miss Dyer was recommended for missionary work when her pastor in Michigan received a communication from a minister in Providence, Rhode Island, "describing an ideal teacher for a school for colored children," and requesting that he suggest such a person. Miss Dyer met the requirements and eagerly accepted the position at a school run by Lydia B. Mann, beginning her work there in 1859. After the war she taught at Roger Williams College in Nashville for a number of years under Dr. Lyman B. Tefft, president of that institution. When Dr. Tefft moved to Richmond, Virginia, to aid in the establishment of Hartshorn College for young women in 1884, she left Roger Williams to go to the new institution and remained at Hartshorn for the rest of her life. She worked under the appointment of the Woman Home Mission Society of Michigan in cooperation with the American Home Baptist Mission Society. She is said to have been a forceful speaker, fully dedicated and that "her advocacy resulted in many dollars in the missionary treasury and for individual work among the freedman."[35]

According to an account given to Dr. C. C. Adams by Mrs. Ora Brown Stokes of Richmond, Virginia, during all the years that Miss Dyer taught, she did not accept any money for a salary. Mrs. Stokes reported:

> But when death came, it was discovered that she had saved from some source the sum of $3,000, and she had made a will to the effect that the money was to be used in the aid and advancement of Negro women. Dr. Tefft was the executor of the will and the money was left in his care to be used for this purpose...Upon the suggestions of Mrs. Stokes, the funds were used to establish a hospital in Africa. This suggestion was joyfully accepted and Miss Mary A. Tefft, daughter of Dr. Tefft, added $2,000 to the $3,000 left by Miss Dyer, making a total of $5,000.[36]

The idea of the hospital finally began to be implemented in 1926 when the ground was broken on an acre of land in Monrovia to be used for a medical facility and additional accommodations to house missionaries located in Liberia as well as those persons connected with the Convention who might come to the capital for business reasons.

The Reverend E. H. Bouey, one of the most energetic missionaries on the field, was given the responsibility of choosing a suitable site for the two buildings and making all the arrangements required for their construction. Early in 1926, Secretary East reported that funds were being sent along with instructions for cement to be purchased for making cement blocks. In addition, he was asked to engage workers skilled in the handling of lumber as well as other aspects of the building trade so that work on the hospital could proceed as soon as possible. In mid-summer 1926, Reverend Mr. Bouey wrote that he had found a location which provided such natural requirements for building purposes as rocks, sand, gravel, water and hard timber.[37]

Reverend E. H. Bouey   *Mrs. E. H. Bouey*

A month later, he reported that construction would soon begin. The blueprints for the hospital and mission home had been forwarded. A cement mixer and a cement block mixer had already been sent. The land had been purchased and there was hope that the building would be under shelter within six months after the rainy season. Reverend Bouey worked diligently to see that the hospital was properly constructed using the best materials available as well as saving as much time as possible. In a letter to Secretary East dated May 1927, Reverend Bouey stated:

> Much has been done, but there is a great deal yet to be done. Unlike in America where there are great lumber yards, brick yards, etc., where materials can be gotten at a moment's notice, here we must put men in the forest to first cut down the trees, saw them into different parts needed and then wait for the parts to be seasoned before they can be put into the building, but thank God we are doing our best and the work is moving on.[38]

Reverend Bouey attributed his ability in building to a former teacher of his at Morehouse College, Professor C. H. Wardlaw, who taught manual training to high school students there. Mrs. Elizabeth Coles Bouey wrote Dr. East about her husband's activity in connection with building a hospital. She said:

> My husband is working day and night. He is first with the carpenters, then with the masons, then seeing to block making, then down at the waterside (where the plank is landed), measuring the plank, then back again to the site. Some days he will go from morning to evening without something to eat.[39]

Great hopes were held for the new hospital. "We aim to make the hospital a real hospital," wrote Dr. East. He was determined that no pains would be spared to finish it neatly, to put a two-story veranda all the way around it, and screen it in and to fill it up as well as he possibly could with the best modern equipment.

The Medical Staff of the Hospital

The Foreign Mission Board took great care in securing competent individuals to serve the hospital. Basic professional staff included a physician, a dentist and a nurse, all of whom sailed for Africa to be there in time for the opening of the hospital.

The physician chosen was Dr. Pauline Dinkins, a native of Alabama whose father was president of Selma University. Dr. Dinkins did her high school work at Selma University and her college work at Hartshorn Memorial College, Richmond, Virginia. She said that she grew up in a home where the children found inspiration for whatever they might attempt to do in later years. Her desire to be a medical missionary began when she was five years of age. Upon finishing college, she was unable, for financial reasons, to go to medical college immediately. She taught for three years at Roger Williams University in Nashville, Tennessee, and developed a love for teaching. She first entered the Meharry Medical College, but transferred to the Woman's Medical College in Philadelphia, Pennsylvania. Upon graduation from medical school, she practiced for six years in Alabama and then took charge of the Brewer Hospital in Greenwood, South

Carolina, where she did outstanding work. The Foreign Mission Board of the National Baptist Convention, U.S.A., Inc., made vigorous efforts to secure her services as a missionary in Africa. Because she had wanted to be a medical missionary to that continent since childhood, it was not too difficult for her to make that decision. In the meantime, however, she had accepted the offer of the Missionary Board of the Congregational Church to go as a medical missionary to Angolaland, West Africa. Fortunately for the Foreign Mission Board, she was able to secure a release from her commitment to work under the Congregational Board in order to take charge of the new hospital in Monrovia.[40]

The nurse chosen for the new hospital was Miss Ruth Occomy of Providence, Rhode Island, who was very dedicated to missionary work abroad. Miss Occomy stated that when she was fourteen years of age she heard an address by a missionary from Africa who described how hungry the people were for a knowledge of God. After being impressed by this address, she stated that, "I promised God in my heart that I would go to Africa." Three

Ruth Occomy

academic terms were spent at the Moody Bible Institute in Chicago. Three years were spent at the Lincoln Hospital and Training School for Nurses, New York City, "where they were kind in giving me the hospital Social Service Scholarship for Teachers College, Columbia University."

Miss Occomy first served as a visiting nurse in New York City and later with the West Virginia Department of Health. For nine months she received further training at the Bellevue School for Midwives in New York City. In a statement published in the *Mission Herald* she said, "It is my dream to see a well-equipped hospital with young women imbued with the spirit and mind of Christ, trained to relieve suffering and prevent diseases, to radiate 'abundant life' in Liberia."[41]

The Foreign Mission Board was fortunate to secure the service of Dr. A. F. I. DeWalt, a native Liberian who had finished his college and premedical studies at Howard University. Dr. DeWalt had worked his way back to Africa and begun teaching but recognized that there was not a single dentist in the whole of Liberia. Accordingly, he worked his way back to America, successfully completed work for the D.D.S. degree, practiced for a while in Philadelphia and then sailed back to Africa under the direction of the Foreign Mission Board. When he sailed, he carried with him $700 worth of dental equipment for the hospital with the understanding that additional materials would be sent to him in due course.[42]

In the meantime, Dr. Pauline Dinkins enrolled at a medical facility in London primarily to study tropical medicine. Miss Ruth Occomy sailed from New York on February 28, 1928, to join Dr. Dinkins in England so that the two of them would be traveling together and would arrive in Monrovia at the same time.

Prior to the sailing, Nurse Occomy and Mrs. S. W. Layton, president of the Women's Auxiliary who was spearheading the drive to raise money for the hospital, participated in several meetings planned for fund-raising. The two visited cities from Boston to Philadelphia raising nearly $3,000 for the new enterprise.

Dr. Pauline Dinkins

Miss Occomy and Dr. Dinkins were a highly effective and dedicated team. They endured many hardships as they carried forward the work to which they were committed. In time both became seriously ill due to the difficulty they had with the tropical environment. But in spite of this, they stayed on the job, resolutely determined to recuperate and continue ministering to the physical needs of those who came to them for help.

In a paper before the Women's Auxiliary of the National Baptist Convention in 1927, Dr. Dinkins addressed the subject, "Carrying Good Health to Africa." This paper was a masterful statement of the philosophy of medical mission as she understood it from the Christian perspective. Among other things, Dr. Dinkins observed that health is not a condition which exists by chance. She pointed out the inevitable effects of good or bad health habits upon the individual. From her point of view, carrying good health to Africa was not only a duty but "a glorious privilege." In her paper, she outlined her conception of a health plan for Africa

Old Baptist Hospital

where superstition in some areas must be overcome by the use of scientific procedures. She stated:

> To develop Africa's heart and head without developing the body in which the heart and head live would be folly indeed. If the development of a human being does not have this three-fold aspect, there is a clash of kingdoms within that individual. It means incapability with himself. The brain with the deepest convulsions and the heart with the greatest fervor must both serve in the fullest way through a strong, active body.[43]

With respect to the relationship between the physical and spiritual aspects of missions, Dr. Dinkins closed her paper with this significant statement:

> A physician is not generally supposed to be qualified to administer to the spiritual needs of his patients and

he might be quite a farce if he attempted to play a clergyman's role; but it is nevertheless true that every physician must deal with hundreds of patients in whom an abnormal physical condition is the reaction to some metaphysical pathology. Doctors' offices are filled with men and women whose physical inability manifests itself in the maximum register of the sphygmomanometer. The cause of it is all too often an insane chase for fame or money, or futile worry over a condition which will make itself right with time, or fierce anger, or a consuming ambition, or the constant nurturing of an old grudge which should have been allowed to starve, or a foolish and expensive vanity which frays one's life at the edges, or a general loss of that mental ballast which insures our spiritual equilibrium. There is a distinct physical ailment; the doctor calls it arterial hypertension, but there is no drug in the pharmacopoeia which can, by itself, effect a permanent cure. The cause is metaphysical and the therapy must be the same. Unless the physician can effect a real mental and spiritual readjustment, any attempt at relief will be ineffectual.

Thus does the physician often turn spiritual advisor, and thus does the hospital become a sanctuary for soul and body. We would have in our hospital in Liberia, a veritable house of hope — a place of healing for all the ills of man — a hospital dedicated to Africa's health.[44]

These sentiments represent a profound analytical mind combined with a deep commitment to contribute to the spiritual as well as the physical needs of those she was going to serve.

It was with much satisfaction that a cargo ship of the West African Steamship Lines sailed from Philadelphia with a large supply of goods for the new hospital. Besides the usual necessary furniture, included in the cargo was a large quantity of medicines, a dental chair and hundreds of yards of material for the new facility.[45]

Dr. DeWalt, the dentist, had already reached Monrovia and was awaiting the arrival of the hospital supplies as well as Dr. Dinkins and Nurse Occomy.

Immediately upon their arrival, the medical crew plunged into work. There was much to be done such as preparing comfortable sleeping quarters and arranging the ward rooms for optimum convenience. In time this was accomplished, and Dr. Dinkins was able to write about the remarkable impact the hospital had made upon the constituency it served. Within a year a training school for nurses was established in the hospital in which the staff took "almost bumptious pride." As described by Dr. Dinkins, this training school:

> Wrought from day to day a wonderful miracle of transformation — the metamorphosis of indifferent girl into reliable womanhood; the growth of an incipient ambition into a hope realized; the change from an embryonic probationer to the full-formed graduate nurse. The practical course ranges from bed-making to "sterile

Dr. A. F. I. DeWalt

95

nurse;" from giving a simple morning toilet to the most painstaking care of a pneumonia patient; from administering a pill to the injection of a saline solution by hypodermoclysis; from manipulation of the internal clyster pipe to the dexterous movements of the masseuse.[46]

In time the constant toil and the rigorous climate took their toll on the dedicated physician and nurse, a situation that was to be repeated more than once. Nevertheless, they insisted upon carrying out their duties in spite of their physical difficulties, until they were compelled to stop. Dr. DeWalt wrote to Dr. East the following impressive account of their situation:

> I want you to know something about the experiences of Dr. Dinkins and Miss Occomy, our nurse. In fact, I feel that all who are interested in this hospital ought to know something about the sacrifices that they are making for suffering humanity. Their sacrifices began on the day of their landing here and have continued until now. One of the most pathetic pictures that I have ever seen was the one which presented itself here last Easter. For several days, Dr. Dinkins and Miss Occomy had been suffering with fever, but it seemed to have come down upon them with all possible force on the Saturday before Easter, and Easter morning found them both prostrate upon their little camp cots in the one little temporary room of the hospital to which they had moved from the beautiful home of Dr. and Mrs. Cassall, where Rev. Bouey had secured accommodations for them. There they lay all day, one unable to pass a glass of water to the other; one scarcely able to hear what the other said. Friends came in and did what they could for them, but still there was suffering and there was sacrifice.[47]

Dr. Dinkins and Miss Occomy served the people and their Lord to whom they were committed with great distinction before they had to discontinue their missionary endeavors entirely. Certainly they sought to inculcate "abundant life" among the people while building a bridge of faith across the sea.

Writing of Nurse Occomy and Dr. Dinkins, Secretary East said:

> In these two young women, both from our best American families, both well-trained in their respective professions, we have a beautiful example of Christian service and self-denial. They leave their homes here of happiness and opportunity for the tropical regions of Africa, where they are to render service, where they will be strangers, and where their health may be endangered; but where they will render service in relieving suffering in and out of the hospital which is erected in Monrovia.[48]

Success In Spite of Difficulties

In 1929, in spite of the difficult economic conditions of the country, Dr. East reported to the National Baptist Convention that the 49th year of the work of the Foreign Mission Board had been "without question the most remarkable year of missionary endeavor ever done by colored people." It will be remembered that this was the year of the crash of the stock market in this country. In addition, there had been a remarkable number of floods and hurricanes that had caused considerable damage in many parts of the country. Yet, in spite of all this, Secretary East reported that record success had been made along many lines. Included in his assessment were the following: more paid workers had been employed; evangelistic efforts had increased; more conversions had been effected; more boarding and day schools had been established; larger numbers of teachers had been employed and a much larger number of children had been brought under the tutelage of the missionary. In addition to these gains, he reported that he had received more contributions of clothing, food stuff, equipment and literature. Moreover, additional buildings had been constructed including churches, schools and mission houses. Among the more satisfying achievements listed by Dr. East was the fact that "more people were treated and healed because of the new hospital." Dr. Dinkins reported during that year that 7,380 treatments had been given, but that if more resources were available, they could give 6,000 treatments per month.[49]

Dr. Ottawa J. Saunders

There have been many times when the hand of God has moved in an unexpected way to meet a need. This was the case when Dr. Ottawa J. Saunders was available to follow the Macedonian Call to go to Liberia and take up the work left when Dr. A. F. I. DeWalt went to his eternal reward at a relatively early age. Dr. DeWalt, the first dentist to serve at the Carrie V. Dyer Hospital, died during the month of May, 1930, of black water fever. He had rendered dedicated and efficient service during the short time he was at the hospital. The Foreign Mission Board was fortunate to have an excellent surgeon/dentist available to both help relieve the physical suffering of so many and to witness to the love of Christ for all people everywhere.

Dr. Saunders was born in Winston Salem, North Carolina, on July 12, 1896. While he was a small child, his parents moved to Bristol, Virginia, where he received his early education. His undergraduate and professional training were received at Howard University in Washington, D.C.

Dr. Saunders carried on his work with efficiency and courage from the time he and his wife reached Monrovia until their retirement from the field. Once again their experience demonstrated the extent of the sacrifices our missionaries were willing to make in Africa. In August 1930, Dr. Saunders wrote to Secretary East. Among other things, he said:

> I thank God that I am able to write once more. I have been very sick, having had two doctors and the careful attention of my dear wife and Miss Turner. I had a severe attack of dysentery and malaria and general debility. I gave up on the advice of Miss Turner, July 19th, and now at this writing, I am weak and have lost seventeen pounds. I don't intend to lose faith and hope and pray to God that I will regain my strength.[50]

Meanwhile the work at the hospital continued despite the difficulties encountered. In July 1933 another nurse, Miss Rosie L. Turner, R.N., who was in charge of the hospital, reported to Dr. East that the previous year had been quite difficult, primarily because the financial conditions of people seriously limited the amount of contributions they could give in return for the aid they received. She was grateful for the funds sent through the Foreign Mission Board which made it possible to keep the hospital doors open. The graduates of the hospital, she reported, had not been idle. All had found useful service either with the Liberian government hospital or in clinics or in private duty nursing. All of this indicated the great contributions made by this facility to the Liberian people.[51]

Accounts of Some Missionaries
The Bouey Family

The story of the Bouey family goes back to the Reverend H. N. Bouey who was sent out as early as 1879 by the South Carolina Black Baptists, and the Reverend J. J. Coles, who was sent out by the Baptist Foreign Mission Convention in 1886. Reverend H. N. Bouey labored effectively for seven years among the Gola tribe at Royesville, Liberia. Upon coming back to this country on furlough, he married and became the father of four sons. Later, under the auspices of the Foreign Mission Board of the National Baptist Convention, U.S.A., Inc., he returned to Africa with two of his sons. He worked at Bendoo for ten years. Upon his second tour of duty there, he took with him his wife and entire family. The Reverend Mr. Bouey died in Africa as did two of his sons, one of whom left two small boys. These boys were brought back to America by the then corresponding secretary L. G. Jordan. They were enrolled at Morehouse College. After graduation, one of these boys, E. H. Bouey, married Miss Elizabeth Coles in 1920. She was the daughter of the Reverend J. J. Coles, a missionary who, upon his return from service in Africa in 1893 (along with his three young babies) had been named corresponding secretary of the Foreign Mission Board. Unfortunately, he died an untimely death just three months after he was elected.[52]

The Reverend E. H. Bouey and his bride, both proud offsprings of missionaries to Africa and a happy couple, sailed for Africa in 1920 as independent missionaries. In a very real sense they were fully committed to the cause of foreign missions. As Mrs. Bouey, who was born in Africa, described it:

> What a happy day it was for us when we found ourselves during the fall of 1920 aboard the beautiful steamer "Carpathia" crossing the Atlantic on our way to that dear land, Africa, where both of us had so long felt the call to go.
>
> Both Rev. Bouey and I being of missionary families, without a doubt had had the mantles of our parents fall on us. It was not for fame; it was not because we could find nothing else to do (for both of us were engaged in school and home mission work); it was not because someone persuaded either of us, but because of our great desire to do all we could to help win the world for Christ; and believing that God had called us as His messengers to that land, we were happy and anxious to go.[53]

Between the time of the Reverend J. J. Coles' return to this country in 1893 and the arrival at Bendoo of his daughter and son-in-law, a radical change had taken place at that mission site. It had been abandoned. The place had become covered with thick growth. It was necessary to clear the land once more, to build buildings and furniture, to seek new converts and to enlist their aid in the re-establishment of the station. "Taking students at once, he took upon himself to make beds, benches, tables — in short, he himself, with the exception of a few chairs, made every piece of furniture."[54]

At Bendoo, nearly 400 souls were converted to Christ through the ministry of E. H. and Elizabeth Coles Bouey. A church was

100

organized, a new chapel built, and many of the converts were transformed into active Christian workers.

After a few years the young Boueys returned to this country. They were persuaded that the goal of completely re-establishing the Bendoo Mission could best be achieved by working under the auspices of the Foreign Mission Board of the National Baptist Convention, U.S.A., Inc. "It re-opened a door in the northern part of Liberia; a call for service."[55]

The David Tyesi Saga

In 1902 the then corresponding secretary, Reverend L. G. Jordan, visited South Africa to inspect the work there. At the request of the Reverend J. I. Buchanan, who had been carrying forward a distinctive missionary endeavor at that station, Dr. Jordan brought back from South Africa four young men to continue their studies in this country. Of these, one died in Louisville, Kentucky; another, the Reverend John Ntlahla, returned to his native land after spending four and a half years studying here. The Foreign Mission Board lost track of the third young man. The fourth, the Reverend David Tyesi, was enrolled at the Virginia Seminary and College in Lynchburg, Virginia. His expenses were paid by the Baptist Sunday School Convention of New Jersey. Tyesi spent a number of years at the seminary and later worked and traveled under the auspices of different Black mission societies, collecting funds for the stated purpose of returning home.

Tyesi tried to return to Africa during Dr. L. G. Jordan's tenure as corresponding secretary. He then attempted without success to return home under the aegis of the National Baptist Convention of America (Boyd Faction), then under the Foreign Mission Board of the Virginia Baptist State Convention, and next under the Lott Carey Foreign Mission Convention.

Upon petitioning the Foreign Mission Board again to send him back to Africa, Dr. East sympathized with him and persuaded the Board to grant his request. He was then authorized to collect funds to travel with his family back to South Africa. There were serious discrepancies, however, amounting to $400, in his financial reports. Members of the Foreign Mission Board urged that he was a nuisance and should be sent back immediately. He and his wife and small daughter sailed on May 2, 1922, charged with the responsibility of taking over the mission station at Queenstown, a station which by that time had not been operating on a regular basis. Apparently he stopped short of going to Queenstown, complaining that there was no church there and no place to live. These statements were called untrue by the Foreign Mission Board.[56] According to reports in the *Mission Herald,* the Reverend Tyesi continued to cause trouble.

It should be said that this kind of experience with a missionary was rare. For the most part, the men and women sent out by the Foreign Mission Board were quite dedicated and honest people, committed to the moral claims of the Gospel.

The Reverend Daniel S. and Flora Malekebu

Daniel S. Malekebu owed his inspiration to be an effective leader, in part, to the mission school established at Chiradzulu, Nyasaland, East Africa, the place of his birth, and especially to Miss Emma B. Delaney who, as we have seen, went there to serve as a missionary in 1902. So impressed was the young Malekebu by what the missionaries had done for him, their wisdom and dedication, that he made an early resolve to go to America, get a good education, and go back to teach and live the Good News of the Gospel to and with his own people.

Daniel Malekebu was probably born about 1890. The exact date of his birth is unknown but he adopted March 1, 1902 as his chronological birthdate. This is the date of his formal commitment to become a Christian. A commitment made much against the wishes of his parents.

Very early he said he had a "vision" to go to America to prepare for a career as a minister, teacher and physician, and to provide a hospital for the physical healing of his people. He began to implement the necessary procedures to reach his ultimate goal when Miss E. B. Delaney, who served as a missionary in Nyasaland (now Malawi) in East Central Africa in the first decade of this century, returned home. She had made an indelible impression upon Malekebu. Accordingly, when Miss Delaney left the mission to return to America he resolved to follow her. The first part of his journey took him 400 miles through jungle territory. He used trees as his sleeping quarters; to scare off wild beasts, he built fires near where he slept at night.

Upon reaching Beria on the East Coast, he persuaded a ship's captain to let him work his way to England, and in England he prevailed upon another captain to allow him to work his way to America. Through the efforts of the Reverend Dr. Adam Clayton Powell, Sr., in cooperation with Miss E. B. Delaney, he was formally admitted to this country and sent to Selma University in Alabama where he achieved an excellent record.

After his graduation from Selma, Malekebu was enrolled at the Meharry Medical College in Nashville, Tennessee. He did his medical internship at the Mudgett Hospital in Philadelphia. He also studied tropical medicine at the University of Pennsylvania. For formal religious training, he attended the Moody Bible Institute in Chicago. In the meantime, he became an ordained minister and married a very popular African young lady who was also studying in this country.

Rev. Daniel S. Malekebu   *Mrs. Flora E. H. Malekebu*

Mrs. Flora E. H. Malekebu

The life of Mrs. Flora E. H. Malekebu, the wife of Dr. Daniel Malekebu, was as equally dramatic as her husband's. Born in the Belgian Congo on December 12, 1898, as a baby she was rescued from a life among a tribe with strange customs by a white missionary, Dr. John P. Morgan, who, with his wife, nurtured and protected her as though she were their own child. When Dr. Morgan's wife died, he gave the child to a missionary alumna of Spelman College, Miss Clara H. Howard, who brought her to the United States and to Spelman College where she grew up and received an education.

The young Miss Zeto, as she was named, was a quick learner, especially in music. She completed the Domestic Science course at Spelman in 1909 and the high school curriculum in 1915 with high honors in piano. In 1916 she completed the Sunday School teacher training course at Spelman. Upon passing the civil service examination with distinction during World War I, 1917-1918, she worked for the United States Government as a Red Cross Reserve. Like her husband-to-be, for a long time she nurtured a deep desire to return to Africa to serve her people. It was, therefore, a fortunate circumstance not only for Flora Zeto and Daniel Malekebu when they met and were eventually married in Howe Chapel at Spelman College, but for the entire cause of foreign missions as the young couple returned to Africa to carry forward an outstanding Christian ministry.

The Malekebus first returned to Africa under the aegis of the Lott Carey Foreign Mission Convention. For some reason that connection did not last. Soon Dr. Malekebu applied for and received a commission to return to his home in Chiradzulu, Nyasaland, East Africa, under the auspices of the Foreign Mission Board of the National Baptist Convention, U.S.A., Inc., to take up the work at this mission which had been discontinued for twelve years (1914-1926).

Established in 1899 by the Reverend John Chilembwe, this station initially had been a success. The Reverend L. N. Cheek had been sent there to assist Reverend Chilembwe in 1901 and

104

remained there until 1907, leaving Reverend Chilembwe to carry on alone. With the outbreak of World War I in 1914, Reverend Chilembwe, having become utterly impatient with the oppressive policies of the British colonials, led an uprising against them. The rebellion was put down and Chilembwe was killed.

This uprising created a suspicion toward Black missionaries on the part of the British, and the mission station was destroyed. For twelve years the grounds were left to grow up in weeds and bushes, and there were some who said that the mission would never be allowed to reopen. Meanwhile, the members continued to worship in secret.

The first efforts made to reopen the mission were met with objections by the British. At last Dr. East was able to persuade the authorities to permit the station to be reopened. The people rejoiced, not only because they would be free once more to worship in their mission, but especially because one of their own would be in charge.[57]

Upon taking over the mission station in 1926, the Malekebus made rapid progress toward restoring its function. According to Dr. East, "the results of their endeavors for the first six months are wonderful. More than 280 have been baptized and there is a membership of nearly 700. Many of the members who have been hiding, far and near, are worshipping the Lord with great joy. Bushes that had grown up around the old church site have been cut down. Their prayers have been answered and they are worshipping their God."[58]

The Reverend Malekebu described the situation as follows:

"Through Divine guidance and wise management, the writer, who is a native of that country and a former student of the mission, who came to America for training to go back to help his people, went back to reopen the mission. There was much misunderstanding and mistrust throughout the country and it was said that the mission could never be opened again. It took faith in God and man to do it. As a result, early in 1926 the work was started: first, by showing to our European friends

105

that we were back in our home country to preach the Gospel of the Son of God, to educate and heal the souls of men. To be sure, these were dark days, but there is no night so dark but that out of it comes a ray of sunlight. We had to work on our own people as well as dispel any suspicion on the part of other people as a whole."[59]

Writing in 1943, the Reverend Malekebu maintained that the reopening of the mission was due to the power of God working through His servants. At first, they held services under a ntunba tree which he had planted approximately twenty years earlier when he was a boy at the mission. Their first task was to clear the land and eliminate snakes and other animals which had found a home on the spot. Then they began to construct buildings. He stated:

Building after building was raised. At this very moment, on this once fearful and weird place, we have eleven brick buildings. One church house that can stand in any man's country anywhere. Two school buildings: one for vernacular or beginners and one for central and station schools. In this latter building, known as "Spelman Hall," English is taught. One hospital, known as the "James East" in memory of the late secretary. It has sixteen brick beds, two wards for women, two wards for men, one medicine room, one examination and treatment room and a nurses' room. One carpenter shop, a mission home, one boys' dormitory, one dormitory for small children, and the other building for teachers.[60]

For many years the Malekebus rendered outstanding service and were among the most effective and highly honored Christian missionaries on the continent of Africa.

Miss Sarah C. Williamson

Another missionary who served long and faithfully at the Suehn Mission in Liberia was Miss Sarah C. Williamson. Miss Williamson went out in 1924 and became not only a very effective worker

106

at Suehn, but was also quite successful in inspiring support of foreign missions on the home front. On occasions when an emergency arose with regard to finances for the field, Miss Williamson would be called home to travel about the country and encourage contributions to the cause. Her efforts always yielded good results. She was responsible for raising thousands of dollars for foreign missions.

Her work at Suehn was outstanding. According to Dr. James E. East, through Miss Williamson's leadership the Suehn Mission took "the lead of all mission work carried on in Liberia. It has required much money, far more than we have been able to supply, and she comes home in the interest of the school for which she is giving her life, to raise funds to pay the debts that have already been made, and also to put up buildings and finance the school in the future. Let us pray that God will be with her."[61]

Sarah C. Williamson

Miss Williamson possessed an unusual combination of ardent dedication and practical, joyous realism. She was a joyous Christian and saw joy in every situation, no matter how difficult or

107

discouraging. After being in Liberia for three years, she returned to the United States to secure funds for the erection of buildings and school supplies. Dr. Adam Clayton Powell, Sr., invited her to speak at the Abyssinia Baptist Church of New York City where he served as pastor. Sister Williamson was happy to comply. During the course of her remarks, she told of the difficulties encountered while traveling in Liberia. Among the worshippers was a Mr. Caspar Holstein, a businessman who was so impressed that after the service he offered to give her an automobile. Sister Williamson immediately accepted though she had never driven a car in her life!

Upon returning to Africa, she spent much of her time reading the manual of the Model T Ford and, soon after landing, sought to drive it up the streets of Monrovia. This caused quite a commotion since it was the first car ever to be driven in Liberia. The natives called it "Ma's house on wheels."[62]

Miss Williamson developed a high school at the Suehn Mission which, at times, had more applicants than it was feasible for her to enroll. Suehn enjoyed an excellent reputation in Liberia and attracted the attention of visitors to that country. "All persons visiting Liberia, whether they are commissions or government officials representing some of the largest governments in the world, whether they are merchants or tourists, representatives of other churches or boards, find time to visit Suehn. Miss Williamson has great credit in Liberia. All merchants will supply the needs of Suehn, even though we do not have the money at all times."[63]

The files of the *Mission Herald* are full of extended and newsworthy letters sent by Miss Williamson. Typical of the letters she wrote is the following:

> Thanks to you for praying for us. I know you are praying. We can feel your prayers. Thanks to you for our salaries and for all the kind things you are doing to make life a little easier in this far-away land. Let us live upon our knees. I want to ask for your very special prayers and for the prayers of all the churches for a trip we are planning for Jesus in the near future. We want, if it is

God's plan, to leave Suehn — Sister and myself — about the first of the new year, for an evangelistic trip through the interior to the French boundary. Secretary Morris has promised to assist us in any way that he can. We don't want to miss a single town, and we are praying that we might shine for Jesus each step of the way. We want to cross over into the French territory and go on to visit some of the missionaries that were in school with Sister. We hope to be gone about two months, at which time the school will be having its summer vacation. Of course, Sister will have charge of the meetings and we hope together God will bless us to radiate the light and love and life of our Savior and Lord and all.[64]

After she retired from service in Africa, Miss Williamson never lost interest in the cause of foreign missions. She continued to frequently write articles and deliver addresses to inspire Baptists to contribute liberally to the work. Fortunately for history, Sister Williamson recorded her memoirs for the Oral History Department of Howard University, Moreland-Spingarn Research Center. Miss Williamson died in Washington, D.C., in 1986 at the age of eighty-six. Corresponding Secretary William J. Harvey, III, delivered the eulogy.

Mrs. Josephine Straughn

As we have seen, from time to time the Foreign Mission Board employed field agents who traveled in certain areas to create interest *in* and support *for* foreign missions. For a period of more than twenty years, Mrs. Josephine Straughn served faithfully and effectively in this capacity until her final illness and death on February 12, 1928.

Mrs. Straughn was a native of South America. She became a Christian under the tutelage of the missionaries in one of the mission stations established in South America by the Foreign Mission Board. Shortly after her conversion she emigrated to the United States and began working as a field agent for the Board. She served first under Dr. L. G. Jordan and later under Dr. James E.

East, both of whom highly praised her for the unselfish and faithful service she rendered. Her efforts resulted in the raising of thousands of dollars for foreign missions.

While she made her headquarters in Sanford, Florida, she spent most of her time traveling across the country in the interest of foreign missions, returning to Sanford only for brief periods of rest. In a statement about Mrs. Straughn by Dr. G. P. McKinney, former president of the Baptist General State Convention of Florida, he said:

> If any person ever worked in season and out of season she did. She traveled day and night in the interest of missions. She went everywhere pleading the cause of those who knew not Christ, and with marvelous results. Through her untiring efforts, Florida today stands second in rank among the whole group of states in the amount annually raised toward foreign missions through the Foreign Mission Board of the National Baptist Convention. At the 1927 session of the Convention held in Detroit, the annual report of Secretary East showed that Florida had contributed through the Foreign Mission Board represented by Mrs. Straughn, during the convention year, more than $8,000. Pennsylvania, the home state of the Board, is the only state that led Florida in contributions.[65]

In a later characterization, Dr. McKinney described Mrs. Straughn as "a foreign missionary on the home field." She regularly attended associations, state and national conventions, and from the time of her affiliation with the national body until the year of her death she never missed a session of the National Baptist Convention.

Secretary East presided at her funeral on February 14, 1928. Mrs. Sarah Williamson Coleman, returned missionary, was also in attendance. Words of condolence came from state and national leaders across the country.

Mrs. Priscilla A. Bryant Jackson

Mrs. Priscilla A. Bryant Jackson was born in Norwich, Portland, Jamaica, West Indies January 12, 1882. It was in Jamaica that she received her early education and embraced Christianity at an early age.

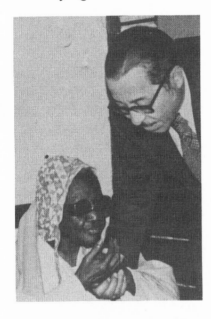

Mrs. Jackson and Secretary Harvey

A love for the Lord and a zeal for His Service compelled Mrs. Jackson to come to the United States where in 1915 she enrolled at the Lincoln Hospital School of Nursing in New York City. On graduating as a professional nurse in 1918, she continued her studies in the Union Missionary Training Institute, Brooklyn, New York. On completion of her Missionary training, Mrs. Jackson went as a Missionary to Liberia, West Africa in the year of 1920. Mrs. Jackson served under the auspices of the Foreign Mission Board of the National Baptist Convention, her first post of duty being at the Bible Industrial Mission, Northeast Fortsville, Grand Bassa County. The work there had been carried on by the late Dr. and Mrs. D. R. Horton.

111

At retirement she lived for a time with Rev. and Mrs. Horton in Monrovia, Liberia. Later, when her eyesight became impaired to near blindness, Rev. John B. Falconer, then Superintendent of Missions for the Foreign Mission Board, brought Mrs. Jackson to the Suehn Industrial Mission where she could receive all the aid and compassion so necessary in the life of a handicapped person. Before total blindness set in, Mother Jackson delighted in teaching English on an elementary level, with teen-age girls serving as her eyes.

When her blindness became total, in addition to her regular pension, the Foreign Mission Board subsidized the persons who took daily care of her. Mother Jackson had no known needs that were not met by the Foreign Mission Board up until her death. Out of gratitude for her services, the Suehn Industrial Mission underwrote expenses of over $800.00 in connection with the funeral activities.

Preparation of Missionaries

One of the continuing concerns on the part of the corresponding secretaries of the Foreign Mission Board has been the adequate preparation of missionaries for the foreign field. Having been a missionary himself, Dr. East was aware that unless a person had the proper understanding of what being a missionary in Africa entailed, he/she would be bound to make some serious mistakes. In his report to the NBC Convention in 1924, he emphasized that the Foreign Mission Board was placing much more emphasis than ever before on the type of missionary employed for the foreign field. Noting that there had been some "colossal failures" with respect to some who had gone to Africa, he stated that the Board was trying to choose "consecrated young men and women in the prime of life who know how to use their hands as well as their tongue and lips to put over the Master's program.[66] In using the term "colossal failures," Dr. East was referring to a type of person who chose to go out as a missionary primarily to spend just enough time there to collect souvenirs and get materials to use in lectures at home. Those persons were never eager to return to Africa and do serious mission work.[67]

A year later, he editorialized in the *Mission Herald* that "...we must exercise more care in selection of our missionaries. No religious cranks or fanatics. Too many people who are burning up to go to Africa are much insane and better suited for an asylum than for a mission field."[68]

This concern for well-trained missionaries resulted in Dr. East taking steps to provide an opportunity for such training at a suitable institution of higher education. In 1929, Dr. East observed that while the foreign mission boards of the predominantly white denominations provide special training for their missionaries, the Black foreign mission boards unfortunately had no such programs. He felt that since practically all of the white boards refused to send out Black missionaries, it would not be desirable to send our missionaries to white missionary schools.

Because of this, Dr. East appealed to the president of Virginia Union University, Richmond, Virginia, to establish a missionary department or a Chair of Missions. Fifty percent of the cost was to be borne by the Foreign Mission Board. After a year's search to find the right person to head this department, they were able to engage the service of Dr. Lyman B. Tefft who had served twenty years as a missionary in India. The department was scheduled to begin instruction in September 1929.[69]

One missionary on the field, Reverend Jasper C. Caston, wrote to Dr. East on this matter:

> To accomplish the work that is necessary here requires a physique that is accustomed to withstanding hardships. Not only are the rigors of the climate to be met, for the work that is to be done requires the expenditure of an excessive amount of energy, but several years of continuous work may be counted upon to tax every organ of the body. Too many persons come to the field without giving proper consideration to their physical condition. They permit their zeal to run away with their common sense. They cannot remain upon the field for sufficiently

lengthy periods with the result that the coffers of the Board are depleted without the work realizing adequate benefits for the expenditure incurred.[70]

Some Unfortunate Appointments

Among the examples of unfortunate appointments Dr. East cited was the case of one Reverend H. B. Brandon who stayed in Africa only fourteen months, but came back and presented the Foreign Mission Board with a bill for $2,869.28 for what he claimed were expenses he had incurred as well as back salary owed him. The matter was settled when Mr. Brandon had to admit his endorsement of the check sent to him for his actual expenses.

Another case was that of Mrs. Corbin who, with her husband, had gone to Africa under the aegis of the Foreign Mission Board. It soon developed that neither she nor her husband were any longer connected with the Board. Actually they were Garveyites who took advantage of the Board in securing the expense of the trip to Africa. After they formally resigned from the Board, they wrote to Dr. East requesting that he send them passage money to return home. This, of course, was not sent.

A third case was that of three missionaries whose loyalty to the Board was questioned. It was charged that these three were doing independent work for themselves, using the support of the Board, but at the same time refusing to go to the assignments given them. Their checks were not paid pending a full clarification of the matter.[71]

One further example of the undesirable type of person seeking entrance to the mission field was pointed out by Dr. East. In the *Mission Herald,* he emphasized that the Board wished to support all the missionaries well, give them adequate pay and support for the furtherance of the work. But, he reported:

> We have had too much trouble with missionaries getting support and yet building something for themselves, deeding property to themselves and not to the Board. Thus we have lost several church houses: one at Pretoria; one at Borksburg (near Johannesburg); one at

114

Kliptown and another at Queenstown, South Africa...We can have no more of this foolishness.[72]

There were several other instances of persons who served in Liberia who were guilty of using their affiliation with the Board for their own aggrandizement. Rather than perpetuate the ignominy of their deeds, they shall remain nameless.

Dr. East was a highly moral man of much sensitivity to matters of right and wrong. These incidents must have pained him greatly. Certainly, these were among the reasons for calling for adequate screening and training of those electing to go to the foreign mission field.

Death of Dr. East

After thirteen years of dedicated service, Corresponding Secretary James E. East passed away on October 2, 1934. He was fifty-three years of age. According to reports, he died "a martyr to his missionary zeal." His funeral was held on October 6, 1934, at Union Baptist Church, Philadelphia, where the Reverend J. E. Kirkland was the pastor. Eulogies were delivered by Dr. J. C. Austin, pastor of the Pilgrim Baptist Church, Chicago, and Dr. W. H. R. Powell of the Shiloh Baptist Church of Philadelphia.

During his eloquent eulogy, Dr. Austin, using as his subject, "A Zealous Servant," said:

> Just one word of four letters tells the story. "ZEAL" — and what did that zeal do? It ate him up. It swallowed all his interest. It motivated his every act. It determined his every thought. And it shook into pieces his frail body, like the blast of dynamite, which shakes the world but loses itself in the service. Zeal is a mixed passion, composed of grief and eagerness, of fervent love and desire. There is no organ, no member of the body, no faculty nor attribute which does not join into the mighty current of a man's zeal. Zeal is psychic fire, spiritual emotion which charges through the entire man, and we find ourselves determining our actions and conclusions in

the light of that something within, which is our zeal...The nature of his work in South Africa, easily rated him as one of the greatest missionaries ever sent out by the Baptist Board, and his program there has in it the basic principles upon which we can build our missionary endeavors and by which Africa can be redeemed.[73]

In his eulogy, Dr. Powell, using as his theme, "He endured as seeing Him who is invisible," (Hebrews 11:27) pointed out that this text is the most fitting epitaph to memorialize Dr. East. In his eulogy, Dr. Powell said:

Let them speak who found light in his teachings, hope in his counsel, deliverance in his message and inspiration in his example! Listen to those whose backs were clothed, whose bodies were healed and whose superstitions were shattered. These will tell you that the labors of James E. East were not in vain! Africa mourns with America the passing of this giant missionary!

Did our brother endure in vain? Go to Heaven — there will you find the answer! Look there among its thousands and somewhere you will find a one-time witch doctor, a devil man, a prisoner, a thief! Look more carefully and there you will find old men and old women to whom the Gospel came late, all but too late in life. You will see little children, black, ragged and dirty once, but now redeemed, cleansed and sanctified! Did James E. East endure in vain? Let the great Daniel answer! "They that be wise shall shine as the brightness of the firmament: and they that turn many to righteousness, as the stars forever and ever."[74]

Resolutions were received from every board and auxiliary of the Convention. The resolution of the Sunday School Publishing Board described Dr. East in these words:

He was an untiring worker, ever ready to carry even more than his part of the burden. Everybody knew him to be "East," who had a firm conviction of what he believed to be right, and he stood hard by it. He was always on the firing line, with musket aimed to defend the right. He could be depended upon in a crisis. He was small in stature, but a giant in the devotion both to his friends and to the best interests of the denomination he served.[75]

Because of his relationship with the Liberian government, it is appropriate to quote the communication to the Home Mission Board sent on behalf of Liberian President Edward J. Barclay:

By instruction of His Excellency Edwin J. Barclay, President of the Republic of Liberia, I am conveying through you to the family of the deceased, the profound sorrow and gloom which has come over the government and people of Liberia in the sudden taking away of Dr. J. E. East. His great services rendered to Liberia in his constant effort to assuage the bitterness and misrepresentation of the enemies of the Republic will never be forgotten and has put the people of the Republic under lasting gratitude to his memory. Not only has Liberia lost a constant friend, but the great Baptist denomination of which he was among the ablest of its advocates. In our opinion, it will be difficult to fill the unique place which he occupied as Secretary of the Foreign Mission Board of the National Baptist Convention.[76]

Because Dr. East spent his missionary days in South Africa, it is fitting to present here some reactions of South Africans to his death.

Buchanan Mission
November 9, 1934

To the Foreign Mission Board
Philadelphia, USA

Dear Brethren:
We the undersigned members of the Deacons' Board

117

of the Native Baptist Church at Middledrift, do hereby wish to express our most sincere and deepest sympathy on the death report of our pastor, father, and brother, Rev. J. E. East, the Board in general, his family and the whole of the brotherhood in America. It was indeed a shock to us, enough to stun us who knew the late Rev. East, his work, his love, his interest in the cause of missions. His place will be vacant for generations to come. Though he may be dead today, yet his works are active, representing James E. East in the pulpit, in the fields, as well as in the home. We will say without hesitation that Africa has lost a friend and America likewise. We are indeed sorry but what he has done we can only say, it's well done, with tears in our eyes.

We beg the Secretary of the Foreign Mission Board to pass some expressions of sympathy to his dear wife and children, since we are not certain of his home address. We are having a special day set aside to pray for the dear family of the late Rev. J. E. East, November 23, 1934. When we, the Baptist Church of Middledrift, come together for the special purpose and further ask God to soon fill the vacancy caused by death. Trust that a noble portion of spiritual disciples will come forward to fill in the most needful post.

Praying for God's guidance to prevail borne from the general church to the family of our late Rev. East and the members of the F.M.B., U.S.A.

Signed: Deacon S. F. Sonjica
         Deacon R. Mampunye
         Deacon A. Somtunzi
         Deacon S. Majola
         Deacon W. Sibini
         Deacon John Mbeia
         Deacon E. F. Hjela, Sec'y.
         F. H. Vockerodt, Pastor[77]

A summary of Dr. East's significant accomplishments was listed in the *Mission Herald* as follows:

(1) Monthly Regulars; (2) Semi-annual Mission Seminars (conventions); (3) THE MISSION HERALD enlarged in size and a Mission Study department added; (4) A fine hospital erected in Liberia, West Coast Africa; (5) Mission schools re-organized, enlarged, and a more efficient staff put over these schools; (6) Mission funds given on the home field greatly multiplied. Before the days of depression, as much as ninety or more thousand dollars contributed by Negro Baptists to foreign mission work in one year, (7) Whatever debts he found when he took over the office as secretary were paid off in little or no time. At the death of Secretary East, the affairs of the Board were left in fine shape.[78]

Dr. J. H. Jackson Elected Corresponding Secretary

During the interim between the death of Dr. East and the selection of his successor, Dr. C. C. Adams, pastor of the New Bethlehem Baptist Church in Philadelphia, served faithfully as acting corresponding secretary of the Foreign Mission Board. Dr. Adams saw clearly the magnitude and significance and necessary qualifications for the person to succeed the late Dr. East. In an editorial entitled, "Who Shall Be Our Next Corresponding Secretary?" Dr. Adams, among other things, said:

No man should allow himself to be voted into this office even by the solicitations and urgings of his friends, no matter how well they may think he is fitted for the position, unless he has first thoroughly searched his own soul and feels there is somewhat in him those qualities of integrity, devotion, intelligence, constancy and determination to follow the hard paths where his Lord leads, and in the full confidence of the fact that he is willing to pay the last drop of devotion.[79]

At a meeting of the Executive Board of the National Baptist Convention held in Louisville, Kentucky, on December 12, 1934, Dr. J. H. Jackson was elected to succeed the late Dr. East as corresponding secretary of the Foreign Mission Board. At the same time, they named former corresponding secretary Dr. L. G. Jordan as his associate. In commenting upon this, Dr. Jackson stated that, "this proved that Baptists, both old and young, are broad enough that God's kingdom cannot be left in the hands alone of aggressive youth, neither to the thorough wisdom and broad experience of our seniors, but both must work together for a common purpose and a common task."[80]

Dr. J. H. Jackson

Dr. Jackson was born in Jonestown, Mississippi. He was educated at Jackson College and at the University of Nebraska. He had held pastorates in Mississippi and in Omaha, Nebraska. At the time of his election, he was pastor of the Monumental Baptist Church in Philadelphia.

When Dr. Jackson took office he was fully aware of the tremendous responsibilities it involved. In spite of the weighty matters with which a corresponding secretary had to deal, Dr. Jordan said that there was a bright side to be considered. Among other things, he stated that it:

> ...offers to the right man a glorious opportunity to walk the path to a blessed immortality. For his is the opportunity to do evangelism on a broad and world-wide scale, by contacting and preaching the Christ in council chambers, round-table conferences to all races and nationalities of earth; and he must learn to speak an international language. In other words, the language of the human heart. For this missionary movement, even under our National Baptist Convention, cannot confine itself in its broadest aspects to Negroes, but must have its counterpart with all those nations and races with whom the destiny of the Negro is bound up in a common solution.[81]

As he faced his new task, Dr. Jackson identified what he said were two immediate and important problems before him. One of these was the necessity for a trip to Africa which, he felt, was urgent and necessary for him to get an overview of the missionary endeavors of the Board on that continent. It is clear that if he was going to be successful in conceptualizing issues, problems and possibilities, it was important for him to make this investigation. He wished to make no changes or modifications in the program until he had a clear understanding of the total situation.[82]

A second problem which he faced was that of clearing up the financial obligations of the Board. These included about $10,000 in back salaries due to the missionaries, $3,000 in floating debts of the Board and mortgages amounting to approximately $10,000 on property held by the Board. It was his feeling that the Board could not carry on the work begun by the late Dr. East until these obligations were paid. It was his hope that about 1,000 churches and auxiliaries would send a minimum of $23 each within the next several months. He felt that it was our "Christian duty" to

121

pay all of our obligations, and that this was an opportunity to reflect the spirit of Jesus. In closing his editorial, he stated that, "We bring to this task not pride, but a righteous purpose; not selfishness, but the salvation which is found in Jesus Christ; not human wisdom, but wisdom which is indeed the will of God. In the language of the great Apostle, "We can do all things through Christ who strengthens us."[83]

In an extended statement entitled "Some Reflections on Modern Missions," Corresponding Secretary J. H. Jackson outlined certain prerequisites for a successful missionary leader. It is important, he said, to have a broad, definite knowledge of the task. He/she needs to have not only a general but a specific knowledge of the people among whom one is to work. Again, one most have a knowledge of the economic status of the country, its assets, liabilities and natural resources and what can be done to raise the quality of economic life for the people he/she serves.

It is important, said Dr. Jackson, for the missionary to have the knowledge and appreciation of the social life of the people. Since many of the customs will be different from our own, one should understand the significance of the mores of the people before denigrating them. In addition, Dr. Jackson observed that we must carefully select those things which we are to oppose so that we will not become embroiled in the nonessentials. Moreover, it was his feeling that the foreign mission enterprises require careful planning on the home base, a balanced budget, a careful selection of workers on the foreign field and a greater attempt at interdenominational cooperation.[84]

Dr. L. G. Jordan's Continued Service

Dr. L. G. Jordan's interest in and work for the convention did not cease with his resignation from his position as corresponding secretary of the Foreign Mission Board. Shortly after his resignation, Convention President E. C. Morris appointed him as Corresponding Secretary of the National Baptist Convention, U.S.A., Inc. However, because some brethren thought this office would be in conflict with the corresponding secretaries of the various boards of the Convention, Dr. Jordan decided not to carry forward any work in that capacity.

In December 1923, he was selected as General Secretary of the Promotion Board, a group formed for the special purpose of directing a drive to raise $37,500 with which to purchase the site for the new publishing house. After that was done, on recommendation from Dr. L. K. Williams, who succeeded President Morris, a Department of History and Research was created and Dr. Jordan was elected Historiographer, a position which he entered upon as of January 1, 1924.[85]

In his first report as the historian, he stated that, "I have gone more than 3,000 miles and often retraced my steps to be accurate as to dates. I have spent several days in the libraries of the Southern Baptist Seminary at Louisville, Kentucky; the Baptist Historical Society at Crosier Seminary, Penn; the Foreign Mission Research Library at New York and the Survey Library Department of the Southern Baptist Convention at Nashville, Tennessee."[86]

It is clear that Dr. Jordan stood very high in the estimate of his peers. He never ceased to cooperate with his successor, Dr. East, in whatever ways he could. In his address to the Illinois State Convention held at Chicago in July 1925, Dr. L. K. Williams, President of the National Baptist Convention, said of Dr. Jordan, "There sits a man...who did the unusual thing, he gave up a position that succeeded and against the protest of his brethren. The foreign mission work under his care was succeeding and had grown to gigantic proportions...I think at some time we should secure a crown, and at some time, in the midst of a session of the National Baptist Convention, stop everything and crown Brother Jordan as one of the unselfish men of his day."

Death of Dr. Jordan

On February 25, 1939, eighteen years after he retired as corresponding secretary, Dr. Jordan ended his earthly career. As we have seen in this study, Dr. Jordan brought to the position of corresponding secretary a tremendous intellect, a profound commitment and effective administrative skills, which for twenty-six years served well the purposes of the Foreign Mission Board and the National Baptist Convention. He was well known for his gifts as a preacher of the Gospel and for the inspiration he gave to ministers of the Baptist churches all over the country. We have already noted that when he took office the foreign missions of the National Baptist Convention were at a low ebb. He accepted the great challenge before him and exhibited great imagination as well as outstanding energy in bringing the work of the Foreign Mission Board to a highly respected level.

In his effort to keep in contact with the foreign mission field, he made four trips to Africa and two trips to South America and to the British West Indies. In addition, he made six trips to Europe to meet with other experts in missions as well as those in political power for the purpose of strengthening our work overseas. Under his leadership, the prominent mission stations in the foreign fields were organized. It was under his direction that the headquarters of the Foreign Mission Board in Philadelphia was secured. Certainly it was due to him that many ministers who at first had no interest in missions became outstanding supporters of the work of the Board.[87]

Shortly before his death, he made the following request: "My desire and request is that as soon as possible after my demise, such churches as will, host a memorial service, take an offering for foreign missions and forward it to the Foreign Mission Board, Philadelphia, Pa., that the work in Africa might be strengthened and carried on."[88]

Some years earlier he had set an example for contributions by giving $500 to the Foreign Mission Board and also by taking out three insurance policies of which the Board was the beneficiary. Unfortunately, however, when he had a nervous breakdown in 1922 and reverses of other kinds, the policies lapsed and because of his age he was unable to renew them.[89]

It was his desire that the $500 given in 1926 be added to the amounts he had previously given for the establishment of the fund from which only the interest would be used for the purpose of helping "worthy young men and women who are preparing for service on the foreign fields of the Christian ministry."[90]

Some months after Dr. Jordan's death, an appeal was made to establish a fund for the purpose of constructing a building in Africa which was to bear his name. Each church missionary society and secondary school was asked to send at least $26 as a contribution toward a Jordan Memorial Fund. This amount was in keeping with the fact that Dr. Jordan had served the Convention for twenty-six years. Eventually, as we shall see, "Jordan Hall" was built at Providence Industrial Mission, Malawi, and today is still serving as a useful and fitting memorial to the work this great man accomplished.[91]

In an editorial about Dr. Jordan, Secretary Jackson stated, "Born under the shadows of slavery and handicapped by the limitations of a fettered people, the early life of this man was spent in the school of adversity. But he possessed a spirit and a mind that made him victor over circumstance, the captain of his own soul, and the master of his emerging future."[92]

Missionary Endeavors Elsewhere Than In Africa

While Africa has always been the primary target of the missionary endeavors of the Foreign Mission Board, attention has not been limited to that continent. The Macedonian Call has been answered in British Guiana and Dutch Guiana in South America, in Trinidad, Barbados, Japan and Okinawa. Secretary Jackson once pointed out that although circumstances have caused the missionary efforts of the National Baptist Convention to be restricted to Africa and peoples of African descent, this factor should not be taken by Black people as proof that Africa is the only target to which missions should be directed. "The entire Western Civilization needs the Gospel of Christ, and unless the Western World abides by the principles of this faith, it is doomed to destruction."[93]

As we have seen, it was through our missionary work in Georgetown, Demerara, British Guiana, that Mrs. Josephine

Straughn was converted some time before she emigrated to the United States. Her zeal for foreign missions was hardly ever excelled. For some reason, however, our support of missions in that part of South America was discontinued, doubtless because the needs for development and improvement were greater in Africa than in British Guiana. In any case, shortly after he took office, Dr. Jackson visited British Guiana and expressed the view that South America offered the National Baptist Convention "a wide field of labor and a great opportunity for service." He found that there was still evidence of the effective work that was done in former days, but that our efforts in that area needed to be renewed.[94]

After being cordially received by the leading citizens of Georgetown, including Dr. Nicholas, president of the Negro Improvement Association of British Guiana, and visiting the Booker T. Washington Institute of British Guiana and the Domestic Science School of Georgetown, Dr. Jackson recommended that the Foreign Mission Board pay the tuition of the students in the school for the following year. This signaled the re-establishment of the Board's work in British Guiana.[95] In 1935 the Baptist church work in British Guiana was carried forward largely by the Reverend F. I. Bunthorne, pastor, and Sister Florence Stanton. Secretary Jackson concluded, however, that, "we must, somehow, recapture the lost ground in Georgetown, Demerara, and meet the need for the type of spirit that our Baptist denomination could infuse into that territory."[96]

In Port of Spain, Trinidad, British West Indies, the Reverend Vincent Quamina served as Baptist pastor. It was the hope that at some time in the future the Foreign Mission Board could establish "a definite and creative relationship with the fine work that Brother Quamina is doing in the Port of Spain."[97]

Secretary Jackson was accompanied on his visit to South America by the Reverend J. A. Younger. Some months after that trip, the Foreign Mission Board received a communication expressing great appreciation for their visit, and a set of resolutions resolving that the churches in British Guiana continue as members of the National Baptist Convention of the United States of America, Incorporated, to use their power and resources to develop the work of the Foreign Mission Board in Surinam, Dutch Guiana; that they be loyal to and governed by the principles of the Foreign Mission Board and that they apprise the Board monthly of their work. These resolutions, dated October 5, 1936, were signed by the Reverend F. I. Bunthorne, pastor of the St. Paul Baptist Church of British Guiana, the Reverend Cecil St. Clair Taylor, pastor of the Ebenezer Baptist Church in Berbice, British Guiana and the Reverend Nellins Neuz, pastor of the Surinam Baptist Church in Dutch Guiana.[98]

Four months after he took office, Secretary Jackson reported certain early accomplishments. Among these were payments on the back salaries of missionaries, a significant reduction of the foreign mission debt (from $23,000 to $16,000), and crowded mission schools. While these were seen as "signs of hope for the future of our missionary enterprise," Secretary Jackson stipulated that the greatest hope was the increased number of young men and women who had made application to the Foreign Mission Board for commissions as missionaries.[99]

Early in 1935, Secretary Jackson reported receiving calls for help by the Foreign Mission Board that could not immediately be provided. Among these were the following:

1. From South Africa: For a young ordained American minister to take charge of religious education work.
2. From Middledrift, South Africa: A call for a much needed school building.
3. From South America: For aid in equipping a house of worship.
4. From St. James, Trinidad: For the National Baptist Convention to take over his mission (buy it).
5. From Grand Bassa: For farm implements and new buildings.
6. From the hospital: A medical doctor, another graduate nurse, a new Delco system, etc.

7. From Bendoo Station: Farm implements, new buildings.

8. From the Gold Coast: To save the station there.[100]

Writing in the September-October 1936 issue of the *Mission Herald,* the Reverend J. A. Younger, Recording Secretary of the Foreign Mission Board, pointed out that whereas the Board owed $10,636.36 in back salaries early in 1934, as of the end of the fiscal year in June 1934, this amount had been reduced to $4,708.32. In addition, the current salaries of all missionary workers had been paid regularly and in advance in most instances. To increase financial efficiency, a policy of operating on a budget was adopted at all mission stations. A further evidence of financial progress was that the Board had been able to operate without having to borrow funds. All of this is significant, especially since, as of early 1934, according to Reverend Younger, "there were about six pending or threatening suits against the Board on the part of active or past missionaries."[101]

The significance of each dollar contributed to foreign missions was set forth in striking terms by Secretary Jackson in an editorial in the spring of 1937. Normally, he said, "the missionary dollar" pays for the travel of missionaries, buys necessities of life for them, aids in healing the sick, tills the fields, trains the hands and "pulls down the idol gods to erect altars to the living God." Moreover, the dollar given to missions functions as "an angel of mercy and a messenger of grace."

On the other hand, however, the missionary dollar is "overworked" because it has to be used to arouse ministers who are indifferent to missions and to encourage them to support the cause. At the same time, funds contributed to missions have to be used to pay for travel, for public relations or to raise money for the cause. For these reasons, the dollar given to missions is said to be "overworked." As more ministers and churches voluntarily contribute to missions, it means that a larger percentage of every dollar is available primarily for work on the foreign field.[102]

The continuing progress of the work of the Foreign Mission Board was cited by Dr. L. K. Williams at the National Baptist Convention in session at Los Angeles in 1937. In his annual address, he praised the Board in glowing terms. "All evidence," he said, "seems to support the conclusion that the Foreign Mission Board of this Convention is in better condition than it has ever been." The evidence cited included the notation that all the debts on the property and past due obligations to the missionaries had been fully settled, and that a new program for the hospital had been put into place, thus establishing the conditions for a close relationship with "noted and interested persons living in Liberia."[103] Moreover, in addition to the above developments, the Foreign Mission Board had received increased cooperation from those on the home front. One example of this was the legacy of a valuable piece of property, willed by a member of the Olivet Baptist Church in Chicago, to be sold and the proceeds used for the promotion of foreign missions.[104]

The Primary Purpose of Missions

One of the continuing issues in the philosophy of Christian missions is that of determining what is the ultimate purpose of the missionary enterprise. Is missionary activity primarily one of saving the souls of those to whom messengers are sent, or is it basically one of transforming a society characterized by economic depression, ignorance, idolatry and all their attendant social ills? To put it another way, should the object of Christian missions be ultimately to bring relief from social and economic problems, or to redeem the souls of men and women for entrance into the Kingdom of God? Should the answer to these questions be "either/or," "both/and?"

Certainly it is of tremendous importance to address the social, economic, medical and educational needs of a people long in bondage to ignorance and economic and political exploitation. Christian missions through the years have continued to meet these needs. But it is important to recognize the fact that a society or an individual may enjoy all the benefits which an advanced civilization can afford, and still be unmindful of, or uncommitted to, the ultimate saving power of the Gospel of Christ. The extent to which an individual or a nation implements that Gospel, to that extent will true salvation be achieved.

Secretary Jackson addressed this issue in an editorial in the *Mission Herald* during his tenure. He said:

> We are convinced that Jesus was more concerned with establishing the principles in the lives of men that would finally destroy all ungodly systems and bring a Kingdom to pass in which justice, righteousness and peace would be the desire and the acceptable rule of social action... A missionary program of relief, in the final analysis, cheapens the personalities both of missionaries and of the people to whom they are sent. It is bad moral discipline for any people to learn to expect others to purchase for them the essential goods of life. To lead any native convert to look to a foreign missionary for his own economic development more than to the resources of his own land, is to teach to sin against his own personality and to lose the needed virtue of self-respect...
>
> Whatever we give or whatever we do, must always be subservient to the great program of Christian redemption. Christ must be central and the Cross our point of departure.[105]

Some Effects of Missionary Endeavors by the Foreign Mission Board

The work of the Foreign Mission Board in Liberia through the years has elicited much praise. Particularly has this been true with regard to the political leaders of that country. These leaders have given our Board their wholehearted support because they have recognized that the missionaries have made a significant impact upon thousands of individuals and upon the country as a whole. In addition, they felt an affinity to Black Americans because of the part their ancestors played in the founding of Liberia.

Consolidating The Gains, 1921-1941

Speaking at the commencement exercises held at the Suehn Mission in November 1936, the Honorable C. D. King, President of Liberia, paid the following tribute to the missionary movement in his country:

To the foreign missionary societies in the United States of America, both Black and white, we owe a debt of gratitude which can never be adequately repaid. Large sums of money have been expended, and many holy Christian lives have been offered upon the great sacrificial altar by those societies to bring the light of Christianity into our dear land and country for the education of our youth. That to this high and noble work these societies are still devoted, our presence here today upon these grounds is an eloquent expression of that fact.

Whatever may be our national aspirations as a Negro State in Africa, we Liberians should never forget the rock from which we were hewn — the rock of Christianity. Liberia must therefore be, first and last, a Christian State — therefore a great state. Great, not necessarily in physical power and in material wealth, as neither of these is of itself evidence of real greatness; but great in spiritual and moral strength. It is the spiritual and moral strength of which the civilized world seems at present to be absolutely devoid.

Are not these conditions (the social and moral and economic collapse of European nations and America) the resulting consequences of the departure on the part of the great nations of Christendom from those high spiritual and moral values upon which their culture and civilization is based? Echo seems to answer: YES. Therefore, let us Liberians read carefully the signs of the times and see to it that we depart not from the landmarks of the Fathers, remembering that no material prosperity and greatness is permanent which takes no account of spiritual and

131

moral values. Religion and education, therefore, always occupy the most prominent place in our national economy.[106]

These sentiments are reflected in communications sent to the Foreign Mission Board by Africans who have benefited from the work of the missionaries. The files of the Board contain many letters which underscore the importance of the work of the Board and serve as a stimulus for continuing and enlarging our efforts. Typical of the expressions received is the following from an African Chief:

Todee Section
Via Monrovia, Liberia
October 4, 1937

Dr. J. H. Jackson, Corr. Sec'y.
National Baptist Mission Board
Philadelphia, PA, U.S.A.

Dear Brother:

I know you would like to know how I come to know you and to write to you. Dr. Townsend is our dentist out here and has done some fine work among our native people in this section and we love him.

I know he is a friend of Ma Watson, so I got her address and yours from him. Ma Watson wrote me a letter but the boy dropped it in the river, so I never saw it. I went down to Monrovia and found how to write.

I am glad to say I am a God man now, and I thank God for it. We have a Baptist church here and we want Baptist churches all through Todee Section, so we are writing to ask you to send us our Ma Watson, because she is the first one that brought Jesus Christ to palaver to us, and we want a mission here so she can sit down here with us native people and be our light. We must have a mission to teach our children God palaver.

Just as much land as your Board want they can have. I am the paramount chief over the whole Todee Section, and all the chiefs here want you to send Ma Watson and other missionaries, because we have plenty children in this section and we want them in our Baptist mission school and in the Baptist Church, for I believe Jesus Christ is the Son of God. Amen.

We are going to support our children in school and help to look out for the mission and the church. God bless you my brother, and the church and make it so we can know more about Jesus Christ. We native people are not asleep; we have our eyes open, but we want someone who has worked with us, knows us, and loves us. We will be so thankful, and I know God will bless you.

I am your brother in Jesus Christ, KYRANA GOBA, Paramount Chief, Todee Section.[107]

Another native African, the Reverend S. W. Martin, who was educated in the United States, for many years carried forward a highly successful ministry in Nigeria. The following excerpt from one of his letters to the Foreign Mission Board indicates some of the progress he had made through the support of the Foreign Mission Board:

Baptist Mission, Issele-Uku
Nigeria, West Africa

May 20, 1938

Dear Dr. Jackson:

May I say, in His name, to you in a humble way, that I have been in Africa for these sixteen years and yet have seen with my own eyes in the blessing of the Lord more than 3,000 converts to the Christian faith, and have with these hands, in the name of the Father, Son and Holy Ghost, baptized at least 450, for which God is to be glorified through the effort that you have been making there. May God bless the Pilgrim Baptist Church, the Board, and all those that have been contributing for the upkeep of our work here...

S. W. Martin[108]

Rev. S. W. Martin

The Effects of World War II

When Adolph Hitler unleashed his legions to invade Poland in 1939, he began a crisis that was destined to affect people and governments around the world. World War II had definite effects upon the work not only of the Foreign Mission Board and other various mission boards in this country, but upon the foreign missionary enterprises everywhere. Our Board was forced to keep at home missionaries who had planned to sail immediately after the convention in September 1939. But because of submarine warfare, travel by water was hazardous. The war not only prevented missionaries from traveling to the foreign fields but

134

also curtailed the travel of those who had worked faithfully at their mission stations for as long as five years and needed to come home for rest and renewal. The war also affected communication by mail. This meant that to communicate with workers in the field, the Board had to do so by cable.[109]

Other difficulties caused by World War II included the destruction of property costing millions of dollars, long lines of refugees without homes and food, and, in many cases, without hope. It is of interest, however, to note that in spite of the difficulties imposed by the war, Secretary Jackson reported that "the interest and enthusiasm for the missionary enterprise seems to be constantly and steadily growing. This may be indicated in part by the widespread concern and willingness on the part of the various groups here in America to sacrifice for the need and suffering of the less fortunate in war-torn countries." Several denominations in America were immediately organizing certain programs and activities for relief work in countries devastated by the war.[110]

New Mission Stations in Uganda

One of the significant developments during World War II was some expansion on the part of the Foreign Mission Board. In late 1939, the Board took over a new mission station in Uganda. This station consisted of 200 acres of land, a five-teacher school and excellent possibilities for educational and religious developments. The principal of the school was Mr. Ernest B. Kalibala, a native of Uganda, who had been trained in the United States. Until he was six years old, he lived the life of the tribe of which his father was the chief and who later became mayor of Kampala. One of the important factors in his development was attending schools operated by the Anglican Missionary Society in Kampala. He also studied in England at Durbyshire and at Selly Oaks, Kingsmead College in Birmingham.

Mr. Kalibala came to the United States in 1925 and studied for a year at Tuskeegee Institute and later at Lincoln University and at Kings Mountain, North Carolina. Following this, he attended City College in New York and New York University where he earned the

Bachelor of Science degree. He married Miss Alta W. Jones, a graduate of Boston University and a daughter of a retired Methodist minister. The Kalibalas returned to Uganda in 1934.[111]

In answer to the question, "Why should the Foreign Mission Board seek to expand at this point in world affairs?" Secretary Jackson stated that the story of Kalibala "impressed upon us the dire need of whatever help could be given at this time. The people need a greater earning capacity and greater knowledge of farm products. They must be given the life of learning so that they might know how to live life at its best, and they need the Christ way of salvation and hope.

"We believe that this is the way to a crowning victory. We work not for ourselves but for the Kingdom of God. That Kingdom is not static; it always moves forward."[112]

In 1939, the Foreign Mission Board elected ten men and women to go to the foreign fields. These were: the Reverend and Mrs. F. H. Austin, Mr. and Mrs. S. B. Coles, the Reverend and Mrs. T. O. Dusuma, Mr. and Mrs. Carleton Wall and Mr. and Mrs. E. K. Kalivala.[113]

60th Anniversary of the Foreign Mission Board

Early in 1940, the Foreign Mission Board observed its 60th anniversary. The Board had a history of which every Baptist could be proud. It represented the initial concern of the founders when the Convention was organized in 1880. That concern was sending the message of faith and hope across the seas. It was appropriate that the 60th anniversary of the Board was observed in Montgomery, Alabama, where the Convention and the Board were first organized. Recognizing that the observance of the 60th anniversary was carried on in spite of the war situation, Secretary Jackson stated:

> While it is in keeping with tradition to observe an historic anniversary by turning our faces toward the past and giving thanks to God for those who have gone before, it is much more significant that we face the future and dedicate and reconsecrate our powers and our gifts to a bigger and better program for Christ. The Foreign Mis-

136

sion Board is in quest of 1,000 churches who will give at least $60 this year in celebration of our anniversary.[114]

Developments at the Carrie V. Dyer Hospital

The Carrie V. Dyer Hospital was built in the fiscal year 1926. In the ten year period between then and 1938, a number of people gave of their time, resources and expertise to make the hospital a vital instrument for raising the quality of health for the people it served. During this period, however, the building went through the normal process of deterioration. At the same time, it was not always easy to keep up with the requirements of modern medical equipment. For this reason Dr. L. Sajous of Monrovia told the Foreign Mission Board it was urgent that the Carrie V. Dyer Hospital secure up-to-date medical equipment and talented physicians and also that the building should be improved or the Board should close down the hospital. This matter became all the more important because the hospital operated by the Liberian government was about to be repaired and the Catholic dispensary was soon to be opened. This meant that these two buildings would make our own hospital look shabby and out-of-date. It was estimated that to carry out the suggestions made by Dr. Sajous, at least $10,000 was required. This was one of several challenges the hospital had to face before, as we shall see, the Liberian government took it over entirely.[115]

It is clear from the records that sending missionaries across the seas to carry the spiritual gifts of the Gospel requires also that material resources must always be provided to make the endeavor a success. Corresponding Secretaries L. G. Jordan and James E. East constantly sought to educate the ministers and their members in the importance of the missionary enterprise and the necessity of sacrificial giving to sustain it. Buildings built in a tropical climate appear to deteriorate more rapidly than those of the same type of material in a temperate climate. One of the primary causes of deterioration of wood structures in the tropics is that of wood-eating ants which can undermine and seriously weaken the foundations and support frames of buildings in a relatively short time. The

Foreign Mission Board had to deal with this problem frequently, and this required constant appeals for missionary giving.

In outlining "Some Basic Needs" in the fall of 1940, Secretary Jackson placed increased financial support at the top of the list. He urged that the operating budget of the Foreign Mission Board be raised from $40,000 to $250,000 a year — an increase of 400%! Among the other material needs identified were more modern buildings and artesian wells and running water in all dormitories. With the proposed increase in the operating budget, the above needs could be adequately met and additional missionary personnel could be commissioned.

Beside the need for an increase in the operating budget, there was expressed the desire for fifty more "strong, courageous young people" willing to accept the challenge of the Macedonian Call. To achieve this end, the Foreign Mission Board would have to do aggressive recruiting in schools, colleges and seminaries, encouraging young people to recognize the spiritual rewards of foreign mission work. It was suggested that the Board itself adopt the policy of paying the tuition of committed youth so that they could secure adequate training for missionary duties. The need for a missionary pension fund was expressed because, "It is un-Christian to demand of people to give all that they have in the service of a great cause and to represent us on foreign fields...and then on their return to neglect and forget them."[116]

Secretary Jackson called for a "missionary statesman" in South Africa sympathetic to both groups there and willing to identify with the people in order to serve their greatest needs. The catalogue of needs set forth in this article included reviving the work of the Board in South America and in the British West Indies, and also opening up work in the Republic of Haiti. It was urged that in this latter instance, the emphasis should be on agriculture.[117]

Death of Dr. L. K. Williams

A native of Texas and born July 11, 1871, L. K. Williams was ordained at the age of twenty-three. Early in his career he combined teaching and preaching, and by 1916 he had become the outstanding religious leader in his home state. In that year, he was called to the pastorate of the Olivet Baptist Church in Chicago, Illinois, where he demonstrated high qualities of administration and leadership. Because of his reputation, he was elected president of the National Baptist Convention in 1922, succeeding the Reverend E. C. Morris. Among the accomplishments attributed to him during the forty-six years of his work as a minister were the following: the organizing of fourteen churches; participating in the organization of twenty-six associations; ordaining 106 deacons; licensing seventeen and ordaining thirty-one ministers, and aiding twenty-six ministers and missionaries in obtaining an education. Throughout his tenure as president of the National Baptist Convention, U.S.A., Inc., Dr. Williams gave much encouragement and support to the Foreign Mission Board.[118] Dr. Williams died in an airplane accident on October 29, 1940.

Dr. L. K. Williams

A few months after the death of Dr. Williams, Dr. Joseph H. Jackson, Corresponding Secretary of the Foreign Mission Board, was called to the pastorate of the Olivet Baptist Church to succeed the late Dr. Williams. In an editorial tribute to Dr. Jackson which appeared in the *Mission Herald,* the following was said of him:

> During his seven years as Corresponding Secretary of the Foreign Mission Board, he has labored untiringly and unselfishly for the cause he held dear and for which he pledged his full measure of devotion. He has never flinched from the most arduous and difficult tasks and problems, but with a determination born of heaven has met them one by one with courage and efficiency and put the work of foreign missions on an unparalled basis of confidence and stability.[119]

With the resignation of Dr. J. H. Jackson, we have the end of an important era of the Foreign Mission Board. This era began with the election of Dr. James East to succeed the missionary giant Dr. L. G. Jordan. Dr. East had come to the position with a background of eleven years as a missionary in South Africa. There he had distinguished himself as a committed messenger of the Gospel and a great organizer and evangelist, bringing many souls to Christ and carrying forward the work of the Foreign Mission Board with tremendous dedication. Dr. J. H. Jackson brought to the task unusual gifts of administration, persuasion, and depth of perception of the philosophy and possibilities of the missionary enterprise. These two men built upon the foundation laid by their predecessors, and extended the outreach of the Foreign Mission Board in its endeavor to be faithful to the Great Commission.

MISSIONARIES AND NATIVE WORKERS OF THE FOREIGN MISSION BOARD, N.B.C., INC. AS OF 1941

SUEHN INDUSTRIAL MISSION
Liberia, West Africa
  Mrs. Mattie Mae Davis, Principal
  Miss Mildred Griffin
  Miss Winifred Borroughs
  Miss Mary Johnson
  Miss Victoria White
  Miss Irene Kennedy
  Miss Thelma Scott
  Miss Victoria Etheridge
  Miss Augusta Dennis
  Emmett Scott
  William Mitchell
  Austin Brown
  Mack Diggs

THE BIBLE INDUSTRIAL MISSION
Fortsville, Grand Bassa,
Liberia, West Africa
  Miss Priscilla A. Bryan, Principal
  Miss Mitchell
  Lafayette Jackson
  Irving Reeves

THE BENDOO MISSION
Cape Mount, Liberia, West Africa
  Rev. J. Smith Cyrus, Principal
  Mrs. J. Smith Cyrus

THE CARRIE V. DYER
MEMORIAL HOSPITAL
Monrovia, Liberia, West Africa
  Miss Susan F. Harris, R.N.

PILGRIM BAPTIST MISSION
Nigeria, West Africa
  Rev. Samuel W. Martin
  R.I. Analgoh
  E.A. Diel
  M.J. Horsfal
  R.N. Ugbolue
  I.E. Onwu
  G.N. Nwobi
  L.C. Chiano
  G.D. Mgbonye
  E.O. Okwuashi
  C.O. Ntinu
  James Ituwe
  J.J. Igborgbor
  Miss Zelma Martin

THE PROVIDENCE INDUSTRIAL MISSION
Nyasaland, East Africa
  Rev. Daniel S. Malekebu, M.D.
  Mrs. Flora E. Malekebu
  Frank Chambo
  Barton Chipuliko
  David Nakhule
  Jordan Njiliyafa
  A. Bizwick Kakbobwe

SOUTH AFRICA
Buchanan Mission Station,
Middledrift
  Miss Martha Hela
  Miss Linda Sonjica
  Miss Florence Yoyo
  Macvicar Mngaza

  Rev. J.S. Mahlangu, Johannesburg
  Rev. E.B.P. Koti, Harding, Natal
  Rev. L.J. Tashalata, Harding, Natal
  Rev. P.M. Mahlangu, Pretoria
  Rev. F.M. Ndezekeni, Mkemani,
  Mt. Frere
  Rev. Henry Nkohla, Tottredge Park,
  Perseverance
  Rev. E. Mgabisa, Flagstaff,
  East Pondoland
  Rev. M. Mate, Lower Umkomaas,
  Natal
  Rev. E.B. Mukena, Basutoland
  Rev. Aron M.G. Cele, Amanzinitoti,
  Natal
  Rev. B. Zwukula, Cape Colony
  Rev. W.J. Spengane, New Anialfi,
  Kokstad
  Rev. Charles S. Pupu, Capetown

SOUTH AMERICA and
BRITISH WEST INDIES
  Rev. P.I. Bunthorne, British Guiana
  Rev. Cecil S. Taylor, British Guiana
  Rev. James A. Welch, British Guiana
  Rev. Nellius Neuz, Dutch Guiana
  Rev. J. Brewster, Barbados, B.W.I.
  Rev. Charles Boyce, Barbados,
  B.W.I.[120]

Notes

1. *Mission Herald,* (February 1924) p. 2.
2. Ibid
3. *Mission Herald,* (September-October 1934), p. 5.
4. *Mission Herald,* (May 1922) p. 10.
5. *Mission Herald,* (December 1924) p. 5.
6. *Mission Herald,* (September 1926)
7. Loc. Cit.
8. *Mission Herald,* (May 1922), p. 10.
9. *Mission Herald,* (April 1926), p. 5.
10. *Mission Herald,* (December 1924), p. 41.
11. *Mission Herald,* (February 1924), p. 9.
12. *Mission Herald,* (April 1925), p. 4.
13. Ibid.
14. *Mission Herald,* (May 1922) p. 3.
15. *Mission Herald,* (September 1925), p. 6.
16. NBC, *Minutes,* 1936, pp. 218 - 220.
17. *Mission Herald,* (September 1926), p. 7.
18. *Mission Herald,* (January 1923), p. 4.
19. *Mission Herald,* (June 1924), p. 5.
20. Ibid., pp. 24-25.
21. NBC *Minutes,* 1925, p. 176.
22. *Mission Herald,* (May 1929) p. 7.
23. Loc. Cit.
24. NBC *Minutes,* 1927, p. 243.
25. Ibid.
26. NBC *Minutes,* 1933, p. 215.
27. Loc. Cit.
28. NBC *Minutes,* 1927, pp. 214-218.
29. *Mission Herald,* (February 1927) p. 17.
30. NBC *Minutes,* 1924, p. 287.
31. NBC *Minutes,* 1926, p. 208.
32. Ibid., p. 209.
33. NBC *Minutes,* 1930, p. 116.
34. *Mission Herald,* (May-June 1947) pp. 6-7.
35. M.E.D. Trowbridge, *History of Baptists in Michigan.* Published under the auspices of the Michigan Baptist Convention, 1909, p. 212.
36. *Mission Herald,* (May-June 1947) p. 7.
37. *Mission Herald,* (August 1926) p. 37
38. *Mission Herald,* (May 1927) p. 34.
39. *Mission Herald,* (March 1927) p. 12.
40. *Mission Herald,* (August 1927) p. 29.
41. Ibid.
42. *Mission Herald,* (December 1927) pp. 3-4.
43. *Mission Herald,* (October 1927) pp. 11-12.

Notes continued

44. Loc. Cit.
45. *Mission Herald*, (March 1928) p. 4.
46. *Mission Herald*, (May 1929) p. 32.
47. *Mission Herald*, (October 1928) p. 29.
48. *Mission Herald*, (February 1928) p. 2.
49. NBC *Minutes*, 1929, p. 163.
50. *Mission Herald*, (October 1930) p. 29.
51. NBC *Minutes*, 1933, p. 74.
52. *Mission Herald*, (September 1970) pp. 7-8. Also *Mission Herald*, (June 1923) p. 7.
53. *Mission Herald*, (June 1925) p. 9.
54. Elizabeth Coles Bouey, writing of her husband, *Mission Herald*, (June 1925) p. 9.
55. *Mission Herald*, (August 1925) p. 5.
56. *Mission Herald*, (September 1923) p. 5.
57. *Mission Herald*, (February-March 1925) p. 7. Also *Mission Herald*, (March-April 1943) p. 16.
58. *Mission Herald*, (November 1926) pp. 8-9.
59. *Mission Herald*, (March-April 1943) p. 16.
60. Loc. Cit.
61. *Mission Herald*, (July 1930) p. 4.
62. Loc. Cit.
63. *Mission Herald*, (August 1930) p. 4.
64. NBC *Minutes*, 1927, p. 232.
65. Cf. George P. McKinney papers in the Florida Memorial College Archives. See also the *Mission Herald*, (May 1928) p. 5.
66. NBC *Minutes, 1924, pp. 209-210.*
67. *Ibid.*
68. *Mission Herald*, (August 1925) p. 5.
69. NBC *Minutes, 1929, pp. 162-163.*
70. *NBC Minutes, 1925, p. 186.*
71. *Mission Herald*, (October 1925) p. 6.
72. *Mission Herald*, (October 1925) p. 7.
73. *Mission Herald*, (September-October 1934) p. 7.
74. Ibid.
75. Ibid.
76. Ibid.
77. Ibid.
78. *Mission Herald*, (November-December 1934) p. 29.
79. *Mission Herald*, (November-December 1934) p. 2.
80. *Mission Herald*, (January-February 1935) p. 21.
81. *Mission Herald*, (November-December 1934) p. 3.
82. *Mission Herald*, (January-February 1935) p. 2.
83. *Mission Herald*, (September-October 0000) p. 3.
84. NBC *Minutes*, 1936, pp. 204ff.

Notes continued

85. NBC *Minutes,* 1925, pp. 163-165.
86. NBC *Minutes,* 1924, p. 142.
87. *Mission Herald,* (March-April 1939) pp. 2-3.
88. Ibid.
89. NBC *Minutes,* 1926, pp. 122-123.
90. Ibid, 1939.
91. *Mission Herald,* (July-August 1939) p. 5.
92. *Mission Herald,* (March-April 1939) p. 2.
93. *Mission Herald,* (May-June 1940) p. 4.
94. *Mission Herald,* (November-December 1935) p. 4.
95. Ibid.
96. Ibid.
97. Ibid.
98. *Mission Herald,* (November-December 1936) p. 38.
99. *Mission Herald,* (March-April 1935) pp. 2-3.
100. Ibid.
101. *Mission Herald,* (September-October 1936) p. 37.
102. *Mission Herald,* (March-April 1937) p. 5.
103. *Mission Herald,* (September-October 1937) p. 8.
104. Ibid.
105. *Mission Herald,* (November-December 1938) pp. 2-3.
106. *Mission Herald,* (March-April 1937) p. 37.
107. *Mission Herald,* (January-February 1938) p. 12.
108. *Mission Herald,* (July-August 1938) p. 20.
109. *Mission Herald,* (September-October 1939) p. 2.
110. *Mission Herald,* (September-October 1940) p. 3.
111. *Mission Herald,* (January-February 1940) pp. 12-13.
112. *Mission Herald,* (March-April 1940) p. 3.
113. *Mission Herald,* (September-October 1940) p. 14.
114. Ibid.
115. *Mission Herald,* (September-October 1938) pp. 3-4.
116. *Mission Herald,* (September-October 1940) p. 17.
117. Ibid.
118. *Mission Herald,* (November-December 1940) p. 2.
119. *Mission Herald,* (May-June 1945) p. 2.

CHAPTER FIVE
AN ERA OF DENOMINATIONAL PRIDE AND WORLD-MINDEDNESS, 1941-1961
The Tenure of Dr. C. C. Adams

Upon the resignation of Dr. J. H. Jackson to assume the pastorate of the Olivet Baptist Church in Chicago, Illinois, the Reverend Dr. C. C. Adams was appointed as Corresponding Secretary of the Foreign Mission Board.

Dr. C. C. Adams

Born in Huntington, Carroll County, Tennessee, on December 12, 1884, Dr. Adams attended Shaw University in Raleigh, North

145

Carolina, and was graduated in 1911 with the degrees of B.Th. and B.A. He had been called to the ministry in 1902 and served churches in North and South Carolina, Tennessee and Pennsylvania. He had served as president of the Pennsylvania Baptist State Convention, and in the interim between the death of Dr. L. G. Jordan and the appointment of Dr. J. H. Jackson as corresponding secretary of the Foreign Mission Board, Dr. Adams served as acting corresponding secretary.

During his twenty-year tenure as corresponding secretary, Dr. Adams served a term as president of the Department of Foreign Missions of the National Council of Churches. Two of the outstanding contributions he made during his administration were the Carrie V. Dyer Maternity Hospital in Monrovia, Liberia, and the expansion of the foreign mission enterprise in Nigeria, West Africa.

Dr. Adams came to the position fully aware of its great responsibilities, having already served in an acting capacity, and apparently with the determination to build upon the foundations laid by his predecessors.

Although from the time of its outbreak, World War II affected the activities of the Foreign Mission Board, nevertheless the Board continued to carry forward its work in Africa despite the difficulties involved. One of the continuing problems was that of sending out new missionaries and bringing missionaries on the field home on furloughs. Because of submarine warfare, it became practically impossible to depend upon safe transoceanic travel between the United States and Africa. This danger was dramatized when a German submarine sank the passenger ship Zamzam. Among the passengers rescued from that sinking were the Reverend and Mrs. T. O. Dosumu, who were on their way to take up a mission post in Liberia. They were interned for more than a year in Berlin, but eventually were released and continued their trip to West Africa. Secretary Adams reported that despite the difficulties imposed upon the Board by World War II, the spirit of missions in the churches were better than ever before.

146

In the fall of 1941, just prior to America's entrance into the conflict, Secretary Adams declared that among his objectives was maintaining and strengthening our faith and morale at home as well as on the foreign field in all the stations operated by the Board. In addition, the Board was determined to build a strong financial reserve so that it would be possible to carry on an expanded building program in Africa when the war ended. Secretary Adams also declared that when the conflict ended, it was his desire to secure and personally lead to Africa a group of young men and women dedicated to Africa's redemption. He wanted them to see the stations and the opportunities for Christian service there. He desired to have a group representing a variety of interests and occupations, including teachers, physicians, dentists, nurses, mechanics, carpenters and those skilled in agriculture.[1]

Undergirding all of these plans was the hope and faith that in spite of the exigencies imposed by the war, there was behind all creation a God who was infinite, absolute in power and love, and whose divine intelligence was directing the forces of the universe toward a righteous and divinely designated objective.[2]

In Liberia, the Bendoo Mission was declared a danger zone after the United States entered the conflict. This added to the anxieties of missionaries and others at that station. Soon they were pleading to be brought home. Because of the dangers involved in transportation by ship, the Board went to great expense to bring the missionaries home on furlough by air. This, of course, imposed a strain on the budget of the Foreign Mission Board.[3]

Death of the Reverend R. J. Langston

In the fall of 1942, the Reverend R. J. Langston, who once served as editor of the *Mission Herald,* passed away. He had been one of the stalwarts of support of the foreign mission enterprise. A graduate of Virginia Union University, he was described as "a ripened scholar, eloquent preacher and a fluent and ready writer." Among the important posts Reverend Langston held were minister of the Bank Street Baptist Church, Norfolk, Virginia;

instructor in religion at Tuskegee Institute, and pastor of the Zion Baptist Church in North Philadelphia, a pastorate he held for sixteen years. In recognition of his passing, the Foreign Mission Board adopted a set of resolutions which included the following tribute:

> Another lesson from his life is the possibility and gain of combining the spirit of conciliation with fidelity to strong conviction. He was a peacemaker both by instinct and on principle, disposed to conciliation and to compromise; but he was not a trimmer. He would yield personal preference or advantage, but not truth or right-eousness. He had a way of seeing a principle of unity in diverse opinions, and thus of grasping the larger truth which is so often distorted by both sides in a controversy. This largeness of spirit was one of the qualities which made him so valued by his associates of the Foreign Mission Board.[4]

Problems On the Home Front

The members of the Foreign Mission Board were well aware of certain problems at home. Among these were keeping up interest and support on the part of some who, while they started contributing enthusiastically, nevertheless began to lag both in their interest and in their giving. Moreover, there was constant concern with respect to those pastors who had never demon-strated any interest in giving to foreign missions. Another prob-lem the Board faced was that of false rumors about what the Board would be able to do in Africa. One rumor was that because of the war, the Board was unable to send money to the workers in Africa, and, therefore there was no need for the churches to send money to the Board. On the contrary, however, Secretary Adams reported that the Board was sending more to Africa than had ever been sent before. An additional problem at home was that of maintaining and keeping the good will of many pastors across the country. Many times invitations came to the corre-sponding secretary to appear at different places on the same date.

148

Because he was unable to accept certain invitations, the persons who invited him felt slighted.

It is clear from the above that during World War II there were not only serious problems with which to deal on the foreign field, but also problems that had to be addressed on the home front. The Foreign Mission Board never became discouraged, but persisted in the endeavor to fulfill its mission as that arm of the church which was charged with the responsibility of sending the Good News of the Gospel to those who were hungering for it in Africa.

Financial Efforts During The War

Underlying the financial drives of the Foreign Mission Board was the view that the one central task of the church that was assigned by Jesus was a missionary one, and that everything else which the church did was subsidiary to this responsibility. The annual Christmas Drives continued to be successful. The purpose of the Drives was to strengthen the belief on the part of ministers and church members that missions should be supported not only by giving, but by prayer, study and reflection. It was also urged that Christian people develop a wholehearted devotion and consecration to the world purpose of the church with the belief that they would be freed from provincialism and their understanding of the world-wide need of Christ would be deepened.

Secretary Adams made strenuous efforts to improve the finances of the Foreign Mission Board. Early in his administration, he began a drive for $100,000 for foreign missions. Following are the reasons given for conducting the drive and the amounts suggested to be contributed by each state:

Why the drive?
$5,000 for emergencies growing out of war conditions.

$45,000 to maintain the status quo of our work, missionaries salaries, upkeep of stations, schools, and the hospital, as well as some work in South America.

$50,000 as a reserve to finance the sending out of new missionaries and the building of an extension program at the close of the war.

How is the drive to be conducted?
By states, with each state given a quota according to numerical strength.

How are the states to be organized?
Under the leadership of an outstanding worker, preferably by the Foreign Mission Board member in each state or section of the state where there is more than one state convention.

How should this leader or board member proceed?
By selecting a group of interested men and women and assigning each to a section of the state, with a quota for his/her state in mind.

What money is to be included in the drive?
All Monthly Regulars, Special Donations, Conventions, Associations and individual gifts.[5]

PRO RATA OF STATES

Alabama	$6,000.00	Missouri	$5,000.00
Arizona	500.00	Nebraska	1,000.00
Arkansas	6,000.00	New Hampshire	100.00
California	5,000.00	New Jersey	4,000.00
Colorado	1,000.00	New Mexico	500.00
Connecticut	1,000.00	New York	7,000.00
Delaware	1,000.00	North Carolina	1,000.00
District of Columbia	7,000.00	Ohio	4,000.00
Florida	6,000.00	Oklahoma	4,000.00
Georgia	5,000.00	Oregon	200.00
Idaho	100.00	Pennsylvania	15,000.00
Illinois	6,000.00	Rhode Island	1,000.00
Indiana	2,000.00	South Carolina	3,000.00
Iowa	500.00	South Dakota	50.00
Kansas	3,000.00	Tennessee	5,000.00
Kentucky	4,000.00	Texas	5,000.00
Louisiana	4,000.00	Virginia	3,000.00
Maryland	2,000.00	Washington	500.00
Massachusetts	3,000.00	West Virginia	1,000.00
Michigan	4,000.00	Wisconsin	500.00
Minnesota	500.00	Wyoming	100.00
Mississippi	5,000.00		

In 1943, the drive for $100,000 for foreign missions was declared a success, but, at the same time, the churches were reminded that just because the drive was a success, they must not stop there. While the churches could very well be proud of reaching that goal, it was pointed out that they could do better and that they must do more than what was collected in this $100,000 drive. The reasons given for this were that the missionaries must be better paid and that the hospitals, the schools and the stations in West, South and East Africa needed to be strengthened and enlarged.[6] In addition to the need for large support for missionary work in Africa, it was necessary to call attention to missionary work outside of Africa, particularly in the Bahamas. This work, formerly in the hands of the Home Mission Board, was taken over by the Foreign Mission Board. Missionary work in the Bahamas, however, was of a different type from that in West Africa because of the relatively more advanced educational and economic status of the islands.

In the fall of 1943, the Reverend Marshall Shepard and Secretary Adams had a conference with president-elect and Chief Justice V. S. Tubman of Liberia at the Waldorf Hotel in New York City. Just as other heads of state and prominent persons in Liberia had done, Justice Tubman expressed a very keen interest in the work that the Foreign Mission Board was carrying forward in Liberia. He praised the work of Mrs. Mattie Mae Davis and her corps of workers. He expressed appreciation for the work of the Carrie V. Dyer Hospital and some of the other stations supported by the Foreign Mission Board. In addition, he pledged his cooperation with the Board in making the efforts of our missionaries in Liberia more effective.[7]

As the war continued, the efforts of the Foreign Mission Board did not lag. In the spring of 1944, Secretary Adams set forth a list of things that the Board had been doing in Africa in spite of attendant difficulties. Among these were the fact that five of the missionaries in Africa had been returned on furlough and that another would sail shortly. New buildings had been erected and a permanent nurses home for the Carrie V. Dyer Hospital in

151

Monrovia was under construction. At the same time, he pointed out that the hospital had been closed and reorganized within the last two years. In addition, the Board was operating a second hospital in Nyasaland, East Africa. New staff workers had been employed abroad and the budget had been increased. The rubber plants which had been set out a few years earlier had yielded a great crop with the chance for a greater yield in the future. Many converts had come forward, and schools and hospitals were crowded. In addition, native nurses were being trained at the hospital and at other mission stations. It was predicted that because of building plans and recurring demands for expansion, it would be necessary for the National Baptist Convention to provide an annual budget of $200,000 for the Foreign Mission Board.[8]

The $200,000 budget adopted for the fiscal year July 1, 1945-June 30, 1946 was listed as follows:

Overheads	$20,000.00
African Missionary Operation	50,000.00
Missionaries' Travel from and to Africa	5,000.00
Emergency Fund	10,000.00
Bldgs. at Suehn, Hospital, Bassa and Bendoo	30,000.00
Survey, Plans and Assembly of Materials	15,000.00
Equipment	12,000.00
Station Wagon & Pick-Up Truck	4,000.00
Food, Clothing & Medicine	5,000.00
Bahama Islands Building & Work	10,000.00
British Guiana	3,000.00
Reserve on 10-Year Bldg. Program	36,000.00
Total	$200,000.00[9]

Some Financial Successes

The persistent call from the Foreign Mission Board urging the pastors to increase their giving for missions had positive results. In 1943, Secretary Adams reported that he was "greatly heartened" by the increased interest on the part of the churches

152

in raising funds through the Annual Christmas Drive. Two years later the following report was made of the contributions from certain of the churches:

Philadelphia	$13,600.00
Tennessee	2,000.00
Newark	900.00
Florida East Coast	1,200.00
Delaware	200.00
Pittsburgh	3,000.00
Boston	500.00
Savannah	182.00[10]

In addition, the Baptists of Louisiana launched a $10,000 drive promoted by Miss Primrose Funches, field director, and the Reverend A. L. Davis, state chairman. This was the fourth annual drive for foreign missions sponsored by the Baptists of Louisiana. Also in 1947, Miss Funches and the Reverend W. M. Walton, executive secretary and director general, launched the first annual spring drive for foreign missions in Mississippi.[11]

Miss Primrose Funches

153

Continuing his efforts to increase support for foreign missions, Secretary Adams initiated a ten-year program to raise $2 million between 1944 and 1954. The challenge was to raise an annual budget of $200,000 — a goal that was achieved in fiscal 1945 and fiscal 1946. During the succeeding years, support for foreign missions continued to increase. In 1953, Secretary Adams reported a "growing interest and support for our foreign mission work. Our special Christmas drives are now in full swing and funds received have been very encouraging. Philadelphia led off by breaking its own record and raising $26,000!"[12]

The Appointment of Major John B. Falconer

The Foreign Mission Board was able to secure the services of a former chaplain in the U.S. Army who was stationed in Africa. He was the Reverend John B. Falconer who held the military rank of Major and had spent more than three years in Africa. Although an American citizen, he preferred to remain in Africa. The Foreign Mission Board gladly employed him to return to Liberia to direct the building program and to assume the general overseeing of all of the foreign mission stations in West Africa. A graduate of Lincoln University, he continued his education at several other schools. The Board was fortunate to have John Falconer in Liberia — a man who was not only well acquainted with that country but was also well received by its citizens. The Board promised to send a builder and a mechanic to work under his supervision.[13]

Four years after Falconer accepted the position, the corresponding secretary wrote that Major Falconer had made an outstanding contribution to the work of the Board in Liberia. As stated by Secretary Adams, under Major Falconer's direction and guidance:

> The work of the Board has been extended into many areas that had been barren through this effort, the joint operation of Ricks Institute in Liberia has been initiated in the training of native preachers. He has also been instrumental in bringing under our Board the Klay Institute in Liberia, a most effective school that has

been operating for forty years under Dr. H. H. Jones. The important building program at Suehn and the Carrie V. Dyer Hospital has been directed by him in an effective manner.[14]

Rev. John B. Falconer

One of the things that Major Falconer did after taking office was to establish a general supply house in Monrovia for the purpose of buying supplies in wholesale lots and thereby saving money. He was able to do this through the Firestone Plantations Company. He reported having saved 1/3 of what he would ordinarily have spent for purchases for the hospital. This involved purchases of food and of hospital, medical and non-medical supplies. In the case of medicine, he reported a savings of more than 50%! All school supplies were ordered on the same basis. This arrangement meant that it was cheaper for the Foreign Mission Board to purchase supplies in Africa than to buy them in America and ship them.

Development of Building Plans

Beginning in 1945, a number of new buildings were constructed under the auspices of the Foreign Mission Board. Among these were the J. H. Jackson Building at the Suehn mission. Funds for this building were contributed by the Olivet Baptist Church of Chicago at the suggestion of Dr. Jackson, pastor of that church and former corresponding secretary of the Foreign Mission Board. Construction began in 1947 at a cost of $35,000. In fall of that year, the permanent building and expansion program of the Foreign Mission Board was reported to be on schedule. The ten-year program began in 1945. In addition to the buildings listed above, some new buildings were constructed in the Bahamas. The main building there was almost completed by the end of 1947 at a cost of more than $35,000. Another building was erected at the W. W. Brown Memorial Station in South Africa, and two more brick buildings were already ordered for 1946. The Nineteenth Street Baptist Church in Washington, D. C., paid the salary of the Reverend J. H. Mahlandu and also contributed to the general work of the W. W. Brown Memorial Station. The Metropolitan Baptist Church of New York City, formerly pastored by Reverend Brown, underwrote the cost of expanding that station.[15]

Also in 1945, a two-story building constructed of rock was erected at the Bendoo Station in Liberia and work on a second building was being planned.

At the Suehn Mission, the construction of a two-story, three-winged girls' dormitory was begun in 1947.

One unfortunate note concerns the damage done to the Carrie V. Dyer Memorial Hospital in Monrovia. The hospital was so seriously damaged by ants or termites that the Board was advised to take it down and rebuild. This was eventually done at great cost to the Board.

Secretary Adams' Visits to Africa

In 1945, Secretary Adams made another visit to Liberia. While there he inaugurated a ten-year building and expansion program for all the missionary stations. He coordinated the work of the

156

Carrie V. Dyer Hospital with that of the National Health and Hospital Programs of Liberia. In addition, he reorganized and added to the personnel of the hospital as well as to the other missionary stations, and traveled to all sections of the country meeting with and preaching to the native tribes. In all, he reported that, "We added to the already goodwill of the Liberian government, to our work, and cemented with President Tubman an agreement by which our Board will help worthy young Liberians come to this country to further their education.[16]

He made another trip to Africa in 1947 and reported that it was clear that all the work in South, Central and East Africa had to be coordinated, "to give a sense of oneness and helpfulness among all the workers and the many new converts." The Reverend D. S. Malekebu was appointed supervisor to represent the work of the Foreign Mission in all of those sections. This responsibility was similar to that given to the Reverend John B. Falconer in West Africa who had charge of supervising the work of the Board in Liberia, the Gold Coast and Nigeria.[17]

Churchmen Visit Africa

In 1950, the Foreign Mission Board began a tradition of sponsoring visits by pastors of the National Baptist Convention, U.S.A., Inc., to mission fields in Africa. This was the first such commission ever sent to Africa by the Convention to study and review the work not only of National Baptists, but also that of other foreign mission agencies regardless of denominational affiliation. Some of these pastors who went to Africa did so at their own expense; others had their way paid by the churches or religious organizations which they represented. The ten churchmen who comprised this first commission were:

> Dr. C. C. Scott, pastor of the Fifth Street Baptist Church, Richmond, Virginia, president of the Goodwill Baptist Convention of Virginia, and chairman of the Commission; Dr. H. H. Coleman, pastor of Greater Macedonia Baptist Church, Detroit, Michigan, president of Detroit Baptist Training Center, and secretary of the Commission;

Dr. J. Raymond Henderson, pastor of Second Baptist Church, Los Angeles, California, official photographer and father of the Commission; Dr. L. G. Carr, pastor of Vine Memorial Baptist Church, Philadelphia, Pennsylvania, and co-photographer of the Commission; Dr. E. C. Smith, pastor of Metropolitan Baptist Church, Washington, D. C., president of Virginia Baptist State Convention and professor in the School of Religion, Howard University; Dr. W. H. Jernagin, pastor of Mt. Carmel Baptist Church, Washington, D. C., and president of the National Sunday School and B. T. U. Congress; Dr. J. C. Austin, pastor of the Pilgrim Baptist Church, Chicago, Illinois, secretary of the Foreign Trade Commission and president of the Illinois Baptist State Convention; Dr. I. H. Henderson, pastor of the Eighth Street Baptist Church, Kansas City, Kansas, and moderator of the Valley Association; Dr. R. T. Harris, Marshall, Texas, president of the B. M. E. Foreign Mission Convention; and your humble servant, leader of the Commission and corresponding secretary of the Foreign Mission Board.[18]

The sending of pastors to the foreign fields was an important step in stimulating interest in and support for the work of the Foreign Mission Board. It was important that our pastors see the actual stations and the personnel in each one which were the targets of their missionary contributions. In every instance, the ministers came away with widened horizons, clearer understandings and a deeper commitment to supporting and enlarging the work carried forward by the Foreign Mission Board.

It will be of interest to report the list of missionaries serving in Africa as of 1953 and listed in the *Mission Herald* during the year. Also included are the names of some of the tribes among whom the Foreign Mission Board served.

158

Names of Some of the Tribes Among Whom the Foreign Mission Board Served

NYASALAND
Yao, Nyania, Lomwe, Ngoni, Chewa, Tumbuka, Tonga, Manglanja, Kholhola, Thakwani, Chukunda.

NORTHERN RHODESIA
Bemba, Biza, Senga,

PORTUGUESE EAST AFRICA
Sena, Shangani, Matoniga, Nyambani.

SOUTHERN RHODESIA
Zezru, Karanga, Makorekore, Toga, Mavenda, Mashone, Manco, Mchakun, Matble, Mklaga.

UNION OF SOUTH AFRICA
Swazi, Zulu, Basuto, Ndeble, Xosa, Shona, Dasotho, Thonga, Ndau, Bechuana, Tswana, Ronga, Venda, Pede.

BECHUALAND PROTECTORATE
Bechuana

TANGANYIKA TERRITORY
Banyakusa

WEST AFRICA
Pele, Bassa, Krew, Pesi, Vey, Mandigo, Ibo, Youraba, Gola

BELGIAN CONGO
Some tribes in the Belgian Congo in whom we are interested but have no direct work other than the leprosarium at Sona Bata, to which we make annual donations of from $300 - $600 are: Azindee, Baluba, Bango, Babomar, Batendo, Bateke, Bakongo, Basenge.[19]

MISSIONARIES AND NATIVE WORKERS OF THE FOREIGN MISSION BOARD, N.B.C., INC.
REV. J. B. FALCONER, Supervisor of West African Missions
REV. D. S. MALEKEBU, M.D.
Supervisor of South, East and Central African Missions
As of 1953

SUEHN INDUSTRIAL MISSION
Liberia, West Africa
 Mrs. Mattie Mae Davis, Principal
  (on furlough)
 Miss Winifred H. Borroughs
 J.B. Wilson
 Miss Virginia Antrom
 Miss Charlotte Jean Levi
 Miss Victoria White
 Miss Theresa Smith
 Miss Cynthia Moore
 Rev. Luke B. Anthony
 Austin Brown
 William E.D. Mitchell
 Victoria Etheridge
BIBLE INDUSTRIAL MISSION
Fortsville, Grand Bassa
Liberia, West Africa
 Mrs. Priscilla Jackson
 Miss Erma Bailey
 Miss Gladys V. East
  (on furlough)
 Mr. & Mrs. John Reid
 Mrs. Frances Jackson
 Miss Mary Diggs
 Mrs. Sarah Finley
 Lafayette G. Jackson
 Matthew Tweigh
 John Wilson
THE BENDOO MISSION
Cape Mount, Liberia, West Africa
 Rev. Rufus Prunty, Principal
 Mrs. J. Smith Cyrus
THE CARRIE V. DYER
MEMORIAL HOSPITAL
Monrovia, Liberia, West Africa
 Magdalene L. Dennis,
  Supervising Nurse
 Henrietta M. Williams
 Eva D. Padmore
 Emma Butler
 Aurelia L. Wocks
 Maria Milton
 Christina E. Morris
 Cora Boykin (on furlough)
 Abigail M. Street
 Julia M. Simpson
 Phoebe M. Outland
 Williette O. Johnson

Bessie M. Seahfe
Nellie C. Rose
Charlie Zeon
Giasenah
Jesse Garnett
Bojah Fuszch
Emmett Zenoga
RICKS INSTITUTE
Monrovia, Liberia, West Africa
 Rev. & Mrs. J.J. McDonald
  Pinkston
KLAY INSTITUTE
Monrovia, Liberia, West Africa
 Rev. H.H. Jones
PILGRIM BAPTIST MISSION
Issele-Uku, Nigeria, West Africa
 Rev. S.W. Martin, Principal
 Prof. Jad Washington
 E.A. Diel
 R.N. Ugbolue
 M.J. Horsfal
 J.C. Chlayed
 Mordi Arn
 Miss G.A. Asheidu
 R.O. Mums
 B.O. Obodoagwn
 E.O. Mooyei
 Miss Zelma Martin
 P.V. Monyei
 Mrs. D.N. Chinyei
 James U. Ituwe
THE PROVIDENCE INDUSTRIAL
MISSION
Nyasaland, East Africa
 Rev. Daniel S. Malekebu, M.D.
 Mrs. Flora E. Malekebu
 Frank Chambo
 P. Chipuliko
 David Nakhule
 Jordan Njiliyafa
 A. Birwick Kakbobwe
SOUTH AFRICA
W.W. Brown Memorial Mission
 Dr. D.S. Malekebu,
  Acting Principal
 Peter Legola
 W.B. Tabetshe
 Seleps

Rev. E.B.P. Koti,
 Box 47, Harding
Rev. L.J. Tashalata, Middewater
 School, Harding
Rev. F.M. Ndezekeni, Mkemane,
 Mt. Frere
Rev. P.M. Mahlangu, Pretoria
Rev. M. Mare, Lower,
 Umkobaas, Natal
Rev. E.B. Tsosane, Basutoland
Rev. G. Cele Itshe, Hlope
 Amaultiutoti
Rev. H.B. Miti, Krugersdorp
Rev. James Peter,
 Harrismith, O.F.S.
Rev. Phielding Yabo, Rooderprt
Rev. E.B. Mgabisa, Flagstaff
Rev. Phillip Ndenzeka, Umatata
Rev. Matillinea, Willowvale

Rev. S.N. Mgqam Lichtenburg,
 Transvaal
BUCHANAN MISSION STATION
Middledrift
 Rev. J. Ndaliso
 Rev. Charles S. Pupu
 Miss Martha Hela
 Miss Linda Sonjica
 Miss Florence Yoyo
 Macvicar Mngaza
CENTRAL AMERICA,
BLUEFIELDS, NICARAGUA
 Rev. D.A. Timpson, In Charge

BAHAMA ISLANDS
Jordan Memorial Training
 School, Nassau
 Rev. T.B. Livingston, Principal
 Mrs. T.B. Livingston
 Rev. A.L. Jarrott
 Rev. Reuben Cooper
 Mrs. M.B. Donaldson
VINE MEMORIAL MISSION
Freetown, Sierra Leone,
 West Africa
 Mrs. Constance Cummings -
  Jobs
NAHA
Okinawa, Japan
 Rev. & Mrs. Yoshlo Higo[20]

160

Missionary Stations Other Than Africa

The Foreign Mission Board, as previously noted, did not limit its attention to the African field. In 1952 it was reported that the Board had built a church in Bluefield, Nicaragua, at a cost of $20,000. This church was dedicated in 1952 by the Reverend J. Raymond Henderson, minister of the Second Baptist Church, Los Angeles, California, and recording secretary of the Foreign Mission Board. Reverend Henderson visited Bluefield early in 1951. This town is located on the Atlantic Ocean and in 1952 had a population of 8,000 comprised of original Indians, Spaniards, Negroes, Creoles and a mixture of Negroes and Indians. The few whites who were there were engaged primarily in business enterprises. Some operated plantations of bananas and rice. Dr. Henderson reported that he found the whites in Bluefield highly prejudiced. They taught the people that "white is supreme to black." He found that housing was far below American standards, "for the most part, a little better than woodsheds." Very few were painted. There was no sewage system, street lighting or water works. There were serious health problems. Although the Zion Baptist Mission in Bluefield had been founded twenty-seven years earlier, Dr. Henderson was the first Baptist from the United States ever to visit there.

The pastor of the church was the Reverend D. A. Timpson, a Creole and described as a man of great zeal and faith. He was a native of Bluefield and was reared as an Anglican Catholic until 1914. In that year, he had a job on a ship which came to this country where he got off and eventually found work near Nashville, Tennessee. There he was converted to the Baptist faith and instructed in Baptist doctrines. In 1921, he went to Managua and secured from the government a gift of 2,000 acres of land for his church. At the time of Dr. Henderson's visit, the land was beginning to produce bananas and rice.

Other denominations in the area included the Anglicans, Moravians and Adventists. The religious organization in greatest number and absolute control of the government was the Roman Catholic Church. Because of their power and influence, it was difficult for non-Catholics to enjoy any kind of political freedom or economic opportunity. Even hospitalization was difficult if one were a non-Catholic.

Before going to Nicaragua, Pastor Timpson was ordained and married by Dr. Mordecai Johnson who was the pastor of the First Baptist Church of Charleston, West Virginia. Although the Foreign Mission Board, under Secretary Adams' leadership, contributed $100 per month to Pastor Timpson's salary, the Board itself had not formally adopted the mission as one of its outposts. Dr. Henderson presented the Board the following recommendations:

Nicaragua Recommendations
To The Foreign Mission Board

1. I recommend that we definitely take over Zion Baptist Mission, located at Bluefields, Nicaragua, Central America, giving to it increased support. It would be better to disclaim all interest in it than to leave it in its embarrassing situation, particularly in its hostile environment.

2. I recommend that the Foreign Mission build a concrete block church there, (aluminum roof because of the climate) which will seat 300 people and equip it with a small organ. This church, with concrete blocks made by the members on a voluntary basis and much unskilled work donated, can be constructed at an estimated cost of $10,000. All materials have to be purchased in the United States and shipped to Bluefields via Tampa, Florida. On Wednesday night, May 23, 1951, Second Baptist Church at Los Angeles, California, of which I am minister, accepted my recommendation that we give $3,000 toward this project. This is aside from the $1,600 we annually give to missions. Our $3,000 is available at any time. With materials high in price and extra shipping charges, it is my belief that the Board might authorize a maximum of $10,000 in addition to ours. The money would be used only if absolutely necessary.

3. I recommend that as soon as possible upon completion of the church, the Board find a young man and his wife from the United States (wife with some knowledge of music) and send them out to take over this work. (This is Reverend Timpson's own idea for reasons which I have explained to Dr. Adams, and with which I agree.)

4. I recommend that when and if our Board sends someone to take Brother Timpson's place, that he be retained as a Missionary and Evangelist among the Indians, in particular. Brother Timpson's knowledge of the country, his ability to preach in English, Spanish and the Indian tongue, makes him a very valuable man.

Should these recommendations be accepted, I offer my services freely to assist the Board in any way possible.[21]

Mission To Okinawa

One of the unusual missionary posts established by the Foreign Mission Board was the Mission to Okinawa. This was established on July 1, 1947, through the cooperation of the Reverend Dr. W. H. Jernagin of Washington, D. C. This operation represented a joint venture with the National Baptist Convention of America (unincorporated).[22]

The pastor in charge of the mission to Okinawa was the Reverend Voshio Higa who was educated in this country but elected to return to the place of his birth to work in the interest of Baptist missions. He began his service in Okinawa on March 15, 1950. In his first letter to the Foreign Mission Board, he expressed thanks for his being sent to Okinawa as its representative "in order to serve the Lord and my people." After a meeting with other missionaries on the island, the decision was made to unite the churches in what was called the Church of Christ in Okinawa. In his letter to Secretary Adams, written on May 5, 1950. Pastor Higa explained his routine as follows:

We have almost no time to rest. Since I came home I myself made already 35 times of preaching and speaking. Every organization in every village and town is planning to invite me to speak. Everyone in Okinawa is just hungry to know what Christianity is. We are happy to report that there are 69 baptized by us since we came here.

We realize that it is necessary to help churches in Okinawa with definite plans. Regular support for pastor's living expenses, construction of church buildings, training of Christian leaders, and many other things should be considered. Therefore, we are going to request the Okinawa Committee to get this help. I wish you would cooperate with the committee so that we could have good harvest in the spiritual field on Okinawa.[23]

Early in 1949, the Foreign Mission Board agreed to pay the salary of the missionary in Okinawa which amounted to $3,000 per year. This work was carried on in cooperation with the Okinawa Committee of the Division of Foreign Missions.

The Foreign Mission Board, under the leadership of the Reverend Marshall Shepard, cooperated with the Division of Foreign Missions in the establishment of the Japanese Christian University. The Board, as one of the founding boards of this university, committed itself to contributing $20,000 over a period of three years to this project. This amounted to $6,660 annually.

Death of Mrs. Sara W. Layton

On January 14, 1950, an outstanding Convention leader passed on to her reward. The constituency of the National Baptist Convention, U.S.A., Inc., and particularly the Women's Auxiliary of the Convention, were greatly saddened at the passing of S. W. Layton. Elected in 1902 as president of the Women's Auxiliary, for forty-eight years Mrs. Layton carried forward an unusually successful program in which she worked closely with the Foreign Mission Board. She was a lady of unusual charm and personality as well as strength of character. Throughout her administration, she demonstrated the highest quality of leadership. Her foresight, dedication and commitment to the cause of Christian work and Christian missions were sources of inspiration to all who knew her. It was, therefore, quite appropriate that the maternity wing of the hospital in Malawi was named in her honor. The impact of the leadership of this great lady will certainly be experienced for many years to come in the history of the Convention.[24]

J. H. Jackson Elected President of the Convention

In September 1953, Reverend J. H. Jackson, former corresponding secretary of the Foreign Mission Board, was elected president of the National Baptist Convention, U.S.A., Inc., in Miami. He succeeded Dr. D. V. Jemison who served as president of the Convention for twelve years. Dr. Jemison's administration was marked by great growth and expansion, peace and brotherly love. His retirement was voluntary and beautiful.[25]

Dr. Jackson, pastor of the Olivet Baptist Church, Chicago, had a distinguished career as has been mentioned earlier in this volume. He carried forward the work of the Foreign Mission Board with imagination and qualities of leadership which made him not only a national, but international figure.

Missionary Stations

The Foreign Mission Board continued its work in the Bahamas where it carried forward a preaching and teaching program. Since the Foreign Mission Board took over work in the Bahamas from the Home Mission Board of the National Baptist Convention, USA, Inc., a new school had been built and they are a part of a fellowship of seventy-two churches. In 1957, Secretary Adams made an inspection trip to Nassau, Bahama Islands and reported that he was happy with what he saw and recognized a new turn in the work of the Foreign Mission Board there. The Reverend Thedford Johnson, pastor of the St. John Baptist Church in Miami, Florida, was appointed supervisor of the work in the Bahamas.

In Liberia, the Suehn Academy continued to make significant progress. Prior to 1955, there had been four principals of the school since it was founded in 1912 by Miss Emma B. Delaney. Following Miss Delaney, other principals included Mrs. Emma Butler, Miss Sarah Williamson and Mrs. Mattie Mae Davis.[26]

The Bendoo Mission, the first station established by pioneer missionaries in the Vai country of Liberia, continued to do well as of 1954, under the leadership of the Reverend Rufus Prunty. Under the leadership of Mrs. Sarah Cyrus, the school, too, did well in carrying on a constructive medical program. The Bendoo Mission has often been referred to as "Holy Ground" because here are buried Mrs. James H. Pressley, the Reverend J. S. Cyrus, the Reverend E. H. Bouey, Sr., one of his sons, and Mrs. W. W. Colley. Because of this heritage, the Bendoo Mission is considered one of the shrines of the missionary movement carried forward by the Foreign Mission Convention.

Bendoo campus includes 325 acres of ground. As of 1960, it was accessible only by boat. The nearest open road was nine miles away. Among the buildings on the campus are the J. S. Cyrus Hall, Indiana Cottage, the boys' dormitory, the mission clinic, the Friendship Baptist Church and residences for members of the staff and mission workers.

In addition to offering formal education at mission schools, the Reverend Mr. Prunty expanded the curriculum to include such trades as carpentry, animal husbandry and agriculture. A standard primary school was also developed. Some of the students of the mission school went on to complete higher levels of learning; many of these students returned to the campus as instructors and workers. Other churches pastored by the Reverend Mr. Prunty were Mt. Zion Baptist at Roberts Port and Mt. Olivet Tailah in Cape Mount County.[27]

Early in his tenure at the Bendoo Mission, Prunty sent the following letter to the Foreign Mission Board which gives an excellent idea of the way in which he carried forward his responsibilities.

*Rev. and Mrs. Rufus
Prunty*

Bendoo Industrial Mission
Cape Mount, Liberia
West Africa
November 19, 1940

Dear Dr. Adams:

God is still blessing us in many ways. We had a successful school year. The students all have shown rapid progress in their work, religiously and intellectually. God is still graciously blessing many who come to Him in the name of His Son Jesus. Their names may be enrolled in the Lamb's Book of Life.

The officials of the Board of Education have asked us to increase our enrollment to not less than 75 students. Our problem is that we have not a sufficient number of buildings to house such a number nor the proper buildings for classes.

167

The spirit of education is moving rapidly through the country of Liberia. The government is compelling the families throughout the country to send their children to school. The Chief informed us just recently (at the close of school) that he and his people are only waiting for us to construct more buildings so that the children may have proper places in which to stay.

The next need is for materials for procuring meat and fish. I would greatly appreciate it if you could send some shells for hunting meat in the bush. My prime object is to reduce the amount of expense for food.

Relative to the church and its work in Cape Mount: I wish to thank you and Rev. Falconer for the privilege of such a glorious opportunity to help increase the speed of the Gospel in this country.

God graciously blesses us each time I go and speak to His people there. I beg your prayers and the prayers of the Board and the Convention in general, that I may always think, speak and live for Christ. I took charge of the church on November 1st.

God has greatly blessed us in our health and strength in that not any of us here on the mission has suffered any serious ailments.

Hoping that you may continue to prosper in all great work for God's cause, as well as in your health, I remain,

Your humble servant in Christ,

S/Rufus Prunty[28]

The Reverend Mr. Prunty, who served as principal of this mission, has been cited as being one of the outstanding missionaries supported by the Foreign Mission Board. He succeeded the Reverend J. S. Cyrus who unfortunately drowned while on a preaching mission. Reverend Mr. Prunty was born in Chatham, Virginia, and was one of twenty children in his family. In his youth, he migrated to Pittsburgh, Pennsylvania, where he attended the Bethany Baptist Church. He enrolled in night school classes and eventually entered Payne Theological Seminary at Wilberforce University from which he was graduated. He also studied at the University of Dayton, University of Rochester, New York University, Hartford School of Missions and at Temple University in Philadelphia. The Reverend Prunty was much loved by his staff and co-workers and highly respected by members of the Foreign Mission Board.[29]

Attitudes of South Africans

When Corresponding Secretary C. C. Adams visited South Africa in 1947, he found a number of conditions which caused him much concern. The Foreign Mission Board had had no American missionary there since Dr. James E. East left in the early 1920s after eleven years of distinguished service. Obviously the racist attitude of the South African government had become increasingly hardened, and all efforts were made to keep the Blacks in that country from being exposed to and influenced by any democratic doctrine or individual who might cause them to foment rebellion.

Dr. Adams found that no American Black was welcome in South Africa, and that he was the first one to be allowed to enter that country since Dr. East left. Severe restrictions applied to American Blacks made it very difficult to secure entrance visas and, even when visas were granted, immigration officers made every effort to inconvenience travellers.

The purpose of Dr. Adams' trip was to visit the W. W. Brown Memorial Station and to examine what was being done by missionary agencies in general. The result of his visit was the opportunity to experience "the deep, heart-searching longings and groanings of our people," to sit where they sit and feel what they feel. He left with a renewed determination to work harder for the redemption of the people in South Africa.

One of the most satisfying aspects of his visit to South Africa was the realization of the high esteem in which native Africans held the National Baptist Convention, USA, Inc. He said:

> It is an inexpressible joy to find out at first hand, as I
> have, that to the remotest recesses of North, South,
> East, Central and West Africa, the name of the National
> Baptist Convention is known with reverence and effec-
> tiveness by its service. The teeming missions of Africans
> look to it and realize it as their rising sun to give a new
> and glorious day to Africa. A religious miracle has been
> wrought in East and South Africa under the leader-
> ship of Dr. D. S. Malekebu. The almost unbelievable has
> happened. There has been organized under the influ-
> ences and patterned after the NBC, the National Bap-
> tist Assembly of Africa, and annually more than 12,000
> happy, singing, praying and paying messengers
> meet...A like movement is in the borning in West
> Africa, with the ultimate hope that the two may have
> mutual fellowship.[30]

In spite of the unhappy conditions which Dr. Adams noted in
South Africa, he did find what he called some bright spots in the
total situation. These were as follows:

> 1. The natives are restless and smarting over the con-
> ditions of being robbed and knowing that they are
> robbed, which is itself a good sign.
>
> 2. They are hungry and anxious for education and
> the blessings of Christianity and ready to respond to
> every opportunity.
>
> 3. There are leaders rising up among them who are well
> educated, fearless and determined.
>
> 4. The government itself has doubled many times what
> it appropriated for native education in the last few years.
>
> 5. Many Negroes, in spite of economic handicaps, are
> becoming well-to-do.
>
> 6. The native farmers have organized farm cooperatives

and are learning better methods of farming. Many of them have large herds of cattle.

7. While the natives do not have direct franchise, they have recently been granted the privilege to vote for their native representatives, two in number, in Parliament, even though the native representatives are white and are supposed to advocate their well-being by securing favorable legislation.

8. At Fort Hair, a splendid college has developed and bright African students have been admitted into Witwatersand University and the University of Cape Town.

9. The enlightened conscience of humanity of the world is focussing the limelight on the government of the Union of South Africa which, in turn, is making it more lenient in its treatment of the natives; and this process is destined to continue.[31]

New Challenge to Missions

The National Baptist Convention, U.S.A., Inc., of course, was not the only denomination carrying forward missionary work in Africa. The zeal with which other religious agencies established and supported missionary work there presented a constant challenge to each of them to make their efforts as effective as possible. This challenge was heightened in 1959 when several denominations with missions in West Africa made plans for expanding their work. In that year, the Catholics announced that they would soon build a university of their own in Nigeria. The National Baptist Convention also announced that they would build a Baptist University in Nigeria with plans to complete it in five years. Moreover, a project of expansive dimensions was begun by the Seventh Day Adventists. This was the ground-breaking ceremonies for a post-secondary educational building at their mission in Ilishan-Remo near Shagamu. The projected cost of the building was $685,915; the name of the building was to be the Adventist College of West Africa. This means that the college was

171

planned to serve all the countries of that area including Nigeria, Ghana, Ivory Coast, Liberia and Sierra Leone. Emphasis was placed by all the denominations upon medical missions. This involved providing better hospital facilities, maternity homes, dispensaries and dental clinics.

The Foreign Mission Board of the National Baptist Convention did not look upon these developments by other denominations at all in a negative way. Rather the Board considered them as complements to the work being done at the Carrie V. Dyer Hospital in Monrovia, Liberia.[32]

R. A. Cromwell, Special Assistant

By 1945, the work of the Foreign Mission Board had been expanded and the responsibilities greatly increased. There was need also for further expansion on the foreign field. All of this meant that the finances of the Board had to be increased. A close and widening contact with the churches was necessary. In response to this situation, the Reverend R. A. Cromwell, pastor of the Mt. Zion Baptist Church in Pensacola, Florida, was appointed as special assistant to the Corresponding Secretary in 1945. The Reverend Mr. Cromwell was a popular preacher in Florida and was well loved by the members of his congregation. To give up these advantages and move north required a profound commitment to sacrificial service. Dr. Cromwell accepted this challenge. He was very effective in communicating the importance of the foreign mission enterprise to pastors and churches across the nation. The description of his work and his editorial comments were sources of inspiration and stimulation to those who read them.[33]

1949 Progress Report

In his report to the National Baptist Convention in 1949, Secretary Adams stated the following achievements:

1. New converts by the thousands.

2. We have sent out and returned twelve missionaries to and from the foreign fields.

3. We have returned eight missionaries for furlough.

4. We have completed thirteen buildings: four in Liberia; two in Nigeria; seven in Nyasaland. We are nearing completion of a girls' dormitory at Suehn and have assembled materials for the reconstruction and enlargement of the Carrie V. Dyer Memorial Hospital in Monrovia.

5. We shall soon be sending out two new missionaries.

6. We have equipped our Baptist headquarters in Monrovia.

7. We have formed a cooperative program in Liberia.

Other accomplishments listed by Dr. Adams included the shipment of about $35,000 in building materials, employing a full-time doctor at the hospital in Monrovia, building and opening a teachers' training college in Nigeria and taking over a new work at Accra, Gold Coast.[34]

Ten Year Assessment of Secretary Adams' Contributions

Ten years after Secretary Adams took office, Dr. Marshall L. Shepard, Chairman of the Foreign Mission Board, summarized some of the contributions made by Dr. Adams during his first years. As corresponding secretary, Dr. Shepard pointed out how, shortly after Dr. Adams assumed his duties, global war occurred which presented special challenges to the entire foreign mission enterprise. One of Dr. Adams' first projects was to reopen the Carrie V. Dyer Memorial Hospital in Monrovia, Liberia, which had been closed for some time. The hospital was placed under new management in 1942 and was able to serve its constituency again. Dr. Shepard also noted the work of Major John B. Falconer, supervisor of the West African Missions of the National Baptist Convention. Under Major Falconer, the hospital was integrated into the larger health program of the Republic of Liberia. As Dr. Shepard indicated, "This has been made possible by the United States Health Mission and President Truman's Point Four Program. The full rights, ownership and management of the hospital is retained by the Foreign Mission Board and our own Mrs. M. L. Dennis remains in her position as superintendent." During Dr. Adams' administration, a ten-year building program was started. This included a new school building and dormitory in the Bahamas, the J. C. Austin Building in Nigeria and the J. H. Jackson Building in Liberia. Moreover, the Foreign Mission Board took over the operation of two Liberian schools, the Klay Institute and the Ricks Institute. In addition, the work in South Africa and in East Africa was reclaimed and re-established.[35]

In 1951, Secretary Adams set forth the program of the Foreign Mission Board as it was conceived at that time. This program is stated as follows:

PROGRAM OF FOREIGN MISSION BOARD FOR THE FISCAL YEAR CLOSING JUNE 30, 1951

1. Integrate the Klay Institute, taken over from Dr. H. H. Jones, into our Liberian work, and bring Dr. Jones to this country to stimulate the churches on the home field with his experience and hope of forty years service in Liberia.

2. To help the Liberian Baptists make a going project of Ricks Institute as a school of ministerial and church leadership training.

3. To complete two new buildings in Liberia and put the remodeled and extended Carrie V. Dyer Memorial Hospital under roof.

4. Repair and paint the buildings at the T. E. Brown Progressive Station at Bassa. This calls for an enlarged staff and increased costs across the board in Liberia alone.

5. Gold Coast, West Africa — This work is centered at Accra, the capital of the country, and extends its reach over much of that country. The school in Accra must be developed and the work in general systematized. This calls for time, patience, thought and money.

174

6. Nigeria, West Africa — The building program at Pilgrim Station is being brought up-to-date and the Teachers' Training College is running so satisfactorily that Dr. and Mrs. S. W. Martin are being brought to America for a year's rest.

7. Sierra Leone, West Africa — A church and school are being set up there in close proximity to Freetown, with another school far out in the Protectorate from Freetown. A school plant with eight buildings has recently been purchased for $8,000.00 and was paid for in cash. A God-send.

8. South and East Africa — This includes the church and school work in the Union of South Africa, Northern Rhodesia and Nyasaland, and constitutes our largest operation on the continent with a hospital, the James E. East Memorial Hospital, at the Providence Station at Chiradzulu, Nyasaland. Dr. D. S. Malekebu is principal and superintendent of all South and East African work. Here we are maintaining a steady but remarkable growth.

9. The Caribbean Area — Here emphasis is placed on the Bahama Islands and Bluefield, Nicaragua. We regret to say that in these fields we experienced greater difficulties in rapid expansion than in all our other fields put together due to so-called local native leadership. Hence, because of physical impossibilities and increasing demands on the Secretary's time and strength, the Board will send Dr. J. Raymond Henderson, pastor of Second Baptist Church, Los Angeles, California, to Bluefield for personal inspection and to make recommendations as to the future of the work there.

10. Our Pacific Interest:

    a. We are sponsoring a joint work in Okinawa through the Okinawa Committee of the

Foreign Missions Conference, now the Division of Foreign Missions of the National Council of the Churches of Christ, U.S.A. Our sponsored missionary there is the Reverend Yoshio Higa.

b. We are sponsoring the founding of a Christian university in Japan proper, with twenty-one other Boards of the above named organization.

11. To implement and assure the future of the above named work, we are presently trying to gradually increase the annual budget so that at the end of the five year period, we will have an underwritten budget of $500,000 annually.[36]

Five years after the above program was published, Secretary Adams prepared a more specific program expressing his philosophy of Christian missions. That statement is as follows:

COMPREHENSIVE PROGRAM, 1956

The work of the Foreign Mission Board, National Baptist Convention, U.S.A., Inc., is established on the continent of Africa in Liberia, Sierre Leone, Gold Coast, Nyasaland, Union of South Africa, Southern Rhodesia, Belgian Congo and Rasutoland, elsewhere in the Bahama Islands, Nicaragua, Okinawa and Japan.

There are eight points in the comprehensive program of the Foreign Mission Board of the National Baptist Convention, U.S.A., Inc., as follows:

1. In order for the program for the redemption of Africa and the heathen to be most effective and far-reaching, it must be comprehensive in approach and application. Salvation through Christ is total for the whole of man, inclusive of all needs and relations.

a. This means more than the conversion and initiation of the new convert in Christian prin-

176

ciples, but also includes the means of perpetuation in the Christian life.

b. Hence it means that the whole of the person must be touched and influenced — his intellect, his hands, his economic and social outlook all must be fitted into the new pattern of life.

2. With the above in mind, the Foreign Mission Board begins with the Bible and the preaching of the Gospel as the foundation, sure and tried, on which to build the character of individuals, races and nations and assure a Godly order.

3. We realize the prime importance of a healthy body. This accounts for our sanitary and health programs, expressed in the work of our hospitals and clinics.

4. We maintain schools and churches in West, South and East Africa, and in the Bahama Islands, for rounded education results.

5. We also have work in Nicaragua, Okinawa and Japan.

6. That the hands may learn the cunning of art, we foster brickmaking, masonry, blacksmithing, carpentry, etc.

7. Knowing that the earth is the mother of all goods and riches, we stress agriculture and the husbandry of plants and trees, and the results are showing in our gardens, farms and rubber plantations.

8. The carrying forward of these things to a fuller success is our task for which we ask larger support from every pastor and church.[37]

Bible Industrial Academy

The Bible Industrial Academy was established at Fortsville, Grand Bassa County, Liberia, by the Liberian Baptists and two pioneer women, Miss Susan Taylor and Mrs. Elizabeth Davis George. In 1917, the Reverend and Mrs. Daniel R. Horton went to this station under the sponsorship of the Foreign Mission Board.

The Reverend Mr. Horton was born in the West Indies and took his higher education at Morehouse College, Atlanta, Georgia. His wife was a native of Philadelphia and finished her academic preparation at Spelman College. Upon his graduation from college, the Reverend Mr. Horton pleaded with the Foreign Mission Board to be appointed to go to West Africa as a missionary. Those who knew him during his student days at Morehouse recommended him very highly, and, accordingly, he was sent to Liberia. At the Bible Industrial Academy, he carried forward a constructive and dynamic missionary enterprise for a number of years.

Rev. Daniel R. Horton   *Mrs. D. R. Horton*

During Reverend Mr. Horton's tenure at the Academy, a large two-story building was constructed which embraced a church as well as dormitories. In addition, an agricultural program was initiated which resulted in large crops of coffee, cassava, corn, sugar cane, potatoes and rice. In 1945 he was cited in the

Mission Herald as one of the "Persons of Mark in Missions." The following tribute was paid to him:

> Dr. Horton is known, respected, trusted and loved from one end of the country to the other. He is a worker and a doer. He has not only preached and taught, but has lived out what he preached. He has shown to the natives the way of self-help in the way of improving breeds of poultry, livestock, etc. He was the first to demonstrate that milk cows could be developed there and the art and benefit of milking cows and churning butter.
>
> To show the way to better advantage, he became a naturalized Liberian citizen and bought land. He owns a beautiful home, cows, hogs, sheep, goats, chickens and a large rubber plantation. Many thousands have been converted by his preaching and taught to buy land, build homes, organize churches, buy sites and build and pay for their own church buildings and schools.[38]

Reverend Horton organized a convention of some twenty churches which raised annually more than $1,000. It was reported in 1945 that he had adopted a five-year plan to raise $25,000 to develop the school and a Christian community center. Among other things that he accomplished was the formation of a beneficial society for the purpose of helping the sick and providing adequate burial expenses in case of death.

In 1955 the school had ninety boarding students. The Antioch Baptist Church there was a center of religious activities from which the older children went, at the close of each mission service, spreading their knowledge of the gospel from village to village.[39]

Eventually the Reverend Mr. Horton discontinued his affiliation with the Foreign Mission Board and worked independently as a Christian missionary.

The Reverend S. W. Martin

One of the significant developments in the missionary enterprise is the training of native people to assume positions of leader-

179

ship. The Reverend S. W. Martin is an example of what can be accomplished by the training of native Africans for mission work in their homeland. He was pastor of the Pilgrim Baptist Mission at Issele Uku, Nigeria, West Africa. This mission is located on an attractive site and has well-constructed buildings, an adequate staff as well as a beautiful church structure. In addition to the main campus, the Reverend Mr. Martin established more than eleven out-stations, all of which were crowded. He developed a successful farm. Under his leadership, the government sponsored an agricultural experiment station to which young men were sent for training.[40]

In 1954, Reverend Mr. Martin reported having a staff of 127 teachers and workers, an enrollment of 3,086 students and a teacher training college. In that year, the physical facilities included ten completed buildings with twenty-three under construction. In 1953, 120 students were graduated.[41]

The Reverend Charles Azu

The Reverend Charles Azu was born in Nigeria. He became the adopted son of the Reverend and Mrs. S. W. Martin who sent him to this country to complete his undergraduate education at Washburn College, Topeka, Kansas. He received his medical education at St. Louis University in June 1959 and served his internship at the Homer G. Phillips Hospital in St. Louis, Missouri. He was then scheduled to return to Africa where there was a great need for his medical skills.[42]

After having an extended conversation with Dr. Azu, Secretary Adams said of him:

> We beheld in him the radiance of Christian personality. We read a "living epistle" of a Christ-made man. Within us something said, "here is a living testimony of the difference Jesus Christ makes in the lives of people." No more a heathen worshipper, no more a scantily dressed pagan, no more committed to backward mores and traditions, and no more wedded to the superstitions of a witch doctor and the curse of evil spirits — He is now

a Christian man, a cultured man and scientifically trained to carry on a healing Christian ministry in the land of his nativity.[43]

Reverend Daniel N. Nwadiei

The Reverend Daniel N. Nwadiei was born in Issele Uku, Benin Province, Southern Nigeria. His father was baptized a Catholic but it is said that he was never really a Christian and died a heathen. His mother was converted to Christianity through the influence of the Reverend S. W. Martin. Originally Daniel was baptized a Catholic but, at eighteen months of age, his parents took him to the Reverend and Mrs. Martin who became his *de facto* parents. Reverend Nwadiei began his education at the Pilgrim Baptist School. Later he was sent to the IWO Baptist day school and lived with a missionary couple, Reverend and Mrs. Brothers, of the Southern Baptist Convention. He attended Arinze Commercial College for one year and then began teaching. After passing the University of Cambridge School Certificate Examination in 1949, he met the Reverend W. L. Muncy of the Central Baptist Theological Society in Kansas City, Kansas. Upon Dr. Muncy's return home, he arranged for Nwadiei to sail for America for further studies. While here, Nwadiei earned the degrees of Bachelor of Theology, Bachelor of Science, Master of Science and Bachelor of Divinity.

In 1959 he wrote to the Foreign Mission Board that he was the assistant manager of Pilgrim Mission Schools, the assistant pastor of Pilgrim Baptist Church and a tutor at the Pilgrim Baptist Secondary School. He reported that since he returned to Africa, he had baptized 472 souls. In writing to Secretary Adams, he expressed appreciation for the inspiration Dr. Adams gave him. He also gave credit for his success to several Baptist pastors in this country.[44]

Dr. Daniel S. Malekebu

Another outstanding native African missionary, Dr. Daniel S. Malekebu, whom we have mentioned several times earlier in this history, continued to make progress in his inspired undertakings. In 1954 he reported that he had a staff of 125 teachers and native workers. Approximately 15,000 pupils were under his guidance as well as 290 established and thriving Baptist churches. In addition, he supervised the James E. East Hospital in which 4,738 patients were treated during 1954. After he returned to the place of his birth in Nyasaland, Chiradzulu, he made significant contributions to the establishment of a sound missionary enterprise.[45]

Carrie V. Dyer Hospital

Several times we have mentioned the Carrie V. Dyer Memorial Hospital which was founded in Monrovia, Liberia, in 1926. The original hospital was relatively small and contained only about twenty-five beds. It was always overcrowded but, nevertheless, rendered valuable service to the community of which it was a vital part. It was said that missionaries, military personnel and Europeans, as well as Africans, were all received and served by this important facility.

In 1950, it was suggested to Secretary Adams by the Liberian government that the hospital should cooperate with the national Public Health Service of Liberia in setting up a maternity and child welfare center. This proved to be beneficial because the hospital widened its possibilities for meeting the medical needs of the community. Shortly after this occurred, however, the hospital was put out of commission by a fire caused by faulty wiring. A new building was erected on the same site. The work was carried out by the mission personnel using the same procedures as were used when the Reverend E. H. Bouey participated in constructing the first building. All of the labor including carpentry, plumbing, masonry and electrical work was done by native Liberians. The new hospital had 100 beds. It also had a large outpatient department and a clinic which gave much needed advice to the patients it served. Also included in the building was a chapel. The Reverend John B. Falconer, West African Supervisor for the Foreign Mission Board, wrote, "It is from this that we hope the spirit of the Great Spirit will be so communicated to the future nurses and midwives that they will build in their own hearts another Carrie V. Dyer which will be open to all who come to them for service." The new hospital was built at a cost of $200,000.[46]

In 1956, Secretary Adams announced that the new hospital had been completed except for some finishing touches. Another catch, however, faced the Foreign Mission Board — that of furnishing the new structure. A total of $35,000 had been pledged for this purpose.[47]

The Foreign Mission Board and African Students

Through the years, the Foreign Mission Board has continuously sought to meet the aspirations of promising African students. This, of course, has been true of all the Christian missionaries. The results of the work of missionaries in African countries have been well demonstrated since the colonial powers released their hold on African countries. Among the heads of state that were listed as products of missionary activity in 1959 were the following: Sekou Toure, Premier of Guinea, West Africa; Houpouet-Boigny, leader of Ivory Coast, West Africa and a cabinet member of the French government; Kwame Nkruma, Premier of Ghana, West Africa; and Namdi Azikiwe, leader of Nigeria's independence scheduled for 1960. These are among the many outstanding Africans who benefited from the labors and teachings of Christian missionaries.[48]

African youths have generally exhibited a keen desire for higher education. They have come to the United States in large numbers, attracted by the democratic principles which are a part of the American dream and by the fact that many of the leaders whom we mentioned, as well as others, have received their higher education in this country. In 1959 the Foreign Mission Board was supporting eight African students in advanced college courses as reported in the *Mission Herald:*

> Six of them graduated this spring, namely: Charles Chukwuemeka Azu, M.D., a Nigerian, graduated from

St. Louis University, Missouri; Anyanaisinuwa M. Mordi and Onuekwuke N. Okwumabua, Nigerians, graduating from Virginia Union University, Richmond, Virginia; S. N. Anazia graduating from Ottawa University, Ottawa, Kansas; Emmanuel Chukwudi Benye, a Nigerian, graduating from Lincoln University, Jefferson City, Missouri; Florence E. Davis, a Liberian, receiving her Masters Degree from the University of Pennsylvania, and Agras Nebo of Liberia graduating from Philadelphia Conservatory of Music. Esther Roberts graduated from Temple University, Philadelphia, Pennsylvania, in February. Miss Roberts is also a Liberian. Mr. Festus O. Aina from Ghana, West Africa, is now pursuing his Doctorate of Philosophy at Edinburgh University, Scotland. Mr. Aina is hoping to take that degree at the end of the next school year.[49]

The contributions to the education of African youths are among the accomplishments of the Foreign Mission Board in which it takes great pride.

In 1959 Miss Florence Davis received the Masters Degree in Education at the University of Pennsylvania and returned to Liberia to work at the Suehn Mission. Mr. Solomon Scott was graduated from the University of Liberia and went back into the Suehn community. Ballah and Florence Davis graduated from the Suehn Mission School. Florence received a scholarship to Cuttington College where she received her degree, while Ballah became a successful farmer. Mr. Charles Russell, who attended Bendoo Mission Episcopal High School and the University of Liberia, was serving as business manager of the supervisor's office in Liberia. These are a few examples of the lives that were transformed and developed through the work of the Foreign Mission Board.[50]

Death of Dr. W. H. Jernagin

Dr. W. H. Jernagin, President of the National Sunday School and the BTU Congress, died in the fall of 1957 at the Mt. Sinai

184

Hospital in Miami Beach, Florida, Dr. Jernagin had held that position for more than thirty years. For over forty years he was pastor of the Mt. Carmel Baptist Church in Washington, D.C. He had a humble beginning but rose to become a recognized and revered leader in the denomination and among our people as a whole. His interests were broad and he was fearless in his support of the principles of the Baptist Church and of the Foreign Mission Board. Born, reared and educated in Mississippi, Dr. Jernagin rose to become a confidant of presidents of the United States — whatever their political party affiliation — and was often sent by them on missions abroad. He gave unstintingly of his energy and time to help extend the Kingdom of God.

Dr. W. H. Jernagin

In a notice of his passing which appeared in the *Mission Herald,* it was said of him:

> No man of his day and generation was more devoted
> to his denomination, race and country, and humanity
> in general. From humble and obscure beginnings, he

185

rose to heights of international and world fame. Indeed, he was a cosmopolitan and stayed active in body and young in mind to the very end. In fact, he fell in harness. Like David of old, he served his day and generation and fell on to sleep. Dr. Jernagin, for a long stretch of years, was the honorable and beloved leader of the Young Baptist People of this nation. Their loyalty to him was unflagging and their love unfeigned.

He was a youth in spirit and did not allow his age to tie him in one place. In fact, he was a leader in the World's Youth Movement and was an active planner in the Youth Congress to be held in Canada in July.[51]

Some months after his death, it was proposed that a joint commission from the National Baptist Convention and the National Sunday School and BTU Congress be appointed to recommend a suitable memorial to Dr. Jernagin, not only as a tribute to him but also as a symbol of service to present and future generations. In commenting on this proposal, Dr. Martin Luther King, Jr., the vice president at large of the National Sunday School and BTU Congress, issued the following statement regarding a memorial to the late Dr. Jernagin:

> The idea of memorializing Dr. W. H. Jernagin which has been projected by the *Mission Herald,* is one that deserves our highest consideration. His commitment to the Christian ideals of love and brotherhood, his sane and wise judgement, and his prophetic vision should be a lasting challenge to every Christian of our day. Moreover, his life should serve as an inspiration to generations yet unborn. Probably no man in our ranks surpassed him in Christian statesmanship. He literally forgot himself into immortality. The Baptists would not only pay a tribute to Dr. Jernagin by memorializing him, but they would pay a tribute to God for making such a life possible.[52]

Dr. Jernagin was truly a great man and a stalwart Christian. His passing was a great loss to the denomination.

Cooperation Conference

In May 1950, a joint conference of representatives of the National Baptist Convention, Inc., the Lott Carey Missionary Baptist Convention and the Liberian Baptist Convention was held and a formal agreement was made for the three bodies to cooperate in bringing about the unification of Baptist work in Liberia. A committee was appointed to work out the details and to put the program into operation. This conference was held in Monrovia, Liberia, and the representatives of the National Baptist Convention of America (Unincorporated) also agreed to this proposal before leaving the country for Africa. This proposal was designed to make for a more efficient operation of the Christian missionary enterprise in West Africa. Unfortunately, the goals of this conference never became a reality.

Crisis in the Foreign Mission Board

For some time a considerable amount of unrest had been observed among some of the pastors in the National Baptist Convention, Inc. This unrest had, as part of its cause, the dissatisfaction of some of the brethren with the policy of tenure with respect to the presidency of the organization. That dissatisfaction was reflected in a sharp decline in the support of the work of the Foreign Mission Board. In 1960 Secretary Adams reported, "In the last three years, for whatever cause, we lost the support of 1,857 pastors and churches while gaining only 399. This is an unhealthy condition that should concern all of us and cause us to bestir ourselves."[53]

Secretary Adams went on to say that at least twenty members of the Board did not give as much as one penny a year or show any interest in the work. Later that year, Secretary Adams expressed disappointment at what he called "a staggering blow" to the financial support of and interest in the work of the Foreign Mission Board. At the meeting of the National Baptist Convention

187

in Philadelphia in September 1960, he reported that "thousands were shocked and stunned and left in total confusion, taking money intended for the Foreign Mission Board back home with them. Our major problem now is how to clear away the confusion." Dr. Adams pleaded for prayers, influence and support to help stem this tide of spirited indifference and confusion.[54]

In the fall of 1960, Secretary Adams wrote an editorial in which he called attention to the increasing dissension in the Baptist ranks. He referred to these as "ominous clouds gathering and overcasting the skies of the home base of our Foreign Mission Board." He pointed out that while some had stood fast, others had gone away or taken shelter. Because of these developments and his faith that the foreign mission work is the work of the Lord, Dr. Adams selected and wrote to 200 pastors called the "Two Hundred Special." These men were asked to redouble their efforts and, where possible, to give twice as much as they did the preceding year.[55]

The confusion that Dr. Adams referred to was based in the concern of Convention members with the electoral procedures as mandated by the constitution which specifically called for an annual election for the officers of the Convention. Instead, an election with each messenger voting for his candidate for a number of years, motions to suspend the rules and vote by acclamation for the offices of the Convention — all had become the custom. When a motion was made to the effect that the election of the officers of the Convention would come at the time designated on the program and that the convention would vote by states, much confusion ensued.[56] Those favoring this motion refused to allow any other motions or amendments to be voted upon. The result was that the Convention agenda could not be followed and the sessions were adjourned. Though the general vote of the Convention was halted due to the disruptive events of the week, all of the auxiliaries and boards continued to carry on their responsibilities during the year 1960-1961 which led up to the next annual convention held in Kansas City, Kansas.

188

Notes

1. *Mission Herald,* (September-October 1941) p. 4.
2. *Mission Herald,* (November-December 1941) p. 2.
3. *Mission Herald,* (May-June 1942) p. 5.
4. *Mission Herald,* (September-October 1942) p. 6.
5. *Mission Herald,* (September-October 1942) p. 2.
6. *Mission Herald,* (September-October 1943) p. 3.
7. Ibid.
8. *Mission Herald,* (May-June 1944) p. 3.
9. *Mission Herald,* (July-August 1945) p. 3.
10. *Mission Herald,* (March-April 1945) p. 2.
11. *Mission Herald,* (March-April 1947) p. 16.
12. *Mission Herald,* (January-February 1953) p. 6.
13. *Mission Herald,* (May-June 1946) p. 19.
14. *Mission Herald,* (November-December 1950)
15. *Mission Herald,* (July-August 1945) p.12
16. Ibid.
17. *Mission Herald,* (September-October 1947) p. 5.
18. *Mission Herald,* (May-June 1950) p. 16.
19. *Mission Herald,* (March-April 1950) p. 21.
20. *Mission Herald,* (May-June 1953) p. 36
21. *Mission Herald,* (July-August 1951) p. 13.
22. *Mission Herald,* (March-April 1947) p. 8.
23. *Mission Herald,* (July-August 1950) p. 13.
24. *Mission Herald,* (January-February 1950) p. 24.
25. *Mission Herald,* (September-October 1953) p. 2
26. *Mission Herald,* (March-April 1955) p. 16
27. *Mission Herald,* (September-October 1960) pp. 7-8
28. *Mission Herald,* (March-April 1950) p. 24.
29. *Mission Herald,* (September-October 1960) pp. 7-8.
30. *Mission Herald,* (September-October 1947) p. 7.
31. *Mission Herald,* (September-October 1947) p. 21.
32. *Mission Herald,* (November-December 1959) p. 8.
33. *Mission Herald,* (September-October 1948) p. 5.
34. NBC *Minutes,* 1949, pp. 176-177.
35. *Mission Herald,* (July-August 1951) p. 6.
36. *Mission Herald,* (November-December 1950) p. 4.
37. *Mission Herald,* (January-February 1956) p. 7.
38. *Mission Herald,* (July-August 1945) p. 12.
39. *Mission Herald,* (March-April 1955) p. 5
40. *Mission Herald,* (January-February 1948) p. 18.
41. *Mission Herald,* (November-December 1954) p. 7.
42. *Mission Herald,* (January-February 1959) p. 7.
43. Loc. cit.
44. *Mission Herald,* (January-February 1959) pp. 7-9.
45. *Mission Herald,* (November-December 1954) p. 7.

Notes continued

46. *Mission Herald,* (May-June 1956) pp. 4-6.
47. *Mission Herald,* (September-October 1956) p. 8.
48. *Mission Herald,* (January-February 1959).
49. *Mission Herald,* (May-June 1959) p. 4.
50. *Mission Herald,* (September-October 1959) p. 11.
51. *Mission Herald,* (January-February 1958) p. 5.
52. *Mission Herald,* (September-October 1958) p. 8.
53. *Mission Herald,* (July-August 1960) pp. 3-5.
54. *Mission Herald,* (September-October 1960) p. 4.
55. *Mission Herald,* (September-October 1960) pp. 2-3.
56. *Minutes,* 1960, p. 53.

CHAPTER SIX
NEW EXPANSION
AND DEVELOPMENT, 1961-1986
The Tenure of Dr. William J. Harvey, III

During the year leading to the annual session, there were many official meetings of the board of directors since the constitution specifically stated that "whatever unfinished business remains after the adjournment of a particular session, it becomes the duty of the board of directors to transact such business and to carry on the program of the Convention (Constitution Article VI). During these meetings Mr. Andrew Means was elected temporary treasurer and the Rev. Mr. I. H. Henderson, Jr., was elected temporary secretary. The board of directors also elected Dr. J. H. Jackson as president.[1] At subsequent meetings, the Board voted that the meeting place of the Convention shall be in the hands of the officials of the Convention;[2] that only delegates are to be seated on the first floor of the auditorium,[3] and that Article XI of the charter would be invoked:

ARTICLE XI

1. In addition to the powers granted to and vested in this corporation by operation of law, this corporation is also hereby given the express and exclusive right, authority and control over the management and properties of the following auxiliary boards which were heretofore created and established by the National Baptist Convention of the United States of America, prior to its

corporation, namely: The National Baptist Publication Board, incorporated under the laws of the State of Tennessee; the Foreign Mission Board of the National Baptist Convention, incorporated under the laws of the State of Kentucky; the Baptist Young Peoples Union Board, incorporated under the laws of the State of Tennessee; the Women's Auxiliary Board, incorporated under the laws of the District of Columbia. That said auxiliary boards and their officers and directors shall have and exercise no power or control over the affairs and properties of said boards independent of this corporation, and said boards shall forthwith amend their charters so as to show that each and all said boards are under and subject to the jurisdiction and control of this corporation. And this corporation shall have the exclusive right and power at its annual session, or at such other time as shall be provided in the by-laws, to nominate and appoint the officers, managers or directors for each and all of said auxiliary boards.

In the 1961 minutes of the Convention, it was recorded that Dr. J. H. Jackson was elected by a vote of 2,732 and Dr. Gardner Taylor received 1,519 votes. Thus ended one of the greatest struggles of the Convention in its history.

Reverend William J. Harvey, III Elected Corresponding Secretary

Following this mandate by the Convention on September 9, 1961, the Reverend William J. Harvey, III, was elected Corresponding Secretary of the Foreign Mission Board to succeed Dr. Adams. This corresponding secretary did not seek the position and, after he was asked to assume the responsibility, he did so only after much prayer and reflection, and with a sense of total commitment to the obligations and possibilities of the Foreign Mission Board. His connection with the Board had begun some years earlier when he served as associate editor of the *Mission Herald* while pastor of the Pinn Memorial Church in Philadelphia. During that period he was able to have a first-hand experience with the important work of the Board.

The new corresponding secretary was born in Oklahoma City, Oklahoma. He was the son of the late Dr. and Mrs. William J. Harvey, Jr. His father was a practicing physician who moved with his family to Philadelphia when the son was quite young. He was baptized at the age of nine by the Reverend W. A. Harrod, pastor of the First African Baptist Church of Philadelphia. He was an honor graduate of Central High School and prior to his gradua- tion won the National Oratorical Contest sponsored by the Improved Benevolent Order of Elks of the World. He was graduated from Fisk University in Nashville, Tennessee, with a Bachelor of Arts degree and received his formal theological train- ing at the Chicago Theological Seminary, University of Chicago, where he earned a Master of Divinity degree. He was licensed to preach under the Reverend Dr. Sandy F. Ray, then pastor of the St. Luke Baptist Church in Chicago. While in the Seminary, he worked at that church and also as pastor of the youth in the Pilgrim Baptist Church, Chicago, under pastor Dr. J. C. Austin.

Rev. William J. Harvey, III

193

Following his graduation from the Seminary, Harvey returned to Philadelphia and, after serving as assistant pastor of the First African Baptist Church for one year, was called to the pastorate of the Pinn Memorial Baptist Church, Philadelphia, a pastorate he held for over ten years. During those years he held various positions including vice president of the Baptist Ministers Conference of Philadelphia, secretary of the Keystone Baptist Association, auditor of the Pennsylvania State Baptist Convention, Negro Baptist representative on the board of directors of the Philadelphia Council of Churches plus numerous positions with other organizations and agencies. He was a frequent speaker at colleges throughout the East.

In 1950 he was called to the pastorate of the Calvary Baptist Church of Oklahoma City, Oklahoma, where he served for three and one-half years. While in Oklahoma, he taught homiletics, church administration and Baptist polity at the Oklahoma School of Religion, Langston, Oklahoma. His other involvements included serving as the first Negro chairman of the Race Relations Commission of the Oklahoma City Council of Churches, the first Negro president of the Oklahoma City Ministerial Alliance and as a member of the board of directors of the Urban League.

In January 1954, he was called to the Macedonia Baptist Church in Pittsburgh. Here, under his pastorate, church membership almost doubled and the church carried forward a remodeling program at a cost of $109,500.

At the same time he became active in the statewide Baptist work. He served as corresponding secretary of the Pennsylvania State Baptist Convention and chairman of the Racial and Cultural Commission of the Pittsburgh Council of Churches.

In 1959 he was chosen to serve as one of five Baptist editors from North America to visit seven countries in South America prior to the Baptist World Alliance meeting in Rio de Janeiro, Brazil, in 1960.

The Challenge of Transition

In 1961 the work of the Foreign Mission Board and the new corresponding secretary faced many challenges. Soon after his election to the office, Dr. Harvey requested a conference with Dr. Adams to arrange for a cooperative transition. In spite of the fact that a definite date and time for the conference had been set, the outgoing corresponding secretary failed to keep the appointment. Nevertheless, the new corresponding secretary offered to place Dr. Adams on pension in recognition of his twenty years of service. Surprisingly, that offer was rejected and a competitive organization founded. This was the Foreign Mission Bureau out of which developed the Progressive National Baptist Convention.

The new secretary also faced two other major problems. The office staff, with the exception of one member, summarily resigned. Correspondence for the preceding year vanished. Regional agents in the deep South and mid-west defected. Many of the leading contributors transferred their allegiance and their gifts. Fortunately, God's work could not be stopped. Members of the National Baptist Convention, U.S.A., Inc., closed ranks; new sacrifices were made; new goals were projected; new materials were written; new mission fields were opened; old mission stations were renewed and mission schools were expanded.

An additional challenge was the need to rethink and reassess the old approaches and methodologies of the missionary enterprise. Foreign mission boards needed to divest themselves of the outmoded garments of approved methods of the past and accept the streamlined approach and methods that would meet the requirements of a new age. The new approach did not necessarily involve a change in the Christian message, for the essence of the Gospel cannot be changed; it is essential, unchangeable and eternally all-sufficient.

Moreover, the sending churches needed to give up the thought and attitude that they were to keep control indefinitely of the leadership of the missions, the churches and the institutions established in foreign lands. The home churches had to recognize and respect the indigenous or native churches' desire and demand to take over and assume the leadership of the native church. Missions had reached the stage of development where it was the plain duty of foreign mission boards to welcome and help the native church to make the transition of leadership from the Foreign Mission Board to the native churches. These observations became part of the comprehensive philosophy of Christian missions of the new corresponding secretary and were set forth at length in the 1966 May-June issue of the *Mission Herald* as follows:

> To state the philosophy of Christian missions is to state the principles and purpose of Christianity. It is basic to all we believe and do in the name of Christ — basic to our preaching, teaching and our plans and policies. This should always be central and distinct as the motivating cause and directing purpose for all we do as Christians.
>
> The source book for missions is the Bible through which, from Genesis to Revelation, the unbroken thread of redemption is unmistakingly woven. Hence, it is accepted as granted that man, by willful and deliberate act, committed a sin; that he transgressed the moral law of God that put all men out of harmony with God and the scheme of divine things. Therefore, all men became sinners, separated from God and helplessly lost, without divine intervention to work the miracle of redemption and salvation. Thus, salvation became a common need of all men, for, "all have sinned or come short of the glory of God." Also, all men fell under the necessity of a common saviour, which has been given by the promise of God and revealed as Jesus, the Christ of God.
>
> The fact that God has given a world plan of salvation and a world Saviour promises that all men are saveable and have a right to a chance of salvation. Hence arises the necessity and duty of the Church of Christ to preach and teach the Gospel to all nations. Not only is it taken for granted by the necessity and duty of preaching the

Gospel to every nation, that some of every nation will accept the terms of the Gospel and be saved, but experience and history have proven that some of all nations will accept the Gospel of Christ.

The Gospel of Christ places a stamp of divine condemnation on the worldly order of things, with the certainty of divine execution, as past and fallen civilizations bear witness, and even as the present civilizations show earmarks.

Therefore, missions is not of human origin, but its source and beginning are of God and woven with the design of God's cosmic purpose in man. Hence, missions has a human and divine necessity. This is another way of saying that man, without the fulfillment of the purpose of missions, cannot attain unto the highest and best good, nor can God realize his creative purpose in man.

The very nature of missions to become operative has a divine side and a human side which make a divine and human partnership in man's salvation and the redemption of God's Kingdom on earth. God's plan of world salvation is simple but comprehensive and all-embracing in statement. Yet that simpleness of statement emphasizes its tremendous importance so that the simplest of people may understand and be made wise. Jesus said that the way is so plain that a wayfaring man, though he be a fool, need not err. But oftentimes this very simplicity of the Gospel causes men to seek to make it more complicated and difficult. Man is prone to want to becloud his situation and, where there is no problem, to make one. He acts as if the Gospel plan is too easy on God's part to save man, and man must add some difficulty on his part to atone for God's easy plan of salvation. The sad fact is that while man seeks to impose on himself a task impossible of accomplishment, he, at the same time, ignores the easy and plain duty of accepting

197

God's way of salvation and goes on groping in darkness to destruction.

The way of salvation is the provision of God; that way is revealed in Christ through the Gospel. The Church is to make that way known through the preaching of the Gospel to all men, and men are saved on the condition of hearing, believing and accepting it. The Church's mission is a world mission with a world message of a world Gospel to the whole world of men. This is the one and only open door of hope and salvation to men and nations. Therefore, the work of the Church of Christ is to preach the Gospel which is a comprehensive expression including all the implications of teaching, healing and building up in Christ. This, effectively and universally done under the dynamic leadership of the Holy Ghost by the undeviating Christ, will bring to end the Gospel dispensation, may make way for the return of Christ and the full ushering in of the Kingdom of God on earth. Such must be the course and end of Christian missions.

So we labor not in vain, nor as those that beat the wind, for we know the nature of our work and see definitely the outline of our goal.[4]

Consecration and First Report of Secretary Harvey

At the consecration service for the secretary-elect held in Hot Springs, Arkansas, at the mid-winter Board meeting following his election, he presented the case for the Foreign Mission Board. Among other things, he pointed out the history of the Foreign Mission Board and described some of the problems it had faced through the years. After being in office for three months, he became acutely aware of the need for bringing certain of the policies of the Board up-to-date. These included raising the salary level of missionaries who were giving their lives as our representatives on the foreign field. He found that most of our missionaries received less than the average welfare check, and it was his conviction that the Convention had a moral obligation to place missionaries on Social Security so that at their retirement they would have some financial security during their remaining years. Moreover, he recommended that hospitalization insurance of missionaries should be taken out and paid for by the Foreign Mission Board. Missionaries, he felt strongly, should not be penalized financially because of their zeal to serve on the foreign field.

When Secretary-elect Harvey took office, he secured as his assistant the Reverend James F. Scott, pastor of the New Bethlehem Baptist Church of Philadelphia and Dr. Charles S. Lee, pastor of the First African Baptist Church also in Philadelphia. With the help of these men, it was possible to reap more effectively many of the demands which the Foreign Mission Board faced.

Secretary Harvey's First Inspection Trip to Africa

The new secretary made his first tour of mission stations in West Africa in January 1962. This first-hand observation made clear the needs of the work and of the missionaries. He found that in Liberia, the missionaries worked and lived under undesirable conditions. The teachers were faced with crowded living quarters, inadequate storage space, roofs that leaked during the six-month rainy season, and floors that were badly in need of repairs. The girls' dormitory was overcrowded with double-decked beds. There was hardly any space for chairs and desks. In spite of their living conditions, he found the children well fed with more than adequate diets.

Moreover, the secretary found inadequate educational materials. Education standards of today require adequate laboratory equipment and supplies for teaching the sciences and industrial arts. In addition, the materials to meet the needs for religious education include Bibles, Bible encyclopedias, concordances, reference books on Christian education and hymn notes. All of these items were either lacking or in scant supply. Also there was a need for an adequate chapel in which to glorify God and worship in an atmosphere of beauty and holiness.

In Nigeria, the secretary visited the Reverend S. W. Martin at Issele Uku, Benin Province. Here he toured a number of schools and held meetings with the trustees of the Pilgrim Baptist Mission and also with the town and clan chiefs, all of whom pledged their continued loyalty to the Foreign Mission Board.

In Accra, Ghana, he met with the membership of the National Baptist Mission Church whose representatives had traveled there from that branch of the church at Asokwa, Ashanti Province. Again he found many conditions which had to be remedied.

During his visit to Africa, Secretary Harvey endeavored to sow the seeds of goodwill among officials of the various countries he visited. During part of his travels he was accompanied by the Reverend John B. Falconer, supervisor of the work in West Africa. In Ghana they found that the congregation at the National Baptist Mission Church was discouraged due to a schism created by the former pastor who sought to have them transfer their allegiance from the National Baptist Convention, Inc., to the Southern Baptist Convention of the United States. Since the congregation insisted on maintaining their relationship with our Convention, the pastor resigned, split the church, and took the matter to court seeking to obtain the land which this church had had for many years (even prior to it being sponsored by the NBC). The Secretary and Rev. Falconer arrived on the same plane as the president of the Southern Baptist Convention, Dr. Herchel Hobbs of Oklahoma. On the first night of worshipping with the congregation, Secretary Harvey had the unique experience of preaching — through an interpreter — in one room, while the competitive brother preached to the other half of this split congregation in an adjoining room! With this uncomfortable experience behind him, Secretary Harvey obtained assurance that the NBC would not lose the acreage in question.

It was in Liberia that the secretary said he felt the deepest sense of belonging, for it was there that the first missionaries from our

Convention started their labors in Africa. Still, he was disappointed when he saw the condition of our mission stations there. At night rats could be heard scurrying across the ceiling. Teachers occupied crowded living quarters with inadequate storage space and termite-weakened rooms. At the Bendoo Industrial Mission in Cape Mount County, sixty-five miles northwest of Monrovia, conditions were better as regards to the physical plant. Yet its very isolation and inadequate educational and religious materials were indications of needs calling out to be met.

On that visit the Liberian government, as a sovereign state, through its Ministry of Public Health, informed the secretary that it desired to own outright the Carrie V. Dyer Memorial Hospital in Monrovia. Under the law, the government had the basic right of eminent domain over everything in its country. Therefore the secretary was grateful that the Liberian government was willing to negotiate with the NBC on the matter. The Foreign Mission Board attorney, A. Leon Higginbotham, negotiated the transfer of the deeds to the Liberian government. The sale price was $350,000 which would be paid over a ten year period at $35,000 per year. The money would be paid into the Foreign Mission Board account at the Bank of Liberia. The Board, in turn, guaranteed that these funds would only be used in Liberia for health services conducted at the Bendoo and Suehn Missions.

Carrie V. Dyer Memorial Hospital

In Freetown, Sierra Leone, Secretary Harvey inspected the Roosevelt School which was basically an elementary and secondary modern school serving over 400 children. This school did not have a single Baptist on its staff of teachers, but pleaded for at least a Baptist minister who might serve as either chaplain, teacher or both. Secretary Harvey concluded that there was nothing in the situation to indicate that this was a Baptist mission school in any sense of the term nor had it ever been in its twelve year history.

Results of the First Visit

Upon returning from his first inspection tour of Africa, the secretary immediately began the task of alleviating some of the unfortunate conditions found at the various missions. Some of the facilities were in deplorable, run-down condition and certainly not adequate to meet the minimum standards of housing which our missionaries deserved. An emergency appeal was made to the home churches and an encouraging response was soon received. As a result the Board was able to send funds overseas to provide for maintenance and a variety of repairs. In addition, some adjustments were made in salaries and a plan was begun to provide such fringe benefits as medical insurance and Social Security for our missionaries. Appeals were made to churches, missionary societies and some individuals to double their gifts, recognizing the obligations of Christians to support the task of building the bridges of faith across the seas.

Mission Stations in Africa
Remain Loyal to the Foreign Mission Board

With the establishment of the Foreign Mission Bureau headed by Dr. C. C. Adams, there was considerable uncertainty at some missionary stations with respect to which of the foreign mission groups they should be affiliated. Most of the mission stations which the National Baptist Convention, U.S.A., Inc., established and supported continued their affiliation with this Convention and wrote to the Foreign Mission Board of their steadfastness. One such communication, typical of others received, read:

Pilgrim Baptist Mission
Of Nigeria, Inc.
Headquarters — Issele Uku

Rev. S. W. Martin, Founder

3rd. Sept. 1962   Ref. 668/28

The National Baptist Convention, USA., Inc.,
C/O Rev. William J. Harvey, III
P. O. Box 3873 Station D
701-03 South 19th Street
Philadelphia, 46, Pa.

My dear Brothers in Christ,

Greetings in the Name of our Lord Jesus Christ, peace be with you all. Though I am not there with you in body but in spirit I am there. I am on this end praying for great success in the Convention of this year. My wife and my co-workers join me in the meeting of this year. Let each one of you in his own heart pray for the will of God to be done this year.

Years have rolled away in bitterness and sweetness in our week here in Nigeria, yet our blessed National Baptist Convention has never for a day left me alone to struggle in vain with the God planned work of the Pilgrim Baptist Mission of Nigeria. I personally owe a great debt of gratitude to the whole members of the National Baptist Convention, particularly to Dr. J. H. Jackson who visited us years ago when our work was naked as the Secretary of the Board. Thanks be to God that it has pleased Him to crown the efforts of the Pilgrim Baptist Mission and the National Baptist Convention with great and notable success. On behalf of the Board of Trustees and members of the Pilgrim Baptist Mission of Nigeria, I say thank you to all lovers of our

203

work who have helped us through these many years in prayers, financially and in a good many other ways. God bless all of you.

The Board of Trustees of the Pilgrim Baptist Mission of Nigeria and my very self, the leader of the group, wish to declare to you this day that we do not and will never have hands in anything that will ever bring confusion and split in this great and blessed Convention. We dissociate ourselves from any act to cause confusion which may lead to a split in our great Convention...

s/S. W. Martin[5]

Despite this statement of loyalty, subsequent events changed the situation. In January of 1962, Secretary Harvey visited Nigeria and the Pilgrim Baptist Mission headed by the Rev. S. W. Martin. Under his leadership, the mission had grown from nothing to an incorporated institution comprised of thirty-eight elementary schools, seven secondary modern schools, one teachers' college, 122 churches, and a maternity home. Further investigations revealed, however, that the Foreign Mission Board held no deeds to any of this property either in fee-simple or fee-conditional, which was the case in every other mission in Africa. Although this mission did not receive all of its support from the Foreign Mission Board, most of its budget was underwritten by the Board on a quarterly basis.

The Foreign Mission Bureau created by Dr. Adams as a competitive organization, needed overseas mission stations to justify its existence. It thus declared the Pilgrim Baptist Mission as its major objective with the ready compliance of Rev. Martin. Thus the Pilgrim Mission became the recipient of two missionary agencies — the Foreign Mission Board and its competitor, the Foreign Mission Bureau.

In 1963, Rev. Martin visited the United States under the auspices of the Foreign Mission Bureau. During his visit he paid a courtesy call to the Foreign Mission Board during a meeting of its executive committee. At that time he was pointedly asked if he realized that by accepting assistance from the Bureau, he was precipitating a split in the ranks of Baptist foreign mission witness. Rev. Martin replied that he preferred the leadership of Dr. Adams and the new organization, many of whom he had known for many years. Following his dismissal from the meeting, the executive committee recommended that further assistance to Pilgrim Baptist Mission be terminated. Further, they proposed to place these recommendations before the National Baptist Convention at its annual board meeting to be held in Bessemer, Alabama, in June 1963. The national Board concurred with the termination of assistance.

Organization of the Audio-Visual Aids Department

The importance of audio visual aids in enlarging the horizon of individuals has long been recognized. The Board decided fairly early in Dr. Harvey's administration to make use of such materials

Rev. William R. Harris

205

to further the interests of the Foreign Mission Board. Accordingly, the Reverend William R. Harris, pastor of the Bethany Baptist Church of Pittsburgh, Pennsylvania, an expert in the field of audio-visual education, was employed by the Board to head-up this department. The results have been effective. Brochures, slides and other materials have been developed which highlight the work of the Board in its various mission fields.

One of the innovations resulting from the formation of the audio-visual aids department was the establishment of an audio-visual booth to be set up at meetings of the National Baptist Convention, U.S.A., Inc., as well as at the meetings of the National Baptist Sunday School and BTU Congress. The first booth was set up at the session of the National Baptist Convention in Chicago, September 1962. This booth, having been carefully planned, became a center of attraction, a department of vital missionary information, and a meeting place and conference center for the staff and missionaries and constituency.

Fortunately, with the cooperation of President J. H. Jackson and the local committee, the Foreign Mission booth was located in the center lane of traffic in the exposition hall of the Coliseum. Because of this location, hundreds of people stopped by the booth, asked questions concerning the work of the Board and the program that the new secretary had in mind. Much helpful material was provided to visitors. A keen interest was shown in the audio-visual presentations of the work on the mission fields. Color slides and transparencies, large paintings and photographs were displayed. These gave visitors a vivid picture of the buildings, activities and work of the missionaries at the various stations. From that time forward, the audio-visual booth has been regularly set up at sessions of the National Baptist Convention, U.S.A., Inc., and has proved to be a valuable means of informing the messengers of the activities of the Foreign Mission Board. As often as feasible, returned missionaries and those on furlough have been invited to spend time in the booth to share with visitors, first-hand, their experiences.

The Foreign Mission Board acquired an adequate supply of film strips and denominational materials which were made available to churches and associations. Churches were also advised that other sources of audio-visual materials could be obtained from such organizations as the American Bible Society and Family Filmstrip, Inc., as well as in many public libraries.

To further spread the good news of the work of this Board, missionaries on furlough have been encouraged to visit conferences, association meetings and conventions. Our mission supporters at home always benefit from seeing and knowing the missionaries who have given so much of themselves to preach and implement the Gospel and thereby extend the Kingdom of God.

The Missionary Worker's Manual

In recent years, the unique contribution of Negro Baptists to the Kingdom of God has come to be widely recognized by National Baptists and the demand for a Missionary Manual written by, and for our people became so insistent that the Foreign Mission Board felt compelled to meet this need. After studying the manual written by Mrs. Cunningham, Secretary Harvey felt that with the addition of historical information pertinent to National Baptists plus other items of a contemporary nature, the manual would be ideal for use among our National Baptist churches. Because of her love for the National Baptist Convention and her lifelong concern for missions, Mrs. Cunningham sold the copyright to the Foreign Mission Board and Dr. Harvey began the intensive work of revision and addition.

Pastors will find their complex leadership responsibility lightened as their missionary society leaders and members apply some of the principles stressed in this book. It was also written to provide suggested sermon stimulators on such subjects as the Biblical basis of missions, soul winning, prayer, stewardship and community service. Missionary workers at all levels will find specific information as to the duties of the officers of a mission group, how to improve the programs, mission study classes and topics, community emphases and programs, suggestions for strengthening youth organizations, the use of men in the missionary societies, the list of missionaries and the locations of the various mission stations. These are but a few of the wealth of topics to be found in the Missionary Worker's Manual.

The Foreign Mission Board was pleased that it did not have to go to another denominational group for guidance in the field of missions. From the day of publication forward, churches could use with pride a missionary manual written by our own people for our own churches within the framework of our own objectives and aspirations.[6]

Cooperative Venture with Liberian Baptists

In 1950, efforts to form a basis of cooperation among all of the Christian missionaries in Liberia were begun. Fifteen years later, President William R. Tolbert of Liberia, speaking at the Fifty-First Session of the Liberian Baptist Missionary and Educational Convention, announced that he had accepted as representative of Liberia the request of the Foreign Mission Board to operate and supply Liberian workers at the Bible Industrial Academy, Fortsville, Grand Vassa, Co., Liberia. Mrs. Priscilla Bryant Jackson supervised the work at this academy for thirty years until her retirement. Throughout its existence, it has made a significant contribution to the civil and cultural life of Liberia. Preachers, teachers and political leaders in that country received their education at this institution.

In 1964, President Tolbert proposed that the Baptist Alliance of Liberia be organized with the understanding that the various Baptist organizations conducting missions throughout Liberia would coordinate their efforts and objectives. The Foreign Mission Board of the National Baptist Convention, U.S.A., Inc., stated that it would be pleased to be the first foreign agency to implement the proposal for a Baptist alliance. This alliance represented a giant step forward in assuring greater efficiency of Christian missionary effort in Liberia.[7]

Providence Industrial Mission

The Providence Industrial Mission was begun in 1900 by John S. Chilembwe who was the first African to come to the United States from what was then known as British Central Africa. The station was destroyed during World War I by the British colonialists and remained closed until June 3, 1926, when Dr. and Mrs. Malekebu reopened the station under the Ntundu tree which was planted by Dr. Malekebu when he was a boy.

During the time the mission was closed, witchdoctors used the tree as a gathering spot to display and use their charms and other materials. It was natural that when the station was reopened the work would begin there even before the buildings were reconstructed. The small fee of six pence ($.12) was charged for medical service at the Ntundu tree clinic. Eventually the people began to appreciate the modern medical skill that Dr. Daniel S. Malekebu practiced. This did away with much of the superstitious fears and practices to which they were accustomed.

As the work developed under Dr. Malekebu, some of the boys were able to pass government examinations to become grade school teachers in English; some found employment in the telephone exchange offices. Students from Providence Mission had excellent training in English and, therefore, were favored by some commercial firms recruiting new employees. Some found employment in law enforcement agencies because they were considered well disciplined and intelligent; others were hired by the Civil Service. Dr. Malekebu observed that, "our girls are the first to prove to the country that African women and girls, as well as African men and boys, can be educated to become teachers. Of primary importance was the fact that a number of students became ministers of the Gospel and went to various parts of the country preaching the Gospel of peace.[8]

The school also had an athletic program including a football team (soccer) that won all the games played against other teams in the country. In addition, Dr. Malekebu emphasized agriculture as a part of the mission's educational program. He organized the Nyasaland Farmers Association. Members of the Association were given instruction in modern methods of farming. In the absence of ploughs and tractors, the men had to use hoes. Following instructions in modern methods, the farmers came to appreciate the new and better ways of producing crops.

Preaching the Gospel, Dr. Malekebu said, was the greatest job of his life. He told of how he walked many days, crossing streams and rivers, climbing hills and mountains and sleeping in the open with only trees for a covering, in his effort to take the Gospel from place to place. Many souls were converted through his efforts.

Organization of the National Baptist Assembly of Africa, Inc.

In 1945, the Reverend Dr. Malekebu realized a dream he had had since his first visit to America as a youth in 1905. In September of that year, he attended the annual meeting of the Convention in Chicago, Illinois. There he saw a large assembly of Black Christians and heard their inspiring preaching and noticed their bearing and piety and was greatly inspired by all he saw and heard. At that time he determined that if he ever got the opportunity, he would eventually have a convention of Baptist churches in his homeland. His years of preparation included the organization of individual churches, preaching, and baptizing many people in different centers and countries. He reported that many times he would baptize from 100-150 candidates on a Sunday. On one occasion he baptized as many as 300 men and women in the Lilongwe District, Central Province. After the church was organized, he would leave a lay preacher to look after the members and conduct prayer services with them. He made future annual visits to those communities to follow-up on the work.

Meanwhile, with the convention idea still in mind, he prepared promising young men for the ministry. Between 1926 and 1944, he was the only ordained Christian minister among his people. In that eighteen-year period, he reported having baptized 19,000 persons and introduced Christian marriage with a total of 306 weddings. As of 1945, he had ordained a few young men who had prepared for the ministry and sent them to various districts as pastors to those areas.

Early in 1945, he began sending out calls to the Christian leaders in each district and country to come to the mission for the purpose of making plans for a convention and drawing up a constitution. This was done and the name chosen, "The National Baptist Assembly of Africa, Nyasaland." The purpose was stated as follows: "To follow an intensive program of evangelism, Christian education and social service in Africa through its institution, Providence Industrial Mission, Chiradzulu, Nyasaland."

In August 1945, the organization was completed and a constitution was adopted. Dr. Malekebu stated what the Assembly meant in the following terms:

What the Assembly has done is wonderful.

Firstly, it has brought different tribes of that region into one great Christian Brotherhood, as no other man-made organization has been able to do.

Secondly, it has created in the minds of the members self-respect, pride and faith within themselves as Christians of God.

Thirdly, it is an Educational Institution where people go to learn many things from preachers, lecturers and teachers.

Fourthly, it is a Spiritual Mountain Top where men and women can speak, sing, preach and pray in their own tongues. You may not understand when they are praying or what they are singing, but you can certainly feel the fire.

Lastly, it is the power and light-house where all the people can see the capabilities and possibilities that are within them to be and to do something by themselves and for themselves in Africa.

The NATIONAL BAPTIST ASSEMBLY OF AFRICA, INC., is a dynamic, unifying force in Africa for which OUR LORD prayed: "THAT THEY MIGHT BE ONE."[9]

Dr. Malekebu was also successful in the establishment of two hospitals. The first one was named the James E. East Memorial Hospital for Men in honor of one of the outstanding corresponding secretaries of the Foreign Mission Board. The second hospital was named the S. Willie Layton Memorial Hospital for Women. This was to memorialize the lady who was the first president of the Women's Auxiliary Convention to the National Baptist Convention, U.S.A., Inc.

In June 1967, Dr. Malekebu was called to the United States to receive the highest award of his Alma Mater, Meharry Medical College, Nashville, Tennessee. This award, called the "President's Award," consisted of a gold plaque presented to him in recognition of his fifty years of service to humanity. Dr. Malekebu was graduated from Meharry in 1917 and was the spokesman for his class. Among the other honors given him during this visit were the following: The Red Carpet Club Award made by the Red Carpet Club which boasts six United States presidents, forty governors and four foreign dignitaries as members; Special Letter of Commendation from the White House; the Mayor's Award from the City of Nashville, embracing Davidson County, Tennessee, which grants honorary citizenship in the city of Nashville and the key to the city of Nashville which extends special courtesies of that city to the recipient; the Governor's Award, presented by the governor of the State of Tennessee, making the recipient an honorary citizen of the state.

The Letter of Commendation from the White House was sent by President Lyndon Johnson to the Honorable Richard Fulton, a member of the House of Representatives from the State of Tennessee. This letter reads as follows:

THE WHITE HOUSE
WASHINGTON
June 9, 1967

Dear Dick:

It is a pleasure to join with you in applauding the achievements of Dr. Daniel Malekebu.

I was deeply moved by your recent account of the remarkable life of this deserving American. His courage and determination are truly inspiring. And the spiritual and medical mission that he carries forth in his native Malawi have earned him our admiration and our thanks.

Please convey my congratulations and my very best wishes for his continued success in perpetuating God's word and work.

Sincerely,

s/Lyndon B. Johnson

Honorable Richard Fulton
House of Representatives
Washington, D. C.[10]

In 1967 Dr. and Mrs. Malekebu retired from the Foreign Mission Board after forty-eight years of missionary service. For forty-five of those years they served in Nyasaland (now named Malawi) at the Providence Industrial Mission, Chiradzulu. Mrs. Malekebu had been bedridden for two years and the Board recognized the need to give them relief from their responsibilities. Upon their retirement, they moved to Atlanta, Georgia, with the hope of enjoying well-deserved peace and relaxation during their remaining years.[11]

Effectiveness of the Indigenous Missionaries

While the work of the American born missionaries in Africa has been demonstrated to be of great importance, the goal has always been to train African born men and women to carry forward the work begun by those who came from across the sea. This goal was achieved in a remarkable way in the career of Dr. Daniel S. Malekebu.

213

We have mentioned others who have spread the Gospel in their native lands, including S. W. Martin of Nigeria. These came to the United States, (often through the assistance of the Foreign Mission Board) obtained a good formal education, and returned to become sources of inspiration to their people and agents for the Gospel of the risen Lord and advocates of His promised abundant life.

Among the advantages of the indigenous missionaries are that they have first-hand knowledge of the various cultural, social, economic and political background of the people they serve. They know the language, and they themselves are living witnesses of what Christianity can accomplish in the life of the individual. They know all the nuances of social relations among the group. They can in no way be regarded as outsiders lording it over those to whom they preach. The Foreign Mission Board has been pleased to be a force in this enterprise, in training native men and women not only to become missionaries, but also to train others of their people to carry the Gospel across the land.

Needs in the Mission Field

In 1965, we recognized the need for general repairs and upkeep in all of our stations. In some instances it was necessary to replace crumbling buildings and, moreover, to increase the salaries of those who were giving their lives unselfishly for a noble cause. It was necessary to make major repairs to our buildings not only because of the need to preserve them, but also because it was desirable to maintain an appropriate image in the community where our mission stations were located. Specifically among the needs in the mission fields in West Africa were the following:

MISSION NEEDS IN THE MISSION FIELD

Our Religious Education needs are manifold:
1. Bibles
2. Reference books
3. Bible encyclopedias
4. Hymnals
5. A chapel for worship

6. Finances for repair of buildings
7. School supplies
8. Needs for the missionaries themselves, money to provide Social Security, hospitalization insurance and increased salaries
9. Books and vegetable seeds
10. Money for medical supplies for the hospital. Medical supplies are needed for small-pox vaccinations and inoculations against yellow fever, typhoid, tetanus, anemia, other diseases and worms. The Carrie V. Dyer Hospital in West Africa, is owned by the National Baptist Convention.
11. Upkeep for one student of Suehn Industrial Academy, $17.50 per month. This includes board, lodging, clothes, tuition, books, medical and dental services.
12. Scholarship for University of Liberia, $250 per year for one outstanding mission high school graduate.

The Reverend John B. Falconer is supervisor of the West African Mission Board of the National Baptist convention.[12]

The Need for New Missionaries

One of the major problems in all of the mission stations sponsored by the Foreign Mission Board was the need for more missionaries. In every instance, our missionaries begged for additional workers to help them.

The Foreign Mission Board kept up a constant effort to enlist new candidates for the Christian missionary enterprise. In 1965, we were fortunate to secure the services of the Reverend Benjamin R. Stephens to serve as a missionary in Liberia. Reverend Stephens was an alumnus of the Western Baptist Seminary at Kansas City, Kansas from which institution he held the degrees of Bachelor of Religious Education and Bachelor of Theology. At the time of his enlistment for missionary service, he was pastor of the First Baptist Church of Nicodemus, Kansas. In addition to his theological training, he was accomplished in the field of agriculture and general mechanics — both of which fields formed a solid background for missionary service in Africa.

He was commissioned to serve at the Suehn Industrial Mission in a supervisory capacity for a three-year tour of duty. An impressive dedication service was held for Reverend Stephens and his family prior to their trip to Africa on which they would be accompanied by Secretary Harvey. A few months after reaching Liberia, he reported to the Foreign Mission Board that all of the past and current bills of the Suehn Mission had been paid and that they had need for repairs on most of the buildings at the mission. He mentioned other needs such as new motors for water pumps and replacement of other appliances.

Rev. Benjamin R.
Stephens

Reverend Stephens also said that one of the hardest adjustments he had to make was that of tribal loyalty. He found that members of a tribe did not think it was wrong to steal so long as one did not steal from members of his own tribe. This was just one of the tribal customs Pastor Stephens had to overcome by trying to get Christian tribesmen to recognize the universality of the Christian Gospel.[13]

The following letter, written by Reverend Stephens, is typical of his commitment to the Foreign Mission enterprise:

Suehn Industrial Mission
Post Office Box 65
Monrovia, Liberia, W
West Africa

Rev. William J. Harvey, III
P. O. Box 3873, Station D
701-03 South Nineteenth Street
Philadelphia, Pennsylvania 19146

Dear Rev. Harvey:

The blessings of God be with you and yours as you undertake the present task of God. All of the workers are well here and trying to do what is required. Your visit was such a refreshing change, even though we were so busy. The work that the National Baptist Preaching Mission accomplished here can never be evaluated to its fullest extent. Liberia is indeed grateful for their suffering and sacrifice.

We were very sorry that we did not see you off as planned. The whole family started for Robertsfield, but the thermostat stuck in the engine and caused us so much trouble that we only got as far as Monrovia, and that was late. Later we learned that Rev. Prunty went with you; we were happy for that.

We are looking forward to the teachers' quarters as well as the other changes. I know that some of the people are already sacrificing, but there is room for more. If our National Baptists are able to see the field, they will know what sacrifice is and what it will accomplish.

I am grateful to the Lord that He has laid it on some of the hearts to give, not once, but many times over. My plea is that these shall be able to endure for, "The race is not given to the swift, nor to the strong; but he that endureth until the end."

Our best wishes and prayers to the Baptists at home who own and support these mission stations here. God be with you until we meet again.

Yours in His service,
Benjamin R. Stephens[14]

The Reverend Benjamin Stephens was able to provide expertise in building mechanical and technical equipment. A major development in his mission was operating an amateur radio with certification from the Ministry of Tele-Communication. With this equipment, he was able to keep in immediate communication with the United States. Thus the Foreign Mission Board could be immediately informed of any emergency in Liberia. This radio communication made it possible for the Board to send emergency funds to meet the need caused by the storm which did much damage at the Suehn Mission in October 1969. In addition, the radio communication network was set up at each mission station in Liberia so that everyday at 5:00 p.m. direct contact was made with the coordinator's office in Monrovia. This system was especially useful in emergency situations involving the illness or injury of missionaries or students.

Mission to India

Earlier in this volume we mentioned the Foreign Mission Board's missionary activity in Bangalore, India. There the Board was interested primarily in supporting an adult literacy educational program. The Board paid the salary of a missionary, the Reverend H. W. Oliver, who went to the post in 1962. As of July

1963, Reverend Oliver reported the goals of his efforts as (1) to contribute to the attack on the evils of illiteracy, ignorance, and superstition, and (2) to work to enable adults to read the written Word. Mr. Oliver expressed the need for additional funds to cover the high cost of producing new literacy materials necessary for a successful attack on illiteracy. He was engaged in training forty-three teachers in the principles and techniques of adult education. He had also trained seventeen writers and had produced and published charts and other materials in two of the native languages. Moreover, he reported that he had preached the Gospel as often as God had given him the time and opportunity. He continued:

Rev. H. W. Oliver

But God has laid a heavy burden upon our hearts for the seventy percent of our fellow church members in India who cannot read and write the precious words of God. How can there be a revival in India (or anywhere) when seventy percent of the body of Christ is receiving no daily spiritual nourishment by way of reading the

Word of God? Now mind you, these people already have the Holy Bible translated into their language — they just can't read it! Must we leave them dumb, blind, and hungry because they cannot read the Word of God for themselves?[15]

Reverend Oliver pledged to seek funds from the officials of the Ministry of Education in India and also from the United States Aid Mission in New Delhi. The Board also pledged to continuing its support to Reverend Oliver's work.

Retreat for Foreign Missionaries

Upon assuming office, Secretary Harvey found that the Foreign Mission Board and the Women's Auxiliary of the National Baptist Convention, U.S.A., Inc., had entered into an agreement to support the operation of a building located at 1922 Maryland Avenue, N.E., Washington, D.C., known as the Retreat for Foreign Missionaries. Purchased during the administration of Dr. Helen Nannie Burroughs at a price of $83,500.00, the building was spacious and commodious, and contained more than eighteen rooms including a kitchen, pantry, wide halls and many baths. The active missionaries at that time had no central place to which they could go for a retreat until their furlough was completed. The Retreat House was designed to meet that need as well as serve as National Headquarters for the Missionary Committees of the Women's Convention and as an interracial and interdenominational fellowship center for foreign missionaries who were home on furlough. The purpose of the Retreat House was stated as follows:

> The Purpose
> 1. To maintain an Interracial and Interdenominational Fellowship center for Foreign Missionaries in active service home on furlough or business.
>   A. A place for Rest and Recuperation; Bible Study, Mission Study (Home and Foreign), Conferences, Fellowship Meetings, Institutes for the

purpose of teaching Social, Racial, Religious
and Political Aspects of Countries of the world;
Specializing in giving a complete course in the
Literacy theory and practice — using Dr. Frank
C. Lauback's simplified method, and
distributing Missionary information to churches
over the country.

B. To serve as National Headquarters for The Missionary Committee of the Women's Convention
Auxiliary to the National Baptist Convention,
U.S.A., Inc.

C. To encourage Spiritual Fellowship for Youth
and Adults in One Day or weekend Retreats.

D. Resident Center for Ministers, Missionaries, and
those engaged in Christian Service.

As of 1966, the basic purposes of the retreat had not been fully
realized; that is, the housing of missionaries on furlough. Nevertheless, under the directorship of Mrs. Sarah Williamson Coleman,
who had served as a missionary at the Suehn Mission in Liberia,
it served as a meeting place for various activities of the churches
of the District of Columbia and also as a residence center for
clergy and local church groups visiting in Washington, D. C. The
Foreign Mission regularly cooperated with the Women's Auxiliary
of the Convention in meeting the financial needs of this retreat.[16]

Inspection Visit of Dr. Jesse Jai McNeil

In December 1962, Dr. Jesse Jai McNeil, pastor of the
Metropolitan Baptist Church, Pasadena, California, and a professor at the California Baptist Seminary at Covina, California,
was invited to attend an all-African Congress on Christian Education at Salisbury, Southern Rhodesia. Upon learning of this, the
Secretary of the Foreign Mission Board requested that he survey
our mission stations in West and East Africa. Dr. McNeil returned
and as a direct result of his enthusiasm regarding what he saw
of missionary activity at our stations, secured the services of two
school teachers to serve at the Providence Industrial Mission in

Chiradzulu, Nyasaland. One of these teachers, Mrs. Doris Allen of Los Angeles, went to Nyasaland at her own expense to serve for one year. The other, Mrs. Christine Benson Newson, went to serve a full three-year term of duty. In addition, Dr. McNeil committed his church to build an elementary school and a teachers' college building for that mission.

Dr. McNeil's report of his visit was printed in the *Mission Herald.* among other things, he said that the people whom he met at the Providence Mission expressed the hope that the missionary activity of the Foreign Mission Board be continued for they wanted their children to get a good education in the true Christian tradition. Dr. McNeil also wanted the benefits of medical services which could be provided only by the availability of doctors, trained nurses, a medical facility and medical supplies. Although he appreciated the work that Dr. Daniel S. Malekebu — the only doctor in the area — was doing, the need for medical personnel, said McNeil, was great. During Dr. McNeil's visit, Dr. and Mrs. Malekebu were on furlough in the United States, yet everywhere Dr. McNeil visited, he heard great praise for the work the Malekebu's carried on among them.

One striking part of Dr. McNeil's report is set forth in the following quotation from his article:

A lone little lady from the Mrewa Reserve, seventy miles away from Salisbury, Southern Rhodesia, walked to the Holy Trinity Baptist Church in Salisbury to hear me speak the Sunday morning after Christmas and to plead with me to convey to the Foreign Mission Board their need of a church in which to worship. She had been with this congregation at Mrewa since its beginning in 1949. Ever since that time they have had to worship under a tree. In 1954 they applied to the Southern Rhodesian government for a permit to build a house of worship. For nine years they waited for the permit to be granted. This year they were able to begin building the house of worship for which they have waited so long. Most of their congregation had fallen away because they

could not understand why it was that the Southern Baptists and the Roman Catholics, both white groups, could
get permits without trouble to build places of worship
and the National Baptist Africans could not. In their simple way they reasoned that the Southern Baptists and
Roman Catholics were true churches and the National

A group of bush children in Malawi.

Revival gathering at Queenstown, Cape Province, South Africa.

Baptists were not. Therefore they simply gave up the faith and tried no longer to follow the way pointed out to them by the National Baptists in Southern Rhodesia.[17]

Dr. McNeil's observations and report shed much light on the status of the missions he visited on that trip. The Foreign Mission Board was reassured of the success of much of its efforts and, at the same time, we were alerted to some of the situations at the missions to which we were encouraged to give more attention.

Suehn Mission Storm

The Suehn Mission, throughout its history, has had to weather many difficulties but, in every instance, has managed to overcome them. One grave difficulty occurred on October 12, 1969, when a severe storm struck the campus and created a considerable amount of damage. The storm blew the roof off three buildings — each a boys' dormitory. Another building, occupied by one of the Liberian teachers, was severely damaged by a falling tree. Many rubber and fruit trees were uprooted and the electrical lines from the generator to several buildings were blown down. Fortunately none of the students or teachers was injured either by the flying objects or the crumbling buildings. Many windows were blown out of the girls' dormitory and the clothing, books and personal effects were damaged by the rains.

Housing was arranged for the boys in the National Baptist College and in the homes of various teachers. Repairs were started immediately under the supervision of the Reverend Benjamin Stephens, supervisor of missions in Liberia. The Foreign Mission Board provided emergency funds so that repairs could begin immediately. The teachers at that time, Miss Gladys East, the principal, Miss Della McGrew, Mrs. Josephine Minter, Mrs. Christine Drew and Mrs. Erma Etheridge, were effective in calming the students and making the emergency adjustments.

Mrs. Christine Drew

Miss Della McGrew

Mrs. Josephine Minter

Mrs. Erma Etheridge

A vivid description of the storm was given by Mrs. Christine Drew:

About 2:30 I decided to go upstairs and close my windows just to be on the safe side. I can get upstairs in

225

about three seconds. I closed the window and then heard the awful sound of gushing waters and gusting winds. I started back down the stairs and saw pieces of clothing, parts of plants, bottles of egg shells (saved for the flowers), and branches from the trees blow past.

I ran downstairs and attempted to reach for the screen door to go in. At the same time, the door blew open and I stepped in and was blown slightly to one side. About this time I met a glass filled with the water and plant off the room divider, and it met the screen door on the rebound and smashed to pieces. Rain was pouring into the kitchen, curtains in an adjoining room had blown down, clothing was blowing around and I was panic stricken. We saw pieces of roof pass through the air and later found that a whole window from one side of my living room was blown out. We could hear the screaming students as they desperately tried to get into their rooms and were beaten back by the wind. One girl with an umbrella up was blown down the hall and out the door. Only the railing kept her from falling to the ground below.

At first it was hard, hard sheets of rain, then suddenly the rain stopped completely and the high winds blew.

Then it was all over.[18]

The Foreign Mission Board was pleased that it could meet the emergency as soon as the news of the storm was received. In 1967, the Board began an emergency fund in anticipation of any natural disaster which might occur in the future.

Miss Gladys East

One of the missionaries who has carried forward the rich heritage of our Foreign Mission Board is Miss Gladys East. Miss East is the daughter of the late corresponding secretary of the Foreign Mission Board, the Reverend James East. She was born

Miss Gladys East

in the Union of South Africa at the Buchanan Mission, Middledrift, where her parents were serving as missionaries under the Foreign Mission Board of the National Baptist Convention, U.S.A., Inc. Later, she came to Philadelphia, Pennsylvania, and finished her high school education at the Overbrook High School. She then entered the University of Pennsylvania where she received the Bachelor of Science degree. She received further training at the Women's Medical College and the Philadelphia Bible College

Miss East was appointed missionary to Liberia in 1944. In the course of time, she became principal of the Suehn Industrial Mission High School where she did outstanding work with the same dedication and commitment her father and mother demonstrated during their years of service in South Africa. In 1977 Miss East retired and returned to Philadelphia where she makes her home.

The Passing of Mrs. Lucinda East

After over a half century of service to Christ, Mrs. Lucinda T.

East, widow of the late Dr. James E. East, passed from labor to reward. Her life had been full and rich with missionary experiences.

In October 1909, Mrs. East accompanied her husband to South Africa where they began their work as missionaries under the Foreign Mission Board of the National Baptist Convention, U.S.A., Inc. For eleven years they served faithfully at this mission before returning to the United States in 1920.

Following the election of Dr. East to the position of corresponding secretary of the Foreign Mission Board, the East family settled in Philadelphia, Pennsylvania. Mrs. East distinguished herself as a devoted and active member of the Mt. Carmel Baptist Church.

With the passing of Dr. East in 1934, Mrs. East did not lose her zeal for foreign missions. She rejoiced that their daughter Gladys was a missionary serving at the Suehn Industrial Mission in Liberia, and she continued to inspire churches and individuals with the message of the overseas work.

Her home was the focal point for missionaries who had served on the foreign field irrespective of their denominational affiliation. During the annual Christmas drives sponsored by the Foreign Mission Board in Philadelphia and vicinity, she was always a willing speaker for the promotion of the cause to which she had given so much of her time and devotion.

When her illness became terminal, her daughter, Miss Gladys East, then principal of the Suehn Mission High School in Liberia, returned home to be with her mother during her final hours.

With the passing of Mrs. East, an era in the development of the work of the Foreign Mission Board came to an end. This was an era which gave the Christian world stalwart souls dedicated to the great commission of Christ: "Go ye therefore into all the world and preach my Gospel." It was an era studded with such names as Emma B. Delaney, W. W. Colley, J. H. Pressley, Richard LaMont Steward, L. G. Jordan, Emma F. Butler, E. H. Bouey, Lillie B. Johns, J. J. Coles, Hattie Pressley, Solomon Cosby, and many other soldiers for Christ who labored in the early years on foreign shores. These are they who held up the cross of Christ to the peoples of benighted lands. These are those who gave their lives that others might see, adore and live through Christ.

Mrs. East lived thirty-three years following the passing of her husband but, as she often said in reminiscence, "my husband lives on because the work he loves lives on. I seek to perpetuate that work so that one day Christ will be known to all men everywhere." This was her dream — a dream still lived in the life and activity of her daughter and countless others who served on foreign shores.[19]

Shortly after Mrs. East's death, arrangements were begun to establish a memorial in her honor. This memorial was founded as a fund to meet the need for trained leaders and workers on the foreign field. The fund was called the Lucinda East Memorial Scholarship Fund. The stated purposes were:

1. To provide funds for the training of ministers for the foreign stations under the Foreign Mission Board of the National Baptist Convention, U.S.A., Inc.

2. To provide funds for the training of teachers and principals for the mission stations under the Foreign Mission Board.

3. To provide funds for the training of other workers such as workers and agriculture workers for the mission stations under the Foreign Mission Board.

The initial officers for this fund were: Mrs. Muriel Lemon, Chairman; Mrs. Olivia Turner, First Vice Chairman; Mrs. Lucille Robinson, Second Vice Chairman; Mrs. Leola Stephens, Treasurer; Mrs. Mary Clifton, Recording Secretary; Mrs. Marie Ewell, Corresponding Secretary; Mrs. Ida Clark, Public Relations Secretary; Mrs. Bessie Holly and Mrs. Trixie Fisher, Members at Large; Mrs. Selton Carter, Chaplain; Mrs. Inez McCullough, Member at Large; Mrs. Violet Beaford, Historian and Mrs. Hattie East, representing the East family.[20]

The fund has had significant growth since it was begun, and has been of great help in assisting in the training of prospective missionaries.

Direct Missions

Over the years, Mission Boards in Evangelical Churches have been faced with the problem of "direct missions" versus missions supported by a board. This problem seldom exists among those denominations whose policy follows an Episcopal pattern. The very nature of their organization precludes the existence of such a situation. Yet, where churches are autonomous and the sovereignty is vested in the local church, Mission Boards often have to contend with the problems that direct missions create.

Those who are adherents of the concept of "direct missions" contend that by supporting a missionary or a mission station directly, they are certain that the funds sent and received are used for the purposes intended. They also feel that it cuts down on the overhead for operating missions and creates a "climate of communication" that engenders greater interest on the part of the local supporting congregations.

While as Baptists we recognize the sovereignty of the local church, we, nevertheless, know that direct missions create a problem of duplication or reduplication of efforts. Direct missions rarely take into account the "total" program of foreign missions and, in some instances, contribute to problems at the mission stations. The Foreign Mission Board has the responsibility of conducting every phase of missionary work on the foreign field. The National Baptist Convention, U.S.A., Inc., depends upon this board to carry forward its program with all the skills and wisdom it has learned over many years of detailed experience. What is needed is a united effort in which all the needs are taken into consideration and there is no duplication of effort.[21]

Growth of Financial Support

One of the satisfying developments since the new administration of the Foreign Mission Board took office is the dramatic increase in financial support from ministers and churches. In September 1961, our total receipts, along with a beginning cash balance, amounted to $129,678.79; total cash disbursements were

$100,752.64. Listed below are copies of the audit of the last three months of the administration of Dr. C. C. Adams:

FOREIGN MISSION BOARD
NATIONAL BAPTIST CONVENTION, U.S.A., INC.
STATEMENT OF CASH RECEIPTS AND DISBURSEMENTS
July 1, 1961 to September 22, 1961

Beginning Cash Balance		$ 92,099.99
CASH RECEIPTS		
Contributions...	$ 21,398.55	
Rents...	172.00	
Book Sales..	16.35	
Subscriptions...	7.20	
Income on Investments ,,,,,,,,,,,,,,,,,,,,,,,,,,,,,,,,,	146.35	
Accounts Receivable	450.00	
Returned Checks	388.35	
Transfer of Funds (contra)..............................	15,000.00	
Total Cash Receipts		37,578.80
Total Cash Available		$129,678.79
CASH DISBURSEMENTS		
Administrative Expense	$ 9,861.13	
Employer's Taxes	471.51	
Secretary's Taxes (C. C. Adams	1,700.00	
Refund on Automobile-Secretary		
(C. C. Adams)...	1,000.00	
Mission Maintenance......................................	59,973.96	
Field Workers Expense	7,035.65	
Printing Plant Expense....................................	2,310.56	
Mission Herald...	561.95	
Notes Payable..	692.00	
Returned Checks	394.35	
Transfer of Funds (contra).............................	15,000.00	
Building Operations	999.47	
Bookkeeping Equipment.................................	609.90	
Special Reserve	58.85	
Accounts Payable and Refunds	83.31	
Total Cash Disbursements..............		100,752.64
Cash Balance, September 22, 1961....................		$ 28,926.15[22]

Financial Progress

Secretary Harvey reports that since he took over the office of corresponding secretary to the present, there has been a continuing increase in the financial well-being of the Foreign Mission Board. In 1963, records showed that the trend toward increased giving was continued in twenty-four out of thirty-nine states contributing to the Foreign Mission Board. In the same year, the states of Oklahoma, Alabama and Indiana raised their contributions 100% over the preceding year. Some churches have given scholarships to African students in our mission stations. Moreover, 192 monthly contributions were added to the list of regular Foreign Mission Board contributors. At the same time, 306 churches which had not contributed in three years, began to make contributions. In 1964, the Board received a total of $163,193.78 in contributions.

In the fiscal year 1969-1970, contributions to the Board totaled $252,788.07 — an increase of $108,894.97 over the income received by the Board in the first year of Secretary Harvey's tenure. Also, in the fiscal year 1969-1970, the Board was able to meet all of the salaries of its workers abroad and to meet its budget three months in advance. In addition, the Board paid the transportation costs of six missionaries either returning to their post of duty or returning to the United States on furlough. At the same time, the Board underwrote the complete individual support of twenty-three students on the elementary and secondary levels in Liberia. In addition, twenty-eight South Africans preparing for the ministry were completely supported pending the reopening of the seminary at Lesotho. In Nicaragua, the Board gave twenty-four students scholarships for elementary school training.

During the fiscal year ending September 1971, fifty churches contributed $1,000 or more. One year later, the number of churches contributing $1,000 or more rose to fifty-seven. Of this number, the Shiloh Baptist Church of New York City contributed $7,950.50. This church was under the leadership of Reverend Leslie E. Wainwright. As a part of this contribution, the church supported twenty children in Africa.

During the fiscal year ending September 1972, contributions to the Foreign Mission Board totaled $302,269.74 — the largest amount ever contributed to the Foreign Mission Board up to that time.

In the fiscal year July 1, 1975-June 30, 1976, the Board received contributions of $530,908.13. This represents a tremendous increase in the support of the work of the Foreign Mission Board in the fifteen-year period since Secretary Harvey took office.

It is clear that more and more churches and pastors were becoming steadily aware of the importance of building bridges of faith across the seas.[23]

Mission Money for Missions

One of the important considerations in the support of foreign missions has to do with determining what percentage of the contributions actually is used on the mission field. It has been the purpose during all of Secretary Harvey's administration, to see that a large percentage of every dollar actually goes to the field. It is with pride and thanksgiving that the Secretary reports that, through expert management, over 70% of all money raised for foreign missions does go to the foreign field.

This has not always been an easy goal to meet and maintain. Each year expenses increase. In order to raise the money needed, money must be spent for promotional materials including posters, convention and association exhibits, and the publication and distribution of the *Mission Herald.*

The mission dollar is divided into four categories: (1) money to and for the field; (2) money for educational expenditures; (3) money for administration, and (4) money for a reserve fund. Actually seventy-three percent of the mission dollar goes to the mission field; seventeen percent goes to education while the remaining ten percent is used for promotion, administration and a reserve fund.[24]

In this connection, it is of interest to point out that at a time when many of the major white denominational bodies were reporting a decrease in foreign mission giving, our National Baptist

Churches increased contributions for foreign missions yearly and, at the same time, there was an increase in applications for overseas service. While major white denominations were experiencing a decline in contributions for foreign missions, some theologians among them suggested that a moratorium be placed on sending missionaries abroad and on supporting overseas missions altogether. Part of this attitude may have represented a subtle racism since most mission areas are in the Third World. It may also have been a reflection of a decrease of concern in Christian witnessing to the whole world. The constant increase of support by pastors, laymen and laywomen of the National Baptist Convention has been a continuing source of encouragement. Those who visit the mission field can see clearly what has been accomplished through the years and what is being done by our people. Nowhere on earth has there been a greater response to the Gospel than in Africa. This has been a continuing stimulus to the Board as it has carried forward the responsibility of building bridges of faith across the seas.

Loyal Boosters Organization

In 1974, an organization named the Loyal Booster Organization was established. This was comprised of women across the country whose purpose was to help underwrite the cost of missions for the Foreign Mission Board. The group sought to increase the success of the Board's financial effort during the summer months when pastors were vacationing and churches were operating on limited schedules. The Loyal Boosters organized special programs and promotions in the endeavor to help the Board maintain a normal cash flow. The specific statements of their aims and objectives are as follows:

Our Aim

To further Christian Fellowship and support the program of the Foreign Mission Board.

To promote "Operation Summer" in order to give an extra financial boost when many supporters are vacationing.

We are organized to offer many opportunities for enlightenment of the work of missions and missionaries supported by our Board.

It is our desire to bring to the attention of the members of our National Baptist Convention the high ideals and the Educational Program for Missionary Societies who are interested in enriching and strengthening their personal service through mission study classes. They may secure literature for all their needs from the Foreign Mission Board.

It is our aim to assist in organizing "Boosters" everywhere, whenever possible and wherever requested.

Will You Be A Booster ?
Enlist The Women Of Your Church
And Community,
And Organize For Service!

Our Objectives

To know more about the people of the world and their spiritual needs.

To be concerned about people everywhere who do not know Christ.

To pray for our Missionaries and Native Workers on the Foreign Field.

To give through our Missionary Programs, and send our gifts through our Foreign Mission Board.

To go, if the Lord calls, to special fields of work in our community, our homeland, or the uttermost part of the world.

First, as always, must come Soul Winning. To bring to Christ those lives that are now lost, and that so sorely need Him, is joy incomparable. For each of our talents there is a place waiting, and God in His infinite wisdom will surely point out the way.[25]

Baptist Women Visit Africa,1972

A significant development in establishing a clearer understanding of our work in Africa was the visit of a group of women from the Woman's Auxiliary of the National Baptist Convention to that continent. A group of twenty-three, headed by Dr. Mary O. Ross, President of the Woman's Auxiliary, responded to an invitation extended by the Woman's Auxiliary Union of the Liberian Missionary and Educational Convention, to meet with them at their annual session in Brewerville, Liberia, West Africa. The entire group utilized the opportunity to visit our Liberian missions and fourteen members of the delegation proceeded from Liberia to

Womens' Group Visits Africa

236

our stations in Malawi and Swaziland. The tour leader was the secretary of the Foreign Mission Board. Among the group were five presidents of Woman's Auxiliaries of five state conventions. These included Mrs. Sudie E. Tatem of Wisconsin, Mrs. Zoie Smith of Indiana, Mrs. Clara Banks of Ohio, Mrs. Lillie S. Weatherspool of Georgia and Mrs. Mary Hackney of New York.

Since the Liberian Woman's Missionary Union was headed by Mrs. William Tolbert, wife of the president of the Republic of Liberia and past president of the Baptist World Alliance, the group was accorded every courtesy from the highest level of the Liberian government. In recognition of outstanding Christian leadership ability on a world-wide scale, President Ross was accorded one of the highest honors conferred by the Liberian government. President Tolbert invested Dr. Ross as a Grand Commander of the Humane Order of African Redemption. This outstanding honor was presented to her at a gathering of Baptists from all over Liberia and was a tribute not only to Dr. Ross, but also to the thousands of Baptist women she had led so capably.

Dr. Mary O. Ross

This group of women visited our mission stations in Malawi and Swaziland. The group gave gifts of over $2,500 to the various missions visited. This was indeed a singular experience for the women of the Auxiliary.[26]

Dr. William R. Tolbert Elected President of the Baptist World Alliance

One of the most significant developments in the history of the Baptist World Alliance was the election of Dr. William R. Tolbert, Jr., vice president of the Republic of Liberia, to the presidency of that group. During a meeting held in Miami Beach, Florida, in June of 1965, Dr. Tolbert became the first Black president of the BWA. A Baptist preacher, Dr. Tolbert was elected without opposition to head this Alliance which then represented 26 million Baptists in 121 nations. At a press conference following his election Vice President Tolbert said, "I humbly commit myself as a servant of God and as an instrument in his hand. I feel I have been summoned by God. I want to say to members of this good Baptist family that I am convinced that this is the mighty work of God."

Dr. William R. Tolbert, Jr., President, Republic of Liberia

238

Dr. Tolbert was president of the Liberia Baptist Missionary and Educational Convention, Inc., with offices in Monrovia, and a past vice president of the Alliance. He said that his election might help the Baptist cause in Africa and pledged to work to erase the idea of some Africans that Christianity is a white man's religion. He also pledged to do everything possible to make it easier for missionaries to return to some countries which at that time prohibited certain missionary activity.

Dr. Tolbert served in this office with great distinction.

Preaching Mission to Africa

In February 1973, Secretary Harvey led a group of Baptist ministers on a preaching mission to Africa. This mission was conducted in cooperation with the Liberian Missionary and Educational Baptist Convention of which Dr. William R. Tolbert was president. Thirteen pastors comprised the team and shared memorable experiences as they traveled throughout the Republics of Liberia, Malawi and the Kingdom of Swaziland. Each team member made a unique contribution to the cause of Christ. All of them knew the joy of preaching the Gospel. All of them experienced the thrill of witnessing souls accepting Christ. Outdoor meetings, indoor meetings, by day and night, the team preached the Gospel to all who would hear. Thousands of miles were traveled and scores of churches and mission stations were visited. Each pastor received personal insights concerning overseas evangelism. Further understanding of daily life in Africa was gained by visiting in the homes of Africans and seeing first hand the circumstances under which they lived. Conferences were arranged with government officials and also with farmers who lived on a subsistence level. Some of the ministers on the team lived in the homes of the native pastors. Others were the guests of people who held responsible government posts. All soon depleted their wardrobes by giving to alleviate some of the poverty they witnessed — a giving born of a deep compulsion from within. Some wept with compassion for the conditions under which their fellow Christians lived. All members of this preaching team were humbly grateful for the opportunity to serve as channels through which the Gospel was proclaimed and Christ exalted.

The thirteen churches who shared their pastors for this preaching mission were extended special thanks by the Foreign Mission Board. Because of their generosity and concern, over 1,400 people openly professed their acceptance of Christ as Lord and Saviour. Hundreds of believers were strengthened in their faith. "God bless our brothers from the United States," was uttered time and time again. There was Christian pride in all of their utterances, but there was racial pride, too. For hundreds of the people in Malawi (formerly Nyasaland) and Swaziland, especially, this was their first exposure to members of our race from the United States. With their own eyes, they saw that the blood of Africa flowed in the veins of their fellow Christians from America and they were proud. "Tell our sister churches in America that we send them our Christian love."

Certainly the experience of the members of this preaching mission was unforgettable. The missionary enterprise was strengthened because they were able to see the results of the work that had been carried on by our missionaries through the years.

The Impact of the Preaching Missions

Ever since the first group of pastors went to Africa on a preaching mission, in 1967 the value of these visits became increasingly and convincingly clear. Until the preaching team visits began, relatively few American Blacks had ever seen the motherland. Blacks at home had only hazy ideas of what life was like in what was often called "The Dark Continent." The first three preaching teams escorted to mission fields by Secretary Harvey went to West Africa and East Africa. They saw, at first hand, the missionaries at work, the conditions under which they labored, and the positive results obtained in lives changed by the saving Gospel of the risen Lord. Each team member became acutely aware of what the Foreign Mission Board had been accomplishing, with limited resources, in giving a needy people a sense of hope, dignity and destiny. The preaching of the team members heightened the aspirations of their hearers wherever they went. The values, importance and imperative demands of the Christian missionary enterprise were made abundantly clear to them.

But what is of greatest importance is that the team members themselves were beneficiaries of their own efforts. They experienced the satisfaction which came from bringing the message of the saving power of Christ to many who had never heard it and who, upon hearing it, became converts to the Christian faith.

At the same time, they were inspired by knowing their preaching reinforced the faith of those who already were practicing believers and helped their hearers deepen their resolve to allow the Gospel of Christ to continue to make a positive difference in their lives. Moreover, during their sojourn on each mission field, as the team members preached, they had the experience of being foreign missionaries themselves, even though for a short period of time. By becoming bridge builders of faith across the sea, each team members own spiritual life was enhanced and each acquired a larger vision of the world of which they were a part. They saw, as never before, the power and potential of Christian missions and resolved to play a larger role in its support.

History was made when nine National Baptist pastors visited the Republic of South Africa to conduct the fourth preaching mission. This was the first time a group of Black American pastors had toured South Africa, preaching in many locations restricted to native Africans. No nation on earth needed their presence more. The repressive laws under which Black South Africans lived led to tremendous frustrations in their endeavor to survive. Other nations visited on this trip were malawi, East Africa, Lesotho and Swaziland.

With the visit of PREACHING TEAM FOUR 1975, the spirit of hope was encouraged among the exploited people. The National Baptist Assembly of South Africa, Inc., was comprised of 123 churches at that time. All of these were located in the settlements restricted to native Africans. Team members preached in locations all over the country. They were joyously received everywhere they went. In most areas, this was the first time the people had ever seen an American Negro. They often remarked about the similarity of color and facial resemblances. "Our Christian brothers from America," was a phrase repeated over and over.

Every member of the team was viewed as a symbol of hope. The native Africans saw in Black Americans what they hoped to become — the freedoms we enjoy, the right to vote, to own property, legal redress, free education on a primary and secondary level, economic opportunity, social security and even welfare for the aged, orphans and the incapacitated. Many accepted Jesus Christ as Saviour and Lord. A feeling of renewal of faith was expressed by the Christians in their testimonies. South Africans continued to look to National Baptists for encouragement and support.

The members of the team were inspired by the experience. As others before them, they saw at first hand the work of the Foreign Mission Board and also witnessed the evangelistic zeal of the people who comprised the missions. Every team member returned with a deeper appreciation of our own country. This comment from a member of the team following the trip is typical of the results. The Reverend Billy V. Bissic of Gramblin, Louisiana, wrote, "Every congregation was very enthusiastic and energetic. They were such lovely people. What they need most is more support from the churches of our Convention. They saw a ray of light and a spark of real hope as we moved among them...Almost unbelieveable, but true, in the midst of the burden of apartheid, the Black people seemed to have found strength in the God they served."[27]

This mission was one of the principal achievements of the Foreign Mission Board in 1975.

The fifth preaching mission visited our stations in Liberia, Malawi and Swaziland. On prior visits to Africa, previous teams spent most of their time preaching in cities, towns and villages. TEAM FIVE, however, spent half of its brief visit at the missions, consulting with the missionaries, talking to the African churches in the various areas, visiting some of the African homes and wrestling with some of the multiple issues which are the day-to-day problems of the average missionary.

One of the first problems emphasized was the cost involved in operating a mission station. This was immediately evident since most of the transportation for the team in Liberia was provided by mission-owned vehicles. There were delays due to problems with automobiles, poor road conditions and the constant need of the mission stations' request for emergency funds to cover the costs of contingencies. Some of the men accompanied the missionaries to the garage for car repairs and were surprised at the high charges and labor costs compared with those in the United States. Gasoline and oil prices exceeded those of the US by at least twenty percent, while food stuffs generally far exceeded similar food stuffs in America.

Rev. Charles Walker

Highlighting the visit of this team was an audience granted by President William R. Tolbert. This meeting was televised and shown throughout Liberia during the broadcast that evening.

243

Another high point occurred when, during this audience, the Reverend Charles Walker presented to President Tolbert the original score of "The Liberian Symphony." This symphony was composed by Reverend Walker and was inspired by his visit to Liberia in 1973. It was a major work for a complete orchestra. President Tolbert expressed deep appreciation for this significant contribution to the cultural and musical life of Liberia and noted that Reverend Walker was blessed to have unusual talents as both a musician and a preacher of the Gospel. He said, "In composing this Liberian Symphony, you are expressing in a musical way, your spiritual ties with Africa, the original homeland of your people. We express our thanks to you on behalf of the Liberian people."

The team was met in Malawi by a representative group of Malawian ministers led by the Reverend L. C. Muocha who was in charge of the Providence Industrial Mission. He expressed that the one theme of the African Baptist Assembly, Inc., is evangelism — bringing souls to Christ and strengthening the church by sharing. As in previous years, the visit concluded with the giving

Rev. L. C. Muocha

244

of gifts. Members of the team were presented chickens, goats, eggs, pineapples, edoes and artifacts handcrafted by the Malawians. Team members gave clothes and Bibles.

The SIXTH PREACHING TEAM of the Foreign Mission Board was comprised of eighteen men who set out for evangelistic work in Liberia, Malawi and Swaziland. One of the great experiences of PREACHING TEAM SIX, which all members appreciated most, was that of speaking in rural native churches. Despite the heat and the dust, the rain and the mud, the bouncing and uncomfortable rides, each team member exhibited great enthusiasm when sharing the Gospel with his African brothers and sisters. Each told the story in his own way. As a result of their sermons, they created a spiritual bond of brotherhood which erased all cultural and language differences which forged a unity toward a goal of world-wide Christian brotherhood. They realized, as never before, that Christian work is not all preaching and singing and praying; often it involves physically hard work, weary travel, lonely hours, and many discomforts. It is moving against the tide of sin and unrighteousness. It is a constant wrestling with principalities and powers that would stifle the light of Christ and profane the righteousness of God. Each team gained these insights and yet each team member also learned that for the missionaries on the field, there is also an inner joy and inner peace as they pursue their labors. Each team member learned how strengthening it is to the missionaries to know that fellow Christians in the US hold up their names and work to the throne of God in prayer and that God hears and gives these missionaries added strength for their tasks. These are the lessons learned from visiting the mission fields as part of a preaching team.

The eighteen preachers who made up PREACHING TEAM SIX met with much success as they proclaimed the Gospel of Jesus Christ in West, East, Central and South Africa during the month of February 1980. Upon returning, they inspired their congregations to a fresh zeal for missions.[28]

PREACHING TEAM SEVEN visited a few of the mission stations supported by the Foreign Mission Board in Liberia, Malawi and Swaziland. One of the highlights of their trip was a visit to the Providence Industrial Mission at Chiradzulu, Malawi. The team was impressed by the hundreds of church members who welcomed them and also by the fervent singing and prayers of the believers in the services of worship. Some of the worshippers traveled over thirty miles to share in these services which made their presence even more inspiring.

The team was also impressed by a visit to the S. Willie Layton Memorial Hospital. In addition, they were able to meet with various pastors of the churches and were surprised to learn that most had from five to twenty churches. They held services every day of the week, either walking or bicycling many miles each day to serve their people.

As usual, following the return of each preaching team, members sent letters to the secretary giving their reactions to the experience. One such letter from the Reverend O. B. Brown of Richmond, Virginia, quoted below, is of special interest:

> Dear Dr. Harvey:
>
> Any Black American, given the opportunity of visiting the "Motherland," must consider himself uniquely blessed in many respects. Likewise, having as a guide on that visit one who is well versed in the political, social and religious climate of places visited adds a dimension that cannot be surpassed.
>
> I am grateful to have been one-eighth of the recent preaching team sponsored by the Foreign Mission Board of the National Baptist Convention, U.S.A., Inc., under the very capable leadership of its executive secretary, Dr. William J. Harvey, III. Seeing foreign mission work and workers close-up gives one a sense of what the mission of the church really is.
>
> To be able to preach the Word in unlikely places to such anxious hearers, is an experience that only mind can recall and lips partially utter.

One of the most exciting experiences which I had was to sit in a room with African church leaders and hear them tell with excitement of the rapid growth of churches in Africa. In the words of one African preacher, "Ta-Ya-Fo" (Go and Tell).

Thank you, Dr. Harvey, for the opportunity to see what God hath wrought.[29]

In 1985, PREACHING TEAM EIGHT, comprised of ten pastors, made an extensive tour which included Liberia, Malawi, Swaziland, Southeast Africa and the Republic of Africa. They were met with warm greetings from representatives of the Liberian government, the Liberian Baptist Missionary and Educational Convention and members of the local clergy.

Miss Roberta Jackson

A memorial service for the late missionary, Sarah Cyrus, was held in the Friendship Baptist Church of the Bendoo Mission in Cape Mount, Liberia. The mission team participated in evangelistic services at the historic Providence Baptist Church, also in Liberia. They paid a special visit to the Providence Industrial Mission at Chiradzulu. The influence of this mission has spread throughout Central and South Africa largely in the countries of Zambia, Mozambique, Tanzania and Angola. This latter mission station played an important role in Malawi's quest for independence. They preached to the Bush people in Swaziland. They were quite pleased with the work being done at our mission station on the Woodlands Estate just outside of Mbabane where an excellent job was being done by Miss Roberta Jackson of the Mt. Zion Baptist Church, Holmesburg, Pennsylvania, principal of our preschool program there. The team did some preaching in the Republic of South Africa under limited circumstances, but all who heard them were impressed by their message.

In 1987, for the ninth time in twenty-one years, a preaching team sponsored by the Foreign Mission Board of the National Baptist Convention, U.S.A., Inc., visited some of our mission stations in Liberia, Malawi, Swaziland and the Republic of South Africa. The team was especially pleased to participate in the dedication of an elementary school building in Baluma Village, Grand Cape Mount County. This building was an outgrowth of the Bendoo Industrial Missions Outreach Evangelistic and Educational Program in the surrounding villages.

The Bendoo Mission was headed by the Reverend V. Alexander Benson, Jr., a native Liberian who served as principal while Mrs. Josephine Minter of Topeka, Kansas, and Reverend and Mrs. Rufus Prunty served as missionaries.

This team also visited the Suehn Industrial Mission headed by Deacon Ballah Davis, principal. The highlight of this visit was the participation of the team in the graduation and commencement exercises of the senior class as well as the dedication of the new boys' dormitory.

Principal Davis, who is also a Liberian senator, arranged for the team to have an audience with the President of Liberia, Dr. Samuel K. Doe. President Doe expressed appreciation for the visit and for the contribution which the National Baptist Convention, U.S.A., Inc., had made to Liberia through the years. He pledged the cooperation of his government toward the continuation of our relationship.

When the team arrived in Malawi, it was met by the Reverend L. C. Muocha and a group of ministers. Soon after their arrival, an intensive preaching schedule for the team members was put into operation. The team visited the S. Willie Layton Hospital for Women where they gave gifts including four bicycles and articles of clothing. Other places visited were Swaziland and Johannesburg, South Africa. Transportation was provided for the team to visit various churches in the Soweto area.[30]

The highlights of each of the visits made by preaching teams to our mission stations in Africa have been an important part of the experiences of the pastors who have had the opportunity to participate in these journeys. This administration has always had as its motto, "An informed people are a giving people." There is no doubt that the various congregations and communities in which the members of each team lived and worked were greatly enlightened by the information and inspiration their pastors brought back.

Laymen Work Team Visits Africa

The growth of interest of National Baptists in overseas evangelism was demonstrated in April 1975 when a request came from the president of the National Baptist Laymen's Movement, Brother Walter Cade, Jr., stating that a group of laymen would like to go on a missionary work service African tour.

Each layman involved had a skill that he would use on the mission tour. They included auto mechanics, plumbers, electricians, bricklayers and carpenters. All of the men would bring their tools and equipment with them so that they could perform much-needed repair work at our stations.

The request was granted. This was the first time in the history of the Foreign Mission Board that a group of laymen visited the mission field with one objective — to worship and work side by

Left to Right...Standing...Mitchell McConnell, James L. Hopkins, Edward Lindsey, Walter Cade, Jr. (on knees), Cleo McConnell, Tommie Williams, Dr. Augustus C. Curry, Fred Berry, Anderson J. Smith, Eura L. Diamond. In front...Left to Right...Harvey Randolph, Ernest O'Polk, Jr., Thee Stevens.

side with their African brothers and sisters. Fourteen members of the Laymen's Movement left on January 31, 1976, accompanied by Secretary Harvey, to witness the activities of the National Baptist Convention in three countries on the continent of Africa.

President Cade served as coordinator of the group. Upon their arrival in Liberia, visits were made to the Suehn and Bendoo Industrial Missions to determine the primary needs. As a result of these preliminary visits, eight men went to work at Bendoo and six at Suehn.

The Liberian Baptists were especially appreciative of the visits of Black Baptists from America. A gracious welcome reception in their honor was given at the Baptist Training Center, Paynesward City, Liberia. Officials of the Liberian Baptist Convention extended greetings.

For five days the laymen worked diligently on the Bendoo and Suehn Missions. One of their immediate impressions was the high cost of general maintenance on a self-contained mission. In each instance, the Suehn and Bendoo Missions were totally dependent upon their own generators for electricity and water. Climatic conditions exact a toll on buildings and motors. Six months of rain and six of dry weather play havoc with roofs, doors, window sashes, vehicle motors and generators. In all of these areas of need, the men worked. Motors on three vehicles were tuned, doors were rehung, electrical fixtures and wiring were overhauled, walls were replastered and painted, and concrete blocks were laid. Sometimes this required parts or materials which the laymen themselves supplied. By doing so, they learned of the extravagant costs in a developing country where import duties tripled and sometimes quadrupled prices. Fortunately, the laymen had provided for this and had funds with them to meet the various costs for materials or parts purchased.

Perhaps for the first time, many of the men came to understand the practical aspects of mission work — the day to day responsibilities of operating a mission with a school and/or health facilities. The needs for funds for educational materials, school desks, blackboards, chalk, flooring, ceilings, science laboratory equipment, athletic goods, ironing boards, irons, beds, mattresses, as well as pews, Bibles and religious education literature, health supplies, medicines — all are vital ingredients in running a mission station. In addition there are needs such as buses, station wagons and jeep maintenance — also necessary to a self-contained mission. Many of the laymen expressed surprise at the enormity of expenses involved for each need.

At the same time, they came to appreciate, to a profound degree, the role of the missionary. The isolation, the sacrifices, the continual responsibility of 24-hour-per-day duties soon became apparent as did the need to adjust to different cultural

251

patterns while still allowing the light of Christian witness and the Gospel of Jesus Christ guide them in every aspect of their service. Being a missionary, the laymen quickly realized, is no easy job. It is not a position which brings profit or advantage. It is, indeed, hard work. Each layman could both sense and witness the dedication of our missionaries as they carried out their various duties. As the week came to a close, the Worship-Witnessing-Work Team expressed regret that they could not stay longer and contribute more of their skills.

The team went from Monrovia to Nairobi. Following an orientation session regarding their forthcoming visit to Malawi and Southern Africa, the men enjoyed a brief visit to the Kenyan Animal Reserves where they saw several species of animals in their natural habitat. Upon arrival in Malawi, they proceeded to the Providence Industrial Mission where over 150 people greeted them with thanksgiving in their own language.

Upon their return from the mission, all of the men wrote letters of appreciation for the unique experience they had had. Two of the letters are quoted below:

Kansas City, Mo.

Dear Dr. Harvey:

I don't have words to express to you just how much this trip meant to me.

Before I go further, let me thank you from the bottom of my heart for your patience, your kindness and all the hard work that you exhibited in order to make our trip an enjoyable one. You are a Prince in my book. I hope you found your family well upon your return home. May God forever bless and keep you in good health, this is my prayer. You are doing an excellent job in Foreign Missions. The trip to Africa meant more to me than I will ever be able to convey in words.

I certainly did appreciate the warm, spirit-filled welcome we received at P.I.M. That great fellowship — I will cherish it as long as I live.

I enjoyed the spirit of worship that they expressed. It was amazing to see them express themselves in giving. Even though they had a little, they were willing to share what they had. That is pure religion. This is Faith in Action. No wonder Jesus said, "He that worships me, must worship me in Spirit and in truth."

There is a great feeling to see the people who want to work, are willing to work and improve their mission, but funds to buy material, they don't have. No one can do a job if they don't have what it takes to do it. For that reason, I have made up in my mind that I am going to give $5 a week toward Foreign Missions, and encourage all members of my church to do likewise. This is what the trip meant to me.

Anderson J. Smith

Kansas City, Kansas

Dear Dr. Harvey:

The people of Africa to me are some of the most loving and cooperative people I have visited. They are very intelligent and most are willing to advance, but the poverty is so that they cannot do many things.

Our Mission Stations in Liberia, Suehn and Bendoo, are doing Great Kingdom Building for God. The missionaries are dedicated Christian workers. Providence Industrial Mission in Malawi is also Kingdom building and teaching the people to help raise their standards of living. National Baptist Mission in Swaziland, the only Black preschool in that land, is a credit to us.

The trip had made me think of how blessed we are living in this country, and how God has blessed me with shoes, clothes to wear, a home to live in and many other blessings, and I pray that I can help my brothers and sisters more who are in a destitute situation.

253

As a member of the National Baptist Laymen, U.S.A., Inc., and a child of the King, I pledge my support to the Foreign Mission Board of the National Baptist Convention, U.S.A., Inc., to the best of my ability and shall tell and ask others to help do our mission task, for it is work that we all can do.

Fred W. Berry[31]

The outstanding result of the "worship and work mission" of the laymen was the fulfillment of a resolution they made while in Africa to underwrite the construction of a building at one of the African missions. Two years after their return, the building they had sponsored, the John L. Webb-Allen Jordan Memorial Chapel of the Friendship Baptist Church, built on the Bendoo Industrial Mission grounds in Grand Cape Mount County, Liberia, at a cost of $65,000, was dedicated. The building was named in honor of two of the past presidents of the National Laymen's Movement. This chapel will continue to be an enduring memorial not only to two of the great leaders of the Laymen's Movement of the Convention, but also as an outstanding example of the

John L. Webb-Allen Jordan Memorial Chapel

Convention's cooperative thrust toward building bridges of faith across the seas.

It was with much pride and joy, therefore, that Secretary Harvey and a delegation from the National Baptist Laymen's Movement went to the Bendoo Industrial Mission to participate in the dedication service of the chapel. It was a grand occasion and was attended by the Liberian Minister of Education, Mr. Fahnbulleh, various officials of government, Paramount Chief Mawbo and many Christian ministers and missionaries. The dedication sermon was delivered by Secretary Harvey.[32]

Some Political Problems

Prior to and including 1970, the Foreign Mission Board felt the effects of unsettled political conditions in some of the West African countries. In Sierra Leone, as a result of a military coup, our missionary, Mrs. Constance Cummings-John, was exiled. She was principal of the Vine Memorial-Roosevelt Secondary School and, at the same time, Mayor of Freetown. This school had operated under the sponsorship of the Foreign Mission Board for over twenty years. In 1972, it had a total of twenty-nine teachers of whom eleven were paid by the Foreign Mission Board, sixteen by the government and two by the Peace Corps. The school functions in cooperation with the Sierra Leone Mission. In 1971, the principal reported an enrollment of 572 girls. Following the exile of Mrs. Cummings-John, the Board appointed Mrs. Elsiemay Kallon, who proved to be an able administrator. Under her leadership, students achieved high ratings in governmental exams. For many students, this was their first exposure to Christian teachings and soon a large majority of them were converted to Christianity.[33]

In Ghana, the work of the Foreign Mission Board was hampered by a law passed in 1970 called the "Compliance Order on Aliens." This denied all aliens the right to own businesses or to be employed. This dealt a serious blow to our work because most of our Baptist strength in Ghana was composed of Nigerians from the Yoruba tribe. Because of this order, these workers were forced to leave Ghana where many had lived and worked for over twenty-five years. The result was a tremendous depletion in the membership of our churches. At Accra, where we had 350 members, only twenty-three were able to remain. A similar situation existed in the Asokwa-Adanse Province.[34]

In Lesotho, a political upheaval caused the closing of our secondary school at Leribe and also the discontinuance of our seminary classes for seven months.

In all of these situations, the Foreign Mission Board had to use delicate diplomacy in order to maintain its stations and continue to carry forward its important programs.

The Tragedy of South Africa

One of the major contributions made by the Foreign Mission Board is that of providing educational opportunities in those areas where there is greatest need. An extended article in the *New York Times* outlines in detail the educational inequalities in South Africa as of March 1970. Among the findings reported in this article were the following:

> A Black African woman earning $192 a year as a domestic servant pays $90 a year to keep her four children in school.

> When schools opened last fall, thousands of Black African pupils were turned away because there was no place for them.

> The average Black African earns the equivalent of $44.80 a month, and many cannot afford the schooling provided by the Bantu Education Department.

> Unlike other racial groups, Black Africans pay for their children's textbooks, writing and handicraft materials, secondary school examination fees and sometimes registration and sport fees. Whites, Asians and Coloreds better able to afford the additional fees, pay few of them unless they send their children to private schools.

> A recent survey in a township in coastal Port Elizabeth

showed that Black Africans pay a third to a half of their wages on educating their children.

Of the 9,500 schools for Blacks, in 1968 only eighty-nine provided a full high school curriculum. There were seven technical secondary schools, thirty vocational training schools and thirty-four teacher colleges.

Of 31,075 Black African teachers outside the Tanskei homeland in 1968, 87% had not even graduated from high school.

An education commission, backed jointly by the South African Council of Churches and the Christian Institute, recently found that school children of all races are being taught that apartheid is the only acceptable policy for South Africa. There are about 3.5 million whites compared with 13 million Blacks.[35]

Secretary Harvey found some signs of hope after the seminary in Leribe was forced to close when the South African seminarians were permitted to continue their studies at the Christian Institute, a white institution in Johannesburg. This institute defied the South African government by permitting these Black students to matriculate. This act was at least one proof that true Christians will defy the highest political authority in order to perpetuate the teachings of the Gospel.[36]

No one can read the above statistics without feeling a sense of indignation at the gross injustice imposed by the white minority upon the Black majority. The white minority doubtless feels threatened by educated Blacks and thus provide minimum schooling for them. At the same time, from the Christian perspective, the Macedonian Call from South Africa becomes increasingly significant. This is indeed one of the basic reasons for sending the Gospel of Christ, the message of abundant life, to those in racial bondage overseas.

Ever since the Reverend R. A. Jackson of Holly Spring, Mississippi, sailed from New York City to open a mission in Cape Town, South Africa in 1897 under the auspices of the Foreign

Mission Board, we have had a continuing interest in and concern for that complex part of the continent. It will be recalled that in 1902, Secretary Lewis G. Jordan visited South Africa and witnessed mission churches established by Reverend Mr. Jackson in twenty-five cities and native townships. Reverend Jackson concluded his work there in 1906. The Reverend James E. East went to that mission in 1909 and spent eleven years there, returning to the United States to become secretary of the Foreign Mission Board in 1921. At that time, there were thirty-six churches and fourteen schools operating in South Africa. The Reverend Mr. East saw prophetically the degrading conditions and the violence apartheid would bring. He constantly urged National Baptists to pray for their South African brothers and sisters who were suffering under the oppressive system. National Baptists not only sponsor the largest mission work in South Africa, but no other Black American denomination has been so involved over the past eighty-three years.

The first group of Black American Baptist preachers to conduct a preaching mission in South Africa was under the auspices of the Foreign Mission Board in 1975. Since then, seven other preaching teams have brought hope to their South African kinsmen. In addition, representatives from the National Baptist Laymen's Movement and the National Baptist Women's Auxiliary have met with representatives of the National Baptists of Southern Africa on two occasions in the last decade in Swaziland.

The question has been asked, "Why haven't these facts been given more publicity?" The answer is twofold. First, too much publicity regarding our mutual affiliations may have created problems for our brothers and sisters in South Africa. Therefore we had to low-key our reports for fear of reprisal from the South African government. Second, our publicity was limited to our only media for information, the *Mission Herald.* Naturally, those who failed to subscribe (then or now), or who failed to read the *Mission Herald,* remained unaware of what was being done on the mission field of the National Baptist Foreign Mission Board. Efforts to ease some of the difficult economic problems faced

258

by the Black South Africans were highlighted by the adoption by some corporations of the Sullivan Principles, introduced by the Reverend Leon Sullivan in 1977 while he was a member of the board of Directors of General Motors. The term, "Sullivan Principles," was a code whereby United States corporations investing in South Africa would form their employment practices to desegregate dining and locker rooms, toilets and work facilities. In addition, they would pay equally for equal or comparable work, would develop training programs to advance Black workers, would increase the number of non-whites in management and supervisory jobs and improve the quality of living conditions for workers. These included improvements in such areas as housing, transportation, education, health care and recreation.

Approximately 350 United States firms were investing in South Africa at the time of the promulgation of the Sullivan Principles. By 1985, only 135 had adopted these guidelines. Supporters of the Principles maintained that the companies which complied with them represented a force for change in South Africa. However, the Principles, even if they were complied with, did nothing about the system of "Grand Apartheid," and the security state which enforces this oppressive system. What was needed was abolition of apartheid which would permit the Blacks, who constitute the large majority of the population, to vote, own or purchase land, be free to choose where they work or live, and whom they marry. It would also eliminate the hated law that Blacks must carry a passbook at all times. (This passbook regulation was eventually eliminated in 1987.)

Because after ten years the main objectives of the Sullivan Principles had not been achieved, the Reverend Mr. Sullivan publicly abandoned them and called for the immediate and total abolition of apartheid and urged all United States corporations to discontinue any financial investments in that nation. It was his feeling that South Africa would not make any changes in its system without strong economic sanctions.

National Baptists and the Foreign Mission Board have felt a continuing responsibility to be involved in the fight for freedom in South Africa. As we have indicated, historically, we have been involved. Our present help to the 152 Black churches and two colored churches; our interest in the 98 Bantustan churches which we either constructed or aided in constructing (seed churches), demand that we intensify our concern through out prayers and gifts.[37]

Secretary Harvey reminded the constituency of the National Baptist Convention, U.S.A., Inc., that today Black Americans must be vitally concerned with the deplorable conditions in South Africa. These concerns, he stated, must not be expressed only in prayerful and financial support for our work there. As important as these forms of support are and as desperately as they need to be kept up and even increased, the concern of Black Americans for the South African situation needs to be expressed through pressure exerted in the local and national community. Pressure, voiced in terms too obvious to be ignored, must continue to decry the inhumane excesses of the South African government.[38]

A South African Minister's Experiences

In the summer of 1979, word was received in the office of the Foreign Mission Board, that the Reverend J. B. Ngubane, who served as an assistant to the Reverend E. D. Ngubeni, our South African supervisor, had to flee South Africa because of false charges that he was engaged in political activities. Through various means, the Reverend Ngubane arrived in Holland and was granted refugee status. In speaking before a group of Christians in Holland who aided in his escape, he described many of his experiences and the conditions under which many of his fellow native Africans had to live. Following are excerpts from that address:

> Our struggle was a common struggle for humanity; our hope is to become our fullest human potential that God has created us to be.

> We should never forget that the new and human course we are pursuing will remain a beautiful dream right

until each one of us is prepared to change the course of his or her own life. We want to assume responsibility...responsibility for living our own lives according to our own estimations of what is value to ourselves and fair to others as well.

To my mind, the passbook is one of the dirtiest things to be carried by any human being; poverty and the breakdown of family life are the results of this book. I hate to speak about this here in Europe because there are many people who support the apartheid policy as the only solution for South Africa.

Thousands and thousands throughout the year are thrown into jails for not carrying a passbook. Daily in South Africa you would hear about illegal Blacks and when you try to follow the story about how this person is illegal, you'll be shocked to hear that he was caught during the night raids in a friend's or relative's house on a visit (without his passbook). This would prove to the world that the Black man in South Africa has (been accorded) no human dignity and that South Africa is a police state.

When the South African government tries to hide its evil treatment of Blacks, you will hear them saying, "Blacks in South Africa are far better off economically than other Blacks in other states." Our complaint is Black people in South Africa have nothing to do with other countries. We say South Africa is rich and we have the right to share its wealth as South Africans.[39]

The Foreign Mission Board continued to send the Reverend Ngubane's salary to South Africa for the subsistence of his wife and children who had no other source of income. Through the World Council of Churches International Refugee Committee, the Foreign Mission Board made efforts to have the Reverend Mr. Ngubane repatriated in Botswana as a worker in a refugee camp.

Vermont Avenue Baptist Church in Zululand

One of the constructive developments in missionary activity has been the sponsoring of a church on the mission field by a church in this country. During July of 1979, a dedication service was held for the Vermont Avenue Baptist Church of Zululand. This church was sponsored by the Vermont Avenue Baptist Church of Washington, D. C., pastored by the Reverend John B. Wheeler. This "seed church" is located in Kwa Mashu, a sprawling Bantu township a few miles from the sea resort town of Durban in the Republic of South Africa.

The Baptists were quite joyous and their pride abounded as they celebrated the dedication of this church. Sitting on corners adjacent to it are two brick church buildings representing different Christian faiths. On the day of dedication, the happiness of our Baptist members was unbounded because they were no longer a church without a building. The structure of their new church is a large brick building formerly owned by the Episcopal Church. It has a seating capacity of nearly 400. With adequate indoor toilet facilities and electric lighting, the modern structure was a great contrast to certain other churches in Africa where we had often preached by the light of oil burning lanterns or the headlights of buses shining through windows and doors.

During our visits to Kwa Mashu, we were treated with much kindness and affection. For example, during the service, each member of our party was called to the front and presented with gifts. Reverend Wheeler decided to become a member of that church and was proud that he was the first American to become a member in its new building. In swift succession, his wife and all other members of our party followed him in joining this joyous congregation.

The construction of this church fills a great need. The Baptists should not fall behind other Christian denominations in their evangelism as well as in the building and/or acquisition of buildings from which to proclaim the Gospel.[40]

Death of Dr. John B. Falconer

After a very successful and impressive term of service to the people of Liberia under the auspices of the Foreign Mission Board of the National Baptist Convention, U.S.A., Inc., the Reverend John B. Falconer passed away on April 5, 1970, while attending the 56th session of the Liberia Baptist Missionary and Educational Convention. He was born in Shubuta, Mississippi, on November 3, 1912. He received his education at Prentiss Junior College, Prentiss, Mississippi, and at Lincoln University in Oxford, Pennsylvania, where he received the Bachelor of Arts and the Bachelor of Sacred Theology Degrees in 1939. The following year he was married to Ann Styles of Savannah, Georgia. To this union was born two children. Following graduation he served as Director of Religious Activity at Prentiss Institute. In 1943, he was appointed as Post Chaplain of the United States Army Contingent stationed at Roberts International Airport in Liberia. After serving three years with the army, he became affiliated with the National Baptist Convention. Recognizing his ability and commitment, the Foreign Mission Board appointed him as supervisor of the work in West Africa. For nine years he was stationed in Monrovia. During that period he was given the added responsibility of administrator and builder of the Carrie V. Dyer Maternity and Child Welfare Center, Bassa Community, Monrovia, Liberia. He was highly regarded as one who possessed profound human concerns as well as compelling skills as a preacher of the Gospel. Among his accomplishments were initiating and completing the following buildings: the Powell Nurses Home, Monrovia; the Mount Galilee Baptist Church, Careysberg, Montserrado County, and the Lott Carey Annex of the Providence Baptist Church. He built himself into the lives of the people whom he served and his memory will be long-lasting. Shortly after his death, the Liberia Baptist Missionary and Educational Convention, Inc., established the annual John B. Falconer Lectures and Ministers Convocation on the campus of the Liberia Baptist Theological Seminary which was founded in 1976. Certainly these lectures have kept his memory vivid in the minds of those who knew him and,

263

at the same time, constitute a source of inspiration for future generations.[41]

Mrs. Josephine Minter

One of the outstanding missionaries in East Africa was Mrs. Josephine Minter of Topeka, Kansas. She was originally assigned to the Bendoo Industrial Mission to assist Mrs. Sarah Cyrus. Upon the retirement of Dr. and Mrs. Daniel S. Malekebu, Mrs. Minter was assigned to the Providence Industrial Mission to carry out that responsibility in cooperation with the Reverend L. C. Muocha who succeeded Dr. Malekebu as chairman of the National Baptist Assembly of Malawi. Mrs. Minter's salary was paid by the Foss Avenue Baptist Church in Flint, Michigan, where the Reverend Avery Alridge was pastor. Mrs. Minter carried forward a successful ministry at the Providence Mission. One illustration of her work and of the enthusiasm she brought to it is indicated by one of her letters written to Secretary Harvey in 1972.

Dear Reverend Harvey:

My return to Malawi seems to be welcomed by all Malawians. Reverend Muocha, Mr. Chipota, Mr. Chiboana, two ministers and Mr. Mahenge met me at the airport at 4:30 p.m. Wednesday, February 23. By the time we reached the mission, it was dark. In spite of the long delay and heavy rain, many people were waiting to welcome me.

It was a very happy reunion with traditional dancing and singing. Friday morning the official welcome was given in the church. Sunday we went to Mulange. Reverend Muocha preached and afterwards the Mt. Hermon members gave me another welcome. They brought many gifts of food. Speeches and demonstrative welcome gestures were brought by senior citizens of the church.

Today was "Martyrs Day," set aside for prayers in remembrance of those who died for freedom. The district

264

commissioner, his wife, the chairman of Malawi Congress Party, two women from the party and a medical assistant, all from Chiradzulu, were here to welcome me and to worship with us. Tomorrow we shall meet with Mr. Muwalo, the minister of state.

I must say a word of thanks to my dear friends at the Suehn Station, Monrovia, Liberia. Mrs. Etheridge got Mr. Davis to drive the bus to the airport. All the missionaries at Suehn stayed up all night to get me to the airport in time. I am grateful to each of them and to the students that went along.

A baby boy was born in the Willie S. Layton Hospital two days after my return. I have been told that this is the first baby born since my departure last year. People are coming from far and near who remembered that I was their nurse just a few months ago. There is much to be done and I shall try very hard to help meet some of the needs; while trying, we shall also be praying for additional missionaries to come and help us.

We are anxiously waiting and looking forward to your next visit. Most of the Malawians know that you will be coming in April with the ladies of our National Baptist Convention.

In closing I must say that I am grateful to the Lord and all of you for another opportunity to serve the people of Malawi.

Yours in Christian Service

Josephine Minter

Mrs. Minter served in that post until she was transferred to Liberia to serve at the Bendoo Industrial Mission.

Dr. Commodore N. Bennett

In July 1974, the Foreign Mission Board appointed Dr. and Mrs. C. N. Bennett of Manassas, Virginia, to serve at the Suehn Mission as supervisor and librarian, respectively. Dr. Bennett, an educator, was born in McDonald, Pennsylvania, a suburb of Pittsburgh. He was educated in the elementary and high school of McDonald from which he graduated with high honors. He received his college education at Virginia Union University, Richmond, Virginia, where he earned the A. B. degree in Social Science. He began his teaching career in the Manassas Industrial Institute. He was also an instructor of history, English, French and mathematics and served as dean of boys at Hackley Hall. Later he served as an instructor and assistant principal in the King and Queen County Training School. Then he worked as an instructor in the public schools of Caroline County, Virginia. After teaching twelve years in Caroline County, he was appointed principal of the A. T. Wright High School in Whitestone, Lancaster County. In 1949, Dr. Bennett returned to the Manassas area to

Dr. & Mrs. Bennett

serve as principal of the Jennie Dean High School. Later he was appointed supervisor of federal programs for Prince Williams County schools.

Dr. Bennett continued his education at several other institutions. He earned the Master of Letters degree at the University of Pittsburgh. Upon receiving a fellowship from the Southern Educational Foundation, he attended the School of Administration at the George Peabody College and Seminary where he earned the Ed.S. degree in Educational Research. The Virginia Seminary and College awarded him the honorary degree of Doctor of Humanities.

Dr. Bennett contributed a number of articles to professional journals and was in demand as a lecturer and panelist as well as a member of various evaluating committees for educational, civic and religious groups. Because of these many activities, he was cited for distinguished service by Virginia Union University and was listed in the 1950 edition of *Who's Who in Colored Americans.* The Foreign Mission Board was fortunate to get someone of Dr. Bennett's experience and expertise to serve as superintendent of the Suehn Mission.[42]

Mrs. Bennett was a certified librarian and teacher of home economics. Upon their retirement from the Virginia school system, both she and her husband volunteered their services to the missionary enterprise. After three months of service which included reorganizing the educational structure of the school and stimulating greater evangelistic emphasis, Dr. Bennett was so inspired that he became convinced God was calling him to preach. The Foreign Mission Board requested that the Liberian Baptist Convention call a Council to ordain him as a minister of the Gospel. He went to Liberia as a Christian teacher; he came back as a Christian preacher.

Brother Cleo McConnel Becomes a Missionary to Africa

One of the results of the Laymen's Worship and Work Team which went to Africa in 1976, was the inspiration of one of the

267

team members to commit himself to a term of service on the mission field. Brother Cleo McConnel of Pacoima, California, committed himself to the Foreign Mission Board for a three-year term as a missionary at the Bendoo Industrial Mission in Liberia.

An officer of the National Baptist Laymen's Movement of the National Baptist Convention, U.S.A., Inc., he contacted a number of churches and laymen's groups across the country in the interest of the missionary enterprise. He took the time to accompany Secretary Harvey to Bendoo in 1978 for the dedication of the chapel which was constructed under the auspices and at the expense of the National Baptist Laymen's Movement.

Brother Cleo McConnel

Brother McConnel was an outstanding example of a Christian layman who was caught up in the activities of his local church, his district association, his state convention and in the Laymen's Movement of the Convention. A native of Vernon, Louisiana, he was graduated from Southern University in Baton Rouge. He and his wife were the parents of six children.

Upon moving to California in 1956, the McConnels joined the Calvary Baptist Church of San Fernando, pastored by the Reverend H. T. Broadus. Brother McConnel served his church in various capacities: deacon, Sunday school teacher, director of the Baptist Training Union, member of the choir and chairman of the Supervisory Committee of the Calvary Baptist Church Credit Union. Outside of the church he served as executive secretary of the laymen's department of the Western Baptist Convention and a member of the board of directors of the National Baptist Laymen's Movement. He received a number of honors and awards from various organizations. He was very active in raising funds for the Webb-Jordan Chapel and traveled at his own expense to Liberia to take part in its construction and dedication.[43]

Mrs. Sarah Cyrus

Among the distinguished emissaries of the Foreign Mission Board, was Mrs. Sarah Cyrus. She had originally gone to Liberia with her husband to serve at the Bendoo Mission. There they both

Mrs. Sarah Cyrus

rendered a great humanitarian service to the people of that area. After her husband unfortunately died in a drowning accident, she decided to remain on the field and continue to minister her nursing skills to the people. Secretary Harvey's visit with her early in 1964 was filled with dramatic experiences illustrative of the importance and influence of the dedicated missionary.

"We first went to Vanzwa, a fifty-three hut village in Montserrado County, Liberia. This is a remote village composed of something over 250 persons belonging to the Vai tribe. The lack of roads and the distance to the city of Robertsport makes this truly an isolated village in the interior. Like all villages in the interior, adequate medical services are at a minimum, and, though the government sends out a medical team once a year to this area, regular medical services are few and far between. Villagers needing such services must either depend upon home remedies and/or the local witch doctor, or trek many, many miles to the Government Hospital in Robertsport.

"It is in this area that missionary nurse Sarah Cyrus constantly met an urgent need. Every week, using Bendoo Mission as a hub, she would radiate out into the surrounding interior. Medical supplies, food and camping equipment were carried by bearers. She was further accompanied by an interpreter, John Hoff, two teen-age nurse's aids, and a representative from the Paramount Chief Mumbo.

"As we neared the village, we could hear the drums announcing our approach. They were expecting us. Sister Cyrus and I were escorted to the town hall. Yellow flowers and palm-like ferns were intertwined around the entrance and the window sills. The whole interior of the square building was bedecked with green garlands and flowers of many hues. We were led to a table and invited to be seated. The village elders were seated toward our right and the subordinate clan and tribal chiefs were to our left. The people milled about outside. Only elderly women shared seats with the elders.

"A young man dressed in a chief's robe addressed us, through our interpreter, in the Vai language. He welcomed us in the name

270

of the chief who was away on government business. He said that, 'Had the chief not been committed to a conference with President Tubman (of Liberia), he would certainly have been present, for the people have long wanted to see the secretary of the Foreign Mission Board from America. Never has a Secretary visited our mission, yet we have been blessed beyond thinking by the services of Mother Cyrus. Because of her, we have heard of your Jesus Christ, and some of our people have accepted him as their personal Savior. When her husband lived, he, too, came preaching Christ. He took our children to Bendoo Mission School and because they learned to read and write English, our village benefited.'

"A tall, gaunt, aged man dressed in a long blue robe with a matching skull cap, then arose. The wrinkled face and the white strands of hair which peeked from beneath his cap, and the work-gnarled hands covered with flaccid flesh, bespoke many, many years. His voice was deep and, though it wavered with each word, the intensity of his speech and the sincerity of his demeanor conveyed to the listener the realization that here was a personality of great strength. To the Foreign Mission Board that sends you here, our greatest thanks. We thank you for life. For before your missionaries came, death was with us every day. Our babies die. Our children die. Our women die. Men die. Chiefs die. Elders die. But with the missionaries coming, we live. Mother Cyrus gives us life. Babies can cry and not be sick. Children grow fat and strong. Women have babies and live. Men do not waste away. Chiefs and elders live to see their increase (progeny). We thank you for life. Tell your people in America what we say. Tell them how we live. Tell them how we need more of them to help the people of this country.

"We love Mother Cyrus who comes to us bringing life. We love Reverend and Mrs. Prunty who teach our children at Bendoo Mission. They give another kind of life so our children may live. We thank you for Christ. Learning of Him, we live again. Our village is yours. Come again. Our welcome is true. Come again. Our love for your missionaries is real. Come again. We thank you for life!'

271

'We spent the night there, and late into the evening we talked of God, Negro Baptists in America, and the work of the Foreign Mission Board in Liberia. From noon until dark Sister Cyrus treated the natives as they came with their many ills. Diseases, from simple stomachaches in adults and croup in infants, to amputation for a gangrenous toe from the foot of a native from a remote village who had heard that Sister Cyrus might visit Vanzwa and was waiting there. Prenatal examinations with the dispensing of vitamins, medicines and advice, were a part of the services.

"At daybreak, we began our journey back to Bendoo. We could not help but thank God that He was using our Board, and through our Board, our missionaries, to meet the spiritual and physical needs of these isolated people. Even at that early hour, many were gathered to bid us farewell. But the words which will ever ring in my mind and heart were — "We thank you for Life!" (See Mission Herald, March-April 1964, pp. 5-7.)

Rev. James S. Cyrus

New Expansion and Development, 1961-1986

It was in 1934 that Sister Sarah Cyrus and her husband, the Reverend James S. Cyrus, were accepted by the Foreign Mission Board of the National Baptist Convention, U.S.A.. Inc., to serve the foreign field in the area of Liberia, West Africa. During the administration of the Reverend James E. East as corresponding secretary of the Foreign Mission Board, the Reverend and Mrs. Cyrus joined the missionary family at the Suehn Mission Station just outside of Monrovia.

The Reverend Mr. Cyrus was versatile and tireless in his efforts as pastor of the church, teaching at the junior high school, running the library, et cetera. In addition, he saved the school much money by doing the cement work on the James E. East Hall.

In 1947 on Fisherman's Lake, the Reverend Mr. Cyrus lost his life while travelling in a canoe to take the Gospel to one of the remote areas on the far side of the lake. It was thought that after this tragic event Sister Cyrus would return home. Instead she continued to serve as school nurse, sewing teacher, and nurse to all the Suehn Mission family and others in the community. Later she was sent to be in charge of the clinic at the Bendoo Mission Station where she nursed the needy souls living in the bush. She became a legend in her own time, personifying the love and dedication of the called of God.

Sister Cyrus was always a main attraction at the annual session of the Convention and would electrify the delegates as she brought greetings from the foreign field. She was largely responsible for the increase in mission contributions as the pastors and people of the Convention churches could see, through her words, the meaningful work she was carrying out in West Africa.

The efforts of Sister Cyrus were widely known and applauded, but no more than in the country of her service, the Republic of Liberia. In 1971, Sister Cyrus was one of two persons who received the William V. S. Tubman Achievement Award. The other was a Liberian, Mrs. Anna E. Cooper, former dean of Liberia College (now the University of Liberia). Each recipient received an award of $1,000. These awards were established in 1967 by the West African Explosives and Chemicals, Ltd., whose president, Mr. Eric

273

R. Davis, and general manager, Mr. James G. Spence, along with their wives, attended the presentation ceremony at the executive mansion.

President Tubman expressed great satisfaction that Mrs. Cyrus decided to remain in Liberia following her husband's death. He praised her for her determination, ability and dynamism, as she contributed to meeting the needs of the sick and disabled, and to the overall health problems of Liberia. This honor was received in March 1971. Sister Cyrus retired in 1982 after having delivered 3,500 babies and given over 200,000 treatments — often in remote areas where she was the only source of medical help.

On December 15, 1984, Sister Cyrus passed on to her reward. She went home at last, having lived a joyful and constructive life. Several people who knew her well wrote tributes to her. Some of these were published in the *Mission Herald,* January-February 1985 issue, following her death.

Funeral services were held on December 20, 1984 at the Nineteenth Street Baptist Church, Philadelphia, Pennsylvania, with the Reverend Charles Walker, pastor, officiating and Secretary Harvey delivering the eulogy.

Retirement of Sister Mattie Mae Davis

After thirty-four years of dedicated service at the Suehn Industrial Mission, Sister Mattie Mae Davis, who was originally appointed principal in 1931, was retired in 1965 by the Foreign Mission Board. During those years, hundreds of Liberian boys and girls were influenced and helped by this missionary who gave of her energy and resources so unselfishly to bring Christ to the people she served. Prior to assuming the principalship of the Suehn Industrial Mission, Sister Davis served as a missionary and teacher at the Lott Carey Mission in Brewerville, Liberia, for ten years. Her competence as a teacher and administrator so commended her to the late corresponding secretary, James East, that he selected her to succeed Sister Sarah Williamson Coleman who had led the Suehn Mission with great distinction. The goodwill created by Sister Coleman was continued under the administration of Sister Davis.

Sister Mattie Mae Davis

Since 1931, the *Mission Herald* is replete with correspondence from Sister Davis. In her letters she tells with Christ-like simplicity of the struggles, the problems, the joys and the spiritual rewards of work in the foreign fields. Throughout all of her letters runs an underlying glimpse of her devout trust in God, her faith in people and her conviction that those who labored for God as He is revealed in Christ, have labored not in vain.

Sister Davis' major interest was in building character. She was especially concerned with orphan and deserted children, some of whom were left after their mothers died in childbirth. Many of these children developed, finished the schooling provided at the mission and went on to hold important positions of responsibility in the Liberian government. Others, after further education, went on to distinguish themselves in medicine, nursing, animal husbandry, tailoring, carpentry, teaching and other fields.[44]

Upon her retirement, Sister Davis was appointed director of "Operation Production" by the Reverend J. H. Jackson, president of the National Baptist Convention, U.S.A., Inc. This project represented a new approach to the foreign missionary enterprise of the Convention. Its basic purpose was to aid and assist Liberians to learn modern methods of agricultural production. This objective was to be obtained by providing pilot projects in various rural (bush) areas in Liberia, under the guidance of missionaries and/or citizens from the United States who were trained in modern methods in agriculture and animal husbandry. This project was begun by the Convention in 1969. At the meeting of the Convention in Jacksonville, Florida, that year, it was recommended that "Operation Production" become another facet of the Foreign Mission Board's program in Africa. It was under the supervision of and operated by the Foreign Mission Board. It was because of Sister Davis' long years of acquaintance with the Liberian scene that she was selected to head this project.[45]

Thirteen years after she retired, Mrs. Mattie Mae Davis went to her final reward. She had chosen to remain in Africa among the people she had loved and served with great dedication. The announcement of her death which appeared in the *Liberia Official Gazette* on March 14, 1978, began as follows:

EXTRAORDINARY

The Government of Liberia announces with pro-
found regrets the death in her ninety-first year of
service:
Mrs. Mattie Mae Banks-Davis
Missionary, Nurse, Educator, Philanthropist and
Mother,
Republic of Africa.

This sad event occurred at the Firestone Medical Center, Harbel, on Wednesday, March 8, 1978, at the hour of two-fifteen o'clock, post meridian.[46]

In the printed eulogy by C. Cecil Dennis, Jr., Minister of Foreign Affairs, and by order of the President of Liberia, a considerable amount of information was given about Sister Davis. She was a native of North Carolina, born on December 12, 1887. She was a student at Oberlin College with the intention of becoming a surgeon, but left college at the close of her junior year to study for missionary service at Nyack Theological Seminary.

Her first missionary assignment was under the auspices of the Lott Carey Baptist Foreign Missionary Convention in Brewersville, Liberia, where she met her late husband, Dr. J. Elwood Davis. She served with the Lott Carey Convention for seven years. In 1930 she returned to Liberia to work at the Suehn Industrial Mission under the auspices of the National Baptist Convention, U.S.A., Inc. There she proved to be an able administrator and educator. Travelling on whatever conveyance was at hand, she established over fifteen village churches. Moreover, she organized the Suehn Native Convention, an annual convention comprised of men and women in the villages.

Because of her educational skills, the Liberian government requested the Foreign Mission Board to release her on loan so that she could develop the government's literacy program. She served in this capacity with efficiency and distinction. She was also instrumental in forming the Dorcas Club comprised of the mothers whose babies regularly attended the clinic.

Mrs. Davis organized the Baptist Training Union in her church, the Bethel Delaney Baptist Church at Suehn, and was a life member of Liberia Baptist Missionary and Educational Convention and of the Baptist Sunday School Convention. Her outstanding service over a long career led President William R. Tolbert, Jr., of Liberia, to award her the Grand Band of the Humane Order of African Redemption.

Her remains were interred in the cemetery at Suehn and, in her honor, the Liberian government ordered the national flag to be flown at half-mast from all public buildings in the township of Suehn from 8:00 a.m. to 6 p.m. on the day of her burial.[47]

STATUS REPORT OF SOME FMB MISSIONS, 1972

Malawi

Our mission work in Malawi has had a long and distinguished history. That country, formerly known as Nyasaland, is about the

277

size of the state of Florida. It is quite mountainous and is bordered on the east by Lake Malawi. Near the lake, the climate is warm and humid; elsewhere it varies with the altitude.

Christian missionaries began work in Malawi at an early date. It became a British Protectorate in 1889 and joined with Rhodesia from 1956 to 1963. It became an independent member of the British Commonwealth in 1964 and a republic in 1966.

In 1970 it had a population of 4.4 million and a projected population of 6.5 million by 1985. The average income per year was $47. About one-third of the population was Christian while two-thirds were Muslim or traditional in their religion.

Mrs. Josephine Minter wrote to the Foreign Mission Board that "with all the little frustrations, setbacks, and disappointments, I love the work. I do not worry about myself for my concern is for these people who are so kind and loyal... They are so in need (yet) they are not looking for handouts...They are a hard-working people. They need someone to teach them how to do for themselves and their families.[48]

The women of the area especially showed deep gratitude and affection for Mrs. Minter. One woman travelled 150 miles to bring eggs to her. Another gave her her last penny. Others brought whatever contributions they could spare.

The National Baptist Assembly of Africa, which was founded by Dr. Daniel S. Malekebu, had a membership of 20,000 and was the most powerful Christian body in Africa.

Malawian Churches Accepted in the World Baptist Alliance

One of the proudest moments in the history of the Foreign Mission Board, National Baptist Convention, U.S.A., Inc., occurred on Tuesday, August 6, 1974, when the executive committee of the Baptist World Alliance, meeting on the campus of the Southern Baptist Seminary, Louisville, Kentucky, formally recognized and accepted into membership the African Baptist Assembly of Malawi, Inc., which was represented by its chairman, the Reverend L. C. Muocha.

The executive committee of the Baptist World Alliance had representatives from twenty-seven countries in attendance and, although the various commissions of the Alliance were finalizing plans for the quadrennial meeting in Stockholm, Sweden, the following year, made time to give particular attention to the acceptance of three new conventions into membership. The Reverend Mr. Muocha was presented to the committee by Secretary Harvey who emphasized that the Assembly was an outgrowth of the work of the National Baptists in Malawi for the past seventy-three years. This is the first overseas convention ever sponsored by Black Baptists in America for membership in the first sixty-nine years of the history of the Baptist World Alliance.[49]

Expansion in Swaziland

The Foreign Mission Board endeavored constantly to put each of its mission stations on a sound economic basis. "We have from time to time considered expanding our work but did not feel justified in doing so until we had reached a moderate standing in the physical plant and services of our present facilities. Having achieved that goal, the Board decided to strengthen its work in Southern Africa. It settled upon the independent Kingdom of Swaziland. This was formerly under British rule as a protectorate and achieved its independence in 1968. Because this new nation followed a policy of freedom of religion, many of our South African members migrated to this land to serve God in an atmosphere of peace and freedom. The Swaziland government allocated to the Mission Board four acres of land so that we would be able to establish a mission church. Four churches in this country made substantial contributions for this purpose. The work in Swaziland has continued to prosper even under often very difficult circumstances.[50]

Harvey Bible Seminary, Lesotho

We have been pleased and honored by the establishment of the Harvey Bible Seminary in honor of the corresponding secretary of the Foreign Mission Board. This seminary is situated in the Republic of Lesotho. It was under the direction of the Reverend E. D. Ngubeni and has carried on a highly successful educational program. In 1968, eighty-seven students were enrolled. Because of the requirements of the authorities, it was necessary to establish a broad curriculum including such subjects as science, mathematics and English, in addition to the theological subjects. Through the generosity of the Mt. Zion Baptist Church of Los Angeles, California, pastored by the Reverend E. V. Hill, a building program was made possible. The local chief donated the land for the seminary. In 1969, a secondary school was established with a student body of 140 boys and girls.[51]

The Bible Industrial Mission

The Bible Industrial Mission at Fortsville, Grand Bassa County, Liberia, was organized by the National Baptist Convention, U.S.A., Inc., in 1917 during the administration of Dr. L. G. Jordan. Many National Baptist missionaries have served on this field. These include Miss Susie M. Taylor, Mrs. Sarah Williamson Coleman, Reverend Henry N. Connor, Mrs. Priscilla Bryan Jackson and Mrs. Nidra Reed. These names will be ever remembered by the Bassa tribesmen among whom they served. Mrs. Jackson served the mission for thirty-four years (1919-1953), until advancing years and incurable blindness forced her retirement. Yet she chose to spend the rest of her years in Liberia where she resided at the Suehn Mission under the benevolent care of Sister Erma Ethridge until God called her home on May 23, 1973.

In 1967, the mission was reopened under the joint auspices of the Foreign Mission Board and the Liberian Baptist Missionary and Educational Convention, with the Liberian Baptists supplying the workers and the Foreign Mission Board supplying their salaries.

Because of the zeal of the Bassa people to rehabilitate the school, the Liberian Convention determined to aid them in the building project. Upon the completion of that building, the Liberian Baptists invited Secretary Harvey to deliver the sermon at the ground breaking ceremonies. This invitation was extended to show appreciation for the contribution made by the National Baptist Foreign Mission Board and the outstanding work of the Board at Suehn and Bendoo Missions. At the conclusion of the services, the Council of Chiefs of the Malloi Clan and Chiefdom of the Republic of Liberia, conferred upon him the title of Honorary Paramount Chief of the Bassa Tribe, with the chairman of the Council of Chiefs, Mr. Oswald S. Dillon, presenting the certificate, the robe and the cap indicative of the honor.[52]

Klay Institute Mission

At the request of Dr. William R. Tolbert, president of the Liberia Baptist and Missionary Educational Convention, the Foreign Mission Board formally relinquished the Klay Industrial Mission to the supervision and operation of the Liberian Convention.

The Klay Industrial Mission was founded in 1929 as an independent mission by the late Dr. H. H. Jones of Mississippi. In 1950, the exigencies of age compelled Dr. Jones to discontinue his active services to this institution. A meeting was arranged with Dr. C. C. Adams, then secretary of the Foreign Mission Board of the National Baptist Convention, U.S.A., Inc., and an agreement was drawn up whereby Dr. Jones would be employed in an advisory capacity. This arrangement continued until his death. The agreement also stated that all of the assets — physical and monetary — would be assigned to the Foreign Mission Board and that the Liberia Baptist Missionary and Educational Convention would continue all of the mission work previously conducted by Dr. Jones. Because of the difficulties involved in securing adequate missionaries and workers to continue the operation of the Klay Mission by the Foreign Mission Board, the Board decided to discontinue all operations in 1956. In October 1969, Secretary Harvey received a communication from Dr. Tolbert stating, "If there are no immediate plans for the area by the Foreign Mission Board, National Baptist Convention, U.S.A., Inc., . . . that the property be turned over to the Liberia Baptist Missionary and Educational Convention so that efforts can be made to have the hopes and expectations of the (former students) realized." The

Foreign Mission Board agreed to turn over all the properties and physical assets it owned at the Klay Mission. This released funds and energies of the Board and its workers to concentrate more effectively on its other mission stations in Africa.[53]

The Child Support Program

In 1967, Secretary Harvey presented a foreign mission support program in the interest of contributing to the welfare of children on the mission fields. He proposed that individuals, churches, or other organizations "adopt" one of the children in our schools for the purpose of providing an education for that child. This program was designed to meet the needs of the many economically deprived children in their effort to get an education. At the same time, this effort would be of great benefit to the mission schools in meeting their budgetary requirements. The expense of each child was estimated at that time as $17.50 per month. Those who adopted a child were asked to give him/her special gifts at birthdays and at Christmas. It was also suggested that they send clothing or other useful items to the child. The program was received with much favor. Some organizations committed themselves to support more than one child. The Shiloh Baptist Church of New York City pledged to provide this kind of support for twenty children.

The Foreign Mission Board sent each benefactor a photograph of the child adopted and other information describing the child including details of his/her background. Unfortunately, although the program was an immediate success, in the course of time, interest began to wane, primarily because of a breakdown in communication between the children and the benefactors in this country. In an endeavor to correct the problem, the Foreign Mission Board made a special effort to see that each adoptive child was located and put in touch with the benefactors. In addition, each mission school was asked to keep the Foreign Mission Board apprised of the child's progress and to inform the Foreign Mission Board of the receipt of whatever gifts were sent for the welfare of the child.[54]

The Bahamas

Reference has been made several times in this volume to our work in the Bahamas. The Bahama Islands, a group of about 700 islands and over 2,000 islets, rocks and cays which extend about sixty miles east of Palm Beach, Florida, to 750 miles southward. Only about twenty of these islands are inhabited. The most prominent are New Providence, of which Nassau is the capital, and Aboco, Andros, Bimini, Eleuthera and the Grand Bahama. As of 1969, the population was estimated to be 173,000, of which half lived in Nassau. The political fortunes of these islands shifted from Spanish to American to British domination. In 1958, a reform movement began which led to the introduction of full internal self-government in 1964.

The Foreign Mission Board has welcomed the opportunity to contribute to the spiritual well-being of these islands. In 1790, Prince Williams, a freed Negro slave, brought the Baptist faith to New Providence, travelling there in an open boat from St. Augustine, Florida. Prince Williams founded the Bethel Baptist Church, one of the oldest in the Bahamas, and, forty years later, the St. Johns Church.

The mission work of the Foreign Mission Board in the Bahamas is traditionally identified by the Jordan Memorial School. This school was named in honor of the late Dr. L. G. Jordan who had a distinguished career as corresponding secretary of the Foreign Mission Board. Our Foreign Mission Board began to work in the Bahamas in 1948.

The National Baptist Convention and the Bahamas Baptist Missionary and Educational Convention worked hand in hand to lift the educational standards in the Bahamas. Among the outstanding participants in the cooperative venture were the late Dr. T. B. Livingstone, headmaster of the Jordan Memorial Training School and Mission, the late Reverend T. E. W. Donaldson, principal of the Prince Williams Baptist High School and president of the Bahamas Baptist Convention and Rev. Enoch Backford, Sr. superintendent of the Bahamas Baptist Union. This collective effort continued until the year 1968 at which time Dr. William

Rev. Enoch Backford, Sr.   *Dr. T.E.W. Donaldson*

J. Harvey, III, corresponding secretary of the Foreign Mission Board, announced a change in the emphasis of the Board's work in the Bahamas. Secretary Harvey described this in a statement made to the National Baptist Convention, U.S.A., Inc., in Atlanta, Georgia, in 1971:

> We are thankful to God that also in the Western Hemisphere, namely the Bahama Islands, the political and economic atmosphere have so changed for the better that we can rejoice in the accomplishments of our fellow Baptists. Twenty-four years ago the Foreign Mission Board entered into an agreement with the Bahamas Baptist Missionary and Educational Convention to aid them in the area of education and outer-island support. This aid grew from a minimum budget of $4,000 per year to a present annual budget of $13,920. These amounts have represented about 4/5 of the total budget of the Bahamas Mission and Education support. In addition to this, an elementary school named after the late L. G. Jordan, was erected and equipped by the Board.

Today, because of a deep sense of responsibility on the part of the Bahamians plus increased government subsidies, the L. G. Jordan Elementary School and Prince Williams High School have a budget which exceeds $144,000. The Foreign Mission Board thanks God for the manner in which our fellow Baptists have shown a proclivity for self-help and self-sufficiency.

With this enlarged income, it is apparent that this group is eminently able to carry on their own work. Therefore, during a recent conference held at a meeting of the S.S. and B.T.U. Congress in Chattanooga, the Bahamas Baptists petitioned the Board to purchase the present grounds and buildings of the L. G. Jordan Elementary School, and stated that the only help they will need in the future relates to the outer-island ministry.

It is now the practice of every foreign mission board in America and Europe that, when evangelism results in the establishment and training of the people to whom they minister to the end that they may carry their own responsibility, then it is the duty of the Board to divert its funds and energies into areas where less developed groups may benefit. When the Bahamas Baptists needed us to aid them in the establishment of an elementary school, we met the need. Now that they are self-sufficient, we can focus our energies and funds on needier areas. The Bahamas Baptists are to be congratulated for this accomplishment.

Since 1968, the Foreign Mission Board has been funding the outer-island ministry in the Bahamas. This program included the cost of maintaining churches and subsidizing pastors' salaries throughout the islands. Three Baptist associations are funded by our Board: the St. John Baptist Association, the Bahama Baptist Union and the Zion Mission Association. Board aid to these groups included, among other things, subsidizing the salaries of 168 pastors.

In 1986, the National Baptist Convention, USA, Inc., contributed $200,000 for remodeling our L. B. Jordan School in the Bahamas. When he was elected president of the Convention, Dr. T. J. Jemison adopted the theme, "The Convention that Cares." That theme was implemented in the preparation and completion of this major remodeling program. The newly refurbished facility was unveiled during an extended session of the 1985 meeting of the National Baptist Convention and Board of Directors held in the Bahamas.

Ever since the Foreign Mission Board became active in the Bahamas, hundreds of students have been educated at the school. Many have gone on to study at the American Baptist Seminary in Nashville, Tennessee. As graduates, these students have returned to the islands and become pastors of churches, thus bringing the mission cycle full circle. The newly-remodeled facility at the Jordan School is a stepping stone to providing future leaders for these small, jewel-like islands.[55]

Jamaica

The interest of the Foreign Mission Board in conducting missionary activities in Jamaica has been of long standing. Already in this volume we have pointed out that George Lisle, the first ordained Black minister in this country, went to Jamaica in 1787, organized a Baptist church and carried forward a mission program — often under great difficulties. The Baptist presence has remained in Jamaica ever since that early beginning. In 1971, in response to pleas coming from Baptists in Jamaica for aid and assistance in carrying on the Lord's work, the executive committee of the Foreign Mission Board commissioned Secretary Harvey and the Reverend Rudolph S. Shoultz of the Union Baptist Church, Springfield, Illinois, to visit the area and study the possibilities.

As a result of their report, the executive committee voted to aid the four pastors and twenty-one churches which were a part of the Jamaica Fellowship Baptist Convention of which the Reverend Lester J. Brown was president. That visit reinforced the determination of the Foreign Mission Board to continue to support the Baptist cause in Jamaica to the extent of the Board's ability.

Barbados

In the effort to reach the yet unsaved souls who remained away from the mainstream of the community, the Foreign Mission Board in 1977 decided to expand its work to the island of Barbados. It was our desire to establish a stronger witness which, at that time, was minimal.

The first known inhabitants of Barbados were the Araks Indians from South America. By the time the first British expedition landed in 1625 and claimed the island in the name of the king of England, the earlier inhabitants had departed. Two years later the first group of colonists, eighty in number, settled in Jamestown. By 1628 Barbados was a thriving colony with a mixed population of Europeans and Negro slaves. A great landmark in the island's history was the abolition of slavery in 1834, followed by the establishment of the first West Indian police force in 1835. The high point in Barbados' history was the attainment of independence within the Commonwealth in November 1966. Although it is one of the smallest independent nations in the world, Barbados took its place as a member of the assembly of the United Nations and in the Organization of American States.

Barbados has been traditionally Protestant in religious outlook, primarily because, for more than three centuries, it was a dependency of England. A sturdy independence of local thought, however, produced many more religious denominations within the island. The largest persuasion on the island is the Anglican Church with eleven different congregations. Other denominations include Roman Catholics, Methodists, Moravians, Seventh Day Adventists, and the Christian Science Church. There are three Baptist churches on the island. The Salvation Army is active there and there are also Hindu and Muslim communities. The Jewish community also has a single meeting place on Barbados.

In 1977, the Foreign Mission Board appointed the Reverend Sinclair Ignatious Rudder as supervisor of missions on the island.

He was educated at Bawden's Mixed School, St. Andrew, Faith Church and the Caribbean Baptist College in San Juan, Puerto Rico, from which he was graduated after three years with a diploma in theology.

Beginning in 1968, the Reverend Mr. Rudder pastored the Packers and Cleveland Baptist churches in Barbados. He founded the Martin Luther King Memorial Society of Barbados, the Customs Institute for the training of customs clerks and the Baptist Home for the Aged. He became a Baptist minister in 1962 and, since that time, his outstanding ability has earned him an excellent reputation. The Foreign Mission Board was fortunate to be able to secure a minister with the Reverend Mr. Rudder's background to carry forward its programs in Barbados.[56]

Rev. & Mrs.
Sinclair Rudder

As of March 1979, the Foreign Mission Board began what was termed a Mission Outreach Program. This program came into being at the urgent suggestion and prayers of the Reverend David N. Licorish who, at one time, served as associate minister of the

Abyssinian Baptist Church of New York. Dr. Licorish, who was a native of Barbados, conferred with Secretary Harvey on the need for Christian expansion in Barbados and suggested ways of extending the work of the Foreign Mission Board on that island. Secretary Harvey, in due time, proposed to the executive committee of the Foreign Mission Board that the work of the Board should be extended to Barbados.

The work began with a three-week workshop conducted by Dr. Licorish at the School of Missions at the Baptist Church in Barbados. The agenda for the workshop centered around the following topics: The History, Structure, and Functional Operations of Baptist Churches in Relation to the Parent Convention; the Program of the National Baptist Convention, U.S.A., Inc., under the Leadership of its President, Dr. Joseph H. Jackson; and Analytical Presentation and Interpretation of the Agencies, Departments, and Institutions of the Convention (including the colleges, seminaries, libraries, and publishing houses in Nashville.)

The convener for the institute was the Reverend Sinclair Rudder, missionary pastor of the Convention. The participating churches were: the Bethel Baptist Church of St. Joseph, the Central Baptist Church of Bridgetown, the Packard Baptist Church of Christ Church and the Cleveland Baptist Church of St. Phillip. All of these churches were members of the National Baptist Convention, U.S.A., Inc.[57]

Nicaragua

After more than twenty-two years of service as supervisor of the Zion Mission Field in Bluefield, Nicaragua, the Reverend F. G. Downs retired in December 1979. A native of Nicaragua, the Reverend Downs followed the Reverend Harry L. Smith as leader in charge of the work in that country. As a result of his efforts, the mission program in Nicaragua gained momentum. On occasion he would visit this country for conferences with Secretary Harvey and members of the executive committee of the Foreign Mission Board. His reports of progress and needs always resulted

289

Rev. & Mrs. F. G. Downs

in more interest in and more money directed toward the work in Nicaragua. It can be said that his missionary service was equal to that of any missionary on any field anywhere. The need for missionary activity was great because of the poverty of the people being served. Reverend Downs was commended for his ability to make progress with the minimum of resources, especially when his work was carried forward in the midst of the Roman Catholic Church, which represented a large pool of resources, and the Moravian church which, along with the Roman Catholics, had

Zion Mission Field

mission stations situated near the large sugar mills where the bulk of the people worked. Because of this great competition from the Roman Catholics and the Moravians for the spiritual allegiance of the people, a competition made easier because these two denominations were able to subsidize the education of children whose families could not afford the expense themselves, Secretary Harvey set up a number of scholarships. These were designated for needy children who demonstrated the desire to learn.

It should be added that Mrs. Downs also rendered great service in support of the missionary undertakings in Nicaragua.[58]

The Seed Church Program

In 1978, the Foreign Mission Board adopted a program called the Seed Church Program in South Africa. The basis of this project was to have US churches in the Convention undertake the sponsorship of a particular church in South Africa. By September 1980, sixty-four National Baptist churches were underwriting South African churches in the Bantustans. (The Bastustans are areas specifically designated for the relocation of millions of Africans who are elderly, physically or mentally handicapped, unemployable or politically suspect. These people have been forced to move to certain remote areas which are invariably underdeveloped and agriculturally unproductive. For all intents and purpose, this relocation to a "Bantustan" is a type of genocide which effectively reduced the Black population through starvation and diseases caused by inadequate health facilities.)

As the participating National Baptist churches adopt and contribute to a church in South Africa through the Seed Church Program, they feel a much closer connection to and relationship with the missionary enterprise. We are especially proud of the results of this most significant program.[59]

The Passing of
Dr. and Mrs. Daniel S. Malekebu

Already we have seen in this history many references to Dr. and Mrs. Daniel S. Malekebu who served for so many years under the auspices of our Foreign Mission Board. Upon their retirement, they moved to Atlanta, Georgia, to rest from their years of long service. Mrs. Flora E. H. Malekebu had been ill for several years prior to their retirement; for awhile, she was completely bedridden. In Atlanta, they were able to get some respite and medical attention. Mrs. Malekebu finally went to her rest in September 1977. Funeral services were held on September 26 at the Auburn Chapel, Atlanta, Georgia. The Reverend William V. Guy, pastor of Friendship Baptist Church of Atlanta, officiated. This was the church in which Mrs. Malekebu had been baptized by the Reverend E. R. Carter during her student days at what was then Spelman Seminary.[60]

Reverend Dr. Malekebu survived his wife by little over a year. Shortly after her passing, he decided to return to his native land, Blantyre, Malawi. The Foreign Mission Board received word that he died on October 8, 1978. His funeral services were held on Tuesday, October 10, in the village of Ntupanyama, his birthplace. Dr. Malekebu had served as a missionary at the Providence Industrial Mission, Chiradzulu, from 1926 until 1971. He was approximately ninety-two years old.

Unfortunately, a strange turn of mind beset Dr. Malekebu following his wife's death. Upon his return to Malawi, he told three of the former ministers of the Providence Industrial Mission that they were under his appointment to serve as trustees of the African Baptist Assembly of Malawi, an auxiliary of the Providence Baptist Mission. That meant that if this were true, they were the legal owners of the mission and the 492 churches and two farms under the mission's auspices. This, of course, created a considerable amount of misunderstanding and tension and represented an utter repudiation of the Foreign Mission Board's ownership and also a repudiation of the Board's missionary in charge, the Reverend L. C. Muocha.

The matter had to be adjudicated in the courts. This necessitated a trip to Malawi by Secretary Harvey to protect the rights of the Foreign Mission Board. Despite an attempt on the part of the opposition to sabotage the verdict by long delays in the trial, the matter was eventually resolved in favor of the Board. Secretary Harvey represented the Foreign Mission Board at the high court proceedings held in Blantyre, Malawi, from July 28 to August 24, 1978, with a nine day recess between August 5 and August 14. During the trial, Secretary Harvey submitted evidence of deeds of ownership dating back to 1902 and the original application of Dr. Malekebu to serve as a missionary under the Board. Further, he submitted duplicates of salary and pension checks paid to Dr. Malekebu plus annual budget checks underwriting the mission dating back sixteen years.

Such evidence proved beyond a shadow of a doubt that Dr. Malekebu and his late wife had in fact been employees of the Board, that his right of appointment ended with his retirement, and that the allegations of the three ministers were null and void. On October 12, 1978, the high court accepted the evidence of the Foreign Mission Board as a true representation of the facts. They agreed that Dr. Malekebu was a retired employee on pension and ruled that the allegations of the three ministers were false and that the Foreign Mission Board of the National Baptist Convention was the true owner of all properties of the Providence Industrial Mission.

293

It was painful to the members of the Foreign Mission Board to be put in the position of having to send the corresponding secretary to Southern Africa in order to protect its interests from being subverted by a retired missionary who, for fifty years, had rendered such outstanding service. We attribute the actions of his last year of life to the infirmities of age which affected his memory and judgement.[61]

Some Progress after Twenty-Five Years

In the twenty-one years just prior to 1982, a total of twenty-five missionaries were sent to the field to serve as evangelists, teachers of religion, teachers in vocational training and in home economics. Three hundred ninety-one churches on the mission fields around the world were supported by the Foreign Mission Board and, as of 1982, there were 947 churches with membership ranging from twelve to 3,000. Thousands of people had accepted Christ as their savior as a result of Foreign Mission Board witness.

In addition, a tremendous growth in financial support was realized. At the end of Dr. Harvey's first year of service in 1961-62, only $143,000 was raised for foreign missions. In 1982, over $1,289,000 was contributed to the cause. In the ten years prior to 1982, over $11 million had been raised and spent for missions.

But beyond these statistical facts is the realization that throughout the National Baptist world, a new awareness of our responsibility to be concerned and supportive of the work grew to the point that no longer could our sister denomination say that we, as Black Christians, were unconcerned about ourselves. No longer could they intimate that we expect others to carry the burden which is our own. No longer could Black Christians in Africa say that Black American Christians were not supporting them in their efforts to evangelize. Our missionaries in South, Central and West Africa were making their impact in the name of Christ. As already indicated, the African Baptist Assembly, Inc. of Malawi, was the direct outgrowth of the work started by our Board in 1900 — a work which by 1982 was comprised of 474 churches with over 40,000 members.[62]

Notes

1. NBC *Minutes,* 1960, p. 55.
2. Ibid, p. 216.
3. NBC *Minutes,* 1961, p. 43.
4. *Mission Herald* (May-June 1966) pp. 3-4.
5. *Mission Herald* (September-October 1962) p. 6.
6. *Mission Herald* (November-December 1969) p. 5.
7. *Mission Herald,* (November-December 1966) p. 2.
8. *Mission Herald,* (January-February 1963) p. 12.
9. Ibid, p. 15.
10. *Mission Herald,* (July-August 1967) p. 9.
11. *Mission Herald,* (September-October 1971) p. 16.
12. *Mission Herald,* (January-February 1965) pp. 3-4.
13. *Mission Herald,* (January-February 1965) p. 4. Also *Mission Herald,* (July-August 1965) pp. 7-8.
14. *Mission Herald,* (March-April 1967) p. 14.
15. *Mission Herald,* (July-August 1963) pp. 10-11.
16. *Mission Herald,* (January-February 1964) p. 5. Also *Mission Herald,* (September-October 1966) p. 4.
17. *Mission Herald,* (January-February 1963) pp. 7-8.
18. *Mission Herald,* (January-February 1970) p. 6.
19. *Mission Herald,* (November-December 1967) p. 6.
20. *Mission Herald,* (December-January 1969) p. 9.
21. *Mission Herald,* (September-October 1965) pp. 3-4.
22. *Mission Herald,* (September-October 1961) p. 8.
23. *Mission Herald,* (September-October 1971) p. 6. *Mission Herald,* (September-October 1972) p. 5. *Mission Herald,* (January-February 1972) p. 5.
24. *Mission Herald,* (January-February 1973) p. 5.
25. *Mission Herald,* (July-August 1974) p. 8.
26. *Mission Herald,* (March-April 1972) p. 12. Also *Mission Herald,* (July-August 1972) p. 3.
27. *Mission Herald,* (March-April 1975) p. 6.
28. *Mission Herald,* (March-April 1980) pp. 3-6.
29. *Mission Herald,* (March-April 1983) pp. 3, 4, 11.
30. *Mission Herald,* (March-April 1987) pp. 3-5.
31. *Mission Herald,* (March-April 1976) p. 9.
32. *Mission Herald,* (March-April 1978) pp. 6-7.
33. *Mission Herald,* (September-October 1971) p. 5. Also, *Mission Herald,* (March-April 1972) p. 14.
34. *Mission Herald,* (September-October 1970) p. 9.
35. Quoted from the *New York Times,* March 1, 1970 in the *Mission Herald,* (March-April 1970) p. 3.
36. *Mission Herald,* (September-October 1971) p. 5.
37. *Mission Herald,* (July-August 1985) pp. 3-4.
38. *Mission Herald,* (May-June 1983) p. 4.

Notes continued

39. *Mission Herald*, (July-August 1979) pp. 9-11.
40. *Mission Herald*, (November-December 1979) pp.5-6.
41. *Mission Herald*, (January-February 1978) pp.10-11.
42. *Mission Herald*, (July-August 1974) p. 12.
43. *Mission Herald*, (September-October 1979) pp. 9-10.
44. *Mission Herald*, (March-April 1965) pp. 3-4.
45. *Mission Herald*, (November-December 1965) p. 2.
46. *Mission Herald*, (March-April 1978) pp. 17.
47. *Mission Herald*, (March-April 1978) pp. 17-18.
48. *Mission Herald*, (March-April 1972) p. 17.
49. *Mission Herald*, (July-August 1974) p. 4.
50. *Mission Herald*, (September-October 1970) p. 10.
51. *Mission Herald*, (November-December 1969) p. 4.
52. *Mission Herald*, (November-December 1976) p. 6.
53. *Mission Herald*, (July-August 1969) p. 16.
54. *Mission Herald*, (July-August 1977) pp. 16-17.
55. *Mission Herald*, (January-February 1986) p. 7.
56. *Mission Herald*, (May-June 1977) pp. 8-14.
57. *Mission Herald*, (March-April 1979) pp. 8-9.
58. *Mission Herald*, (January-February 1980) pp. 7-10.
59. *Mission Herald*, (September-October 1980) p.5
60. *Mission Herald*, (September-October 1977) p. 14.
61. *Mission Herald*, (January-February 1979) p. 12
62. *Mission Herald*, (September-October 1982) p. 4.

CHAPTER SEVEN
REVIEWING THE PAST—
ANTICIPATING THE FUTURE

Centennial Observance

Each decade during the first century of the Foreign Mission Board's history has witnessed some unusual achievements on the various mission fields. The complete story of the zeal and enthusiasm of the missionaries, their sacrifice and dedication for the cause of Christ, can only be told in segments.

Once the Gospel had been preached and souls converted, the necessity to "study to show themselves approved unto God" became a natural corollary. Thus, schools were started on a primary level and later on a secondary level. The healing aspects of the Christian Gospel was also mandatory. In mission areas, diseases were so rampant and medical services so meager, the missionary saw the further need for ministering to the sick. Invariably, missionaries were appealed to by the native persons for help. Thus, the art of ministering to the sick and diseased became a regular responsibility of the missionary. Out of meeting these needs developed health clinics and hospitals.

In each decade as needs arose, missionaries, through the Foreign Mission Board, sought to meet them. Many times the resources of the Board were insufficient, yet, the missionaries made "a way out of no-way." If textbooks were unavailable, our missionaries composed their own. If housing was in short supply, our missionaries did without. If medicines were scarce, our missionaries used what they had and depended upon the healing

297

Christ to make the difference. And the missions grew. So, too, did the support received by the Board from our churches. These increased funds meant increased resources for missionaries and missions.

During the last two decades we have been able to carry forward significant developments at practically all of our stations in Sierra Leone, Liberia, the Republic of Lesotho, Jamaica, Swaziland, Barbados, the Bahama Islands and in Nicaragua. We have erected new buildings and carried on successful evangelism and educational programs. Only in Ghana has the work been at a standstill due to litigation initiated in 1961 over the ownership of the property. A series of government changes so disrupted the judicial system that the settlement of the issue has continued to be delayed.[1]

Preparation for the celebration of the first 100 years of the National Baptist Convention, U.S.A., Inc., was begun early in 1978. Dr. J. H. Jackson, then president of the Convention, called attention to the fact that in two years the Convention will have been in operation for 100 years. He listed the following objectives of the celebration:

1. An occasion of thanksgiving to God for the work of our founding fathers and for the blessings He has bestowed upon us.

2. To inspire our young people to commit themselves anew to the ideals and principles of the Christian religion.

3. To revive the interest of all Americans in the Christ way of life. We hope we will begin with ourselves in giving Christ the right-of-way.

4. To encourage the nation to turn from the sins of materialism, to cease negating herself, and to turn to a positive study and appreciation of the great values that have made this nation great.

5. To embrace the economic philosophy that would eliminate poverty without destroying the productive genius of those who are the captains of industry.

6. To affirm all the great freedoms for which the nation has stood — freedom of speech; freedom of the press; free enterprise cleansed of the evils that would enslave the minds and bodies of all groups; and freedom of religion.[2]

In 1980 the Convention celebrated the 100th Anniversary, which coincides with the Centennial of the Foreign Mission Board. During this, our first century of service, many miracles of change were witnessed. Working through hundreds of dedicated men and women, the Foreign Mission Board was able to reach out to our fellow Black man in eleven areas of overseas mission.

With the scars of slavery still on their backs and minds, Black missionaries, impassioned by their love for Christ and their burning zeal to share that love, answered the Macedonian Call. From the humble beginning of the ministry of one such impassioned spirit arose the schools, hospitals, clinics and churches of which the Foreign Mission Board has been so proud for 100 years. While we took pride in the work accomplished, we dared not become complacent; there was still much work to be done.

In honor of its 100th Anniversary year in 1980, the Foreign Mission Board set a goal of $1 million. This was a goal thought worthy of a century of missions. It was not set arbitrarily but in direct response to the five most pressing needs of our mission fields:

1. Southern Africa — To plan 200 seed churches for the spread of the Gospel.
2. Malawi — Providence Industrial Mission: to build a seminary to train lay-leaders and clergy for 472 churches.
3. Liberia — Bendoo Industrial Mission: to build a new dormitory and classroom facilities for the boys primary school.
4. Liberia — Suehn Industrial Mission: to build a new dormitory and classroom facilities for the secondary school which was then educating 167 children and could have helped more if space had been available.

5. Promote rehabilitation of all mission station facilities.

In launching this $1 million drive, Secretary Harvey pointed out that the denomination was at the crossroads, that we could not turn back, that too many of our brothers and sisters lived in darkness and that thousands cried out to us to "come over and help." Through this appeal, the churches, ministers and church workers responded in a very favorable way.[3]

Dependence or Interdependence

One of the questions raised in connection with the observance of the 100th Anniversary of the National Baptist Convention was, "have we been in any one place in Africa long enough?"

This was indeed a pointed question and one that many denominational boards of foreign missions have had to study and conclude. Historically, the modern missionary movement in the last 200 years has seriously altered its basic concept of the enduring purpose of missions. In obedience to the Great Commission given by our Lord and Savior Jesus Christ, all believers were to "go into all the world preaching the Gospel." The book of Acts vividly tells the story of the spread of Christianity through the missionary efforts of the early believers. William Carey, often credited with being the Father of Modern Protestant Missions, was inspired to carry the Gospel to the Far East and established a church which refuses to die.

But the church established by Carey is not the church in Burma. The rise of nationalism in Burma was accompanied by the desire of the Burmese to operate and maintain their own church without the domination of any outside group. When Burma virtually deported all Western missionaries, the foreign mission boards of the various denominational groups operating in Burma predicted the death of Christianity in Burma. But such has not been the case. The indigenous believers continued the faith and the Church of Christ still thrives in that developing nation.

This fact holds true in many areas of the world and has caused many mission boards to rethink their attitudes toward overseas

300

evangelism in general. Interestingly, National Baptists have always maintained that our primary purpose is to preach Christ and aid the believing Christians to develop, in their own unique way, the faith once delivered to the saints. The role of National Baptists has been that of being "our brother's brother," aiding him in establishing a church, assisting in educating, training and building the household of faith to the end that they could continue the spread of the Gospel in their own land and the Board could then move to a new area. Concrete examples of this may be seen by the Board's work with the native churches in the rural areas of Liberia and Nigeria, and also in the field of education in the Bahama Islands.

This was the technique employed by the early Christians. The Apostle Paul aided in the establishment of many churches throughout Asia Minor. In every instance the indigenous believers continued the work so nobly begun. So vigorous were their evangelistic efforts that the course of human history was changed from B.C. (Before Christ) to A.D. (Anno Domini — in the year of our Lord).

In the years of modern Protestant missions, however, there are those who have usually expressed one of three opinions regarding churches established in foreign lands. There are those who believe in establishing the church and forever after paternalistically sponsoring it. Any act of independence on the part of the native people served is viewed as disloyalty or ingratitude. They believe that the native church must always be a carbon copy of the sponsoring church and often would rather the church die than express any attitude of independence.

A second group feels that the missionaries' goal should be only to establish an indigenous church. Usually the phrase they use is "to build self-governing, self-propagating and self-supporting native churches." With Paul, they feel that the basic responsibility of missions is to preach the Gospel and establish Christ-minded, Christ-loving and Christ-supporting churches which are free from the evils of a selfish nationalism which views all outsiders as aliens.

The third approach can only be that of interdependence. Independence can mean isolation and, often, death. But interdependence means mutual dependence — Christians working together to exalt Christ, Christians helping each other mutually, beyond race, class, economic conditions or nationality — mutually working together to make the kingdoms of this world the Kingdoms of our God and His Christ. This is the goal of the Foreign Mission Board of the National Baptist Convention, U.S.A., Inc. May nothing or no one ever swerve us from this objective![4]

Development of Churches in Central and Southern Africa

One of the satisfying developments in the work of the Foreign Mission Board has been the rapid expansion of churches in Malawi. In 1983, the Foreign Mission Board witnessed by word and deed on the fields that God entrusted to our care. Church development received a significant thrust in Malawi, Central Africa. Twenty more churches were added to the 472 already in place throughout that country.

Church development showed progress in Southern Africa as well. In Lesotho there were 19 churches; in Swaziland, nine and in the Republic of South Africa there were 152 churches, one colored church and 94 seed churches.

In 1897 when the Board sent the Reverend R. A. Jackson of Holly Springs, Mississippi, to open a mission in Capetown, South Africa, the intense discrimination now experienced did not exist. Through the help of the Foreign Mission Board, the struggling churches in South Africa were encouraged. They needed our prayers and gifts. Thus, as of 1984 there was a total of 781 churches under our supervision on the continent of Africa.

Since the beginning of our work in foreign lands, education has been another evangelistic thrust. Our third major evangelistic thrust was the improvement of health care. The S. Willie Layton Memorial Hospital, discussed earlier in this volume, was completed at a total cost of $185,000. The Board is proud to report that as of 1984, every item had been completely paid off.[5]

Revolution in Liberia

On April 12, 1980, at 3:30 a.m., President William R. Tolbert, Jr. of the Republic of Liberia, was assassinated in the executive mansion, Monrovia, Liberia. In addition to being president of Liberia, Dr. Tolbert was chairman of the Organizations of African Unity, an organization composed of approximately forty-two independent African countries.

President Tolbert's assassination marked the first coup in the 133-year history of the nation founded by ex-slaves from America. President Tolbert encouraged foreign investments such as the significant contracts with the Firestone Tire and Rubber Company. He also allowed Liberia to serve as a convenient port of registry for international shipping, another way to attract foreign investment.

In 1979, the government proposed a hike in the price of rice from $22 to $30 for a 100-pound bag. The average wage of the Liberian soldiers was $85 per month. A student-led group of demonstrators headed toward the executive mansion. The police and soldiers shot into the crowd. Forty people were killed and hundreds injured. This led to riots and looting and eventually gave rise to opposition groups known as the Movement for Justice in Africa and the Progressive Alliance of Liberia. After a lengthy legal battle, the Alliance gained legal status as an opposition party under its new name, the Progressive People Party.

The government overthrow was engineered by Samuel K. Doe, a master sergeant in the Liberian Army. Sergeant Doe declared that he had overthrown the Tolbert regime because of "its rampant corruption and continuous failure" to solve Liberia's problems. Following the coup, many of the outstanding leaders in the Tolbert government were executed.

Secretary Harvey kept in close touch with the missionaries by cable via the American Embassy in Monrovia, Liberia. It was reassuring to know that they were safe and well although their supplies were limited.[6]

The revolution occurred on the eve of the 100th anniversary of the founding of the Liberia Missionary and Educational Baptist

Convention. In fact, President William R. Tolbert attended the preconvention musical on the very evening he was assassinated.

As president of the Liberia Missionary and Educational Baptist Convention and former president of the World Baptist Alliance, Dr. Tolbert was always associated with Baptist work around the world. Because of this, many of those who opposed his political administration also opposed his religious connection.

During the first night of the revolution, the Baptist headquarters building was severely damaged and vandalized. This building housed most of the records of the Liberian Convention, including historical items which had been collected at the 100th anniversary.

Unfortunately, many of the officers of the convention were either slain or jailed. This created a great problem for the continuance of the work of the Liberian Baptists. Fortunately, the life of Reverend Eric David, Executive Secretary of the Liberian Convention, was spared and, though he was detained for a time, he was eventually released and proceeded to reorganize the convention. According to Reverend Mr. David, forty-five to fifty percent of the Liberian Baptists were thrown out of work. The homes of many were destroyed and their property taken. The leadership of the Convention was decimated and the funds depleted.

Much of the Convention's funds were invested in preparation for the Centennial celebration which was to have taken place in April 1980. The Liberians had anticipated raising nearly a million dollars for the various objectives of the Convention. These developments necessitated a clear understanding on the part of the members of our National Baptist Convention of the opportunities and responsibilities they had in helping the Liberian Baptists.

Because of the concern of the Foreign Mission Board for the safety of the missionaries serving in Liberia during the revolution, the Board sent the Reverend Charles Walker, pastor of the Nineteenth Street Baptist Church in Philadelphia, Pennsylvania, to make an assessment of the situation. Reverend Mr. Walker was given the authority to make immediate decisions regarding personnel and the work of the Board. Unfortunately, a potentially dangerous incident occurred.

Reverend Walker was attempting to take photographs of the Baptist headquarters building when he was accosted by a uniformed Liberian who berated him for taking pictures, dragged him across the street by the necktie, threw him to the ground and took his watch and camera. He was then made to undress down to his underwear in front of a crowd of approximately 200 people.

A car bearing soldiers from the executive mansion drove by, stopped, and one of the executive mansion soldiers berated the uniformed man for his treatment of Reverend Walker. These soldiers then escorted Reverend Walker to the American Embassy which had already been alerted that an American was being manhandled.

Upon arriving at the embassy, Reverend Walker learned that the United States Marines had been dispatched to the scene and had promptly arrested the offending Liberian and escorted him to the Ministry of Defense where he was remanded to the authorities. The embassy reported that the person responsible for Reverend Walker's treatment had been punished and that several members of the government had expressed their deep and sincere regret over the incident.

The embassy praised Reverend Walker's courage, fortitude and strength in the face of adversity and danger. They stated that his conduct brought tremendous credit on him as an individual and on his church.[7]

Following the report of the revolution that took place in the Republic of Liberia, the Foreign Mission Board was inundated with inquiries regarding the status and safety of missionaries serving in that troubled nation. As the situation developed, all reports indicated that the new government was not opposed to the continuance of mission work in Liberia. In the first broadcast the head of state and chairman of the Peoples Redemption Council of the Armed Forces of Liberia, Master Sergeant Samuel K. Doe, made to citizens and residents in Liberia, he outlined the causes which led to the policies and objectives of his government. In his address to the people, he stated that while Liberians would use their own resources in building up their country, they would seek the help of foreign investors in solving their burning problems.

Telephone conversations with our missionaries confirmed that there were few, if any, incidents of molestation or harassment that occurred and that their services were especially needed during the adjustment period.

Political Transitions

Revolutions occurred in other countries served by the Foreign Mission Board. The first took place in Ghana with the overthrow of Nkrumah, the sponsor of Pan African ideology. This was followed by the coup in Sierra Leone. In each instance, our work was not seriously affected.

Independence came to the Bahamian Islands without any problems for our Board, while the change in political emphasis in Jamaica only intensified the needs of the people we were serving. A violent revolution occurred in Nicaragua and, although our churches were not affected, certain pronouncements by the new government regarding mission schools created concerns about their future.

It is in periods like this that the church had to be prayerfully cautious and always alert to the guidance of Almighty God. Since the advent of Christ, kingdoms have waxed and waned, political and economic systems have developed and declined. Every conceivable type of government known to man has felt the influence of Christ. This is our faith, and in that faith, the Foreign Mission Board has carried on its work in spite of revolutions.[8]

One of the outgrowths of the revolution that occurred in Liberia was the impact it had on the economic situation of that country. Without any prior notice, the Bank of Liberia was closed by the Liberian government and all of its deposits were frozen. The Suehn Industrial Mission had over $6,000 of its operating funds on deposit, while the Foreign Mission Board had over $4,000 in an emergency fund for the Liberian missions. Since both funds were frozen, the Board had to deposit immediately the Suehn funds in another bank to enable them to meet their monthly expenses.

We are pleased to report that although the new government of Liberia came in by very violent means, the head of state, Sergeant Samuel Doe, was sympathetic to the work of our missionaries in that country. On more than one occasion, Secretary Harvey, along with other Americans who accompanied him, were received in a friendly manner by Mr. Doe. It is the Board's expectation that this attitude will continue, especially in light of the tremendous contributions the Foreign Mission Board has made to Liberia since their first missionaries went there in 1882.

Dr. T. J. Jemison Elected President

For nearly thirty years, the eminent Dr. Joseph Harrison Jackson gave effective leadership to the great National Baptist Convention, U.S.A., Inc. The Convention can point to and take pride in the many achievements which came about under the leadership of Dr. Jackson. It is quite possible that had he continued as a leader of this great Convention, other achievements would have been realized. But the era of his reign closed and the baton of leadership was passed to another.

The factors leading up to the election of Dr. Jemison were long-standing issues. A primary reason for the change of leadership was the feeling of many younger, well-trained ministers that they were being left out of leadership roles for an indefinite period of time. For several years prior to the election of Dr. Jemison, there had been many instances of demonstrated dissatisfaction. One of the most dramatic of these occurred when a group of younger dissenters led a movement to take charge of the platform where the officers of the Convention were seated. The ultimate result of this movement was the failure of Dr. C. C. Adams to be re-elected as corresponding secretary of the Foreign Mission Board and, later, the organization of a third national Baptist convention among Negroes titled "The Progressive National Baptist Convention." This new organization came into being in 1962, however it did not entirely eliminate the dissatisfaction among some of the brethren who remained with the old Convention.

307

Certainly the election of Dr. T. J. Jemison to head the Baptist organization of more than seven million members represented one of the highlights in the history of the Convention. Dr. Jemison took office at the annual session meeting in Miami, Florida, in September 1982. For some time, behind the scenes sentiment for a change in administration had been growing. Certain leaders of Convention organizations, as well as a large number of influential pastors, had carefully organized the campaign to elect Dr. Jemison. They had distributed attractive flyers to many members of the Convention, pointing out the excellent leadership that had been carried forward by President Jackson but, at the same time, making the argument that the time had come for a fresh approach to the work of the Convention.

An interesting feature of Dr. Jemison's election was that it was contrary to the usual voting procedures at these annual sessions. It had been the custom that, following the annual address of the Convention president, someone would rise and move that the rules be suspended and that the president be immediately reelected by acclamation. At the convention in Miami, however, this procedure was defeated and it was determined that the election of the president be by delegates according to the individual states they represented. When at long last the votes were tallied, it was found that Dr. Jemison had won by a large margin. This represented a clear mandate from the Convention constituency for a fresh and dynamic leader. An important feature of the campaign was emphasis upon a limited tenure for the office of president — a provision which had been supported originally by Dr. Jackson but which had later been rescinded.

Early in his tenure, Dr. Jemison showed signs of a departure from customary routine and commitment to a more progressive type of activities for the organization.

Dr. Jemison came to the office out of a tradition of Christian leadership. His father, the late Dr. David V. Jemison, was the eleventh president of the National Baptist Convention, U.S.A., Inc. Dr. Jemison rarely spoke without alluding to this great tradition and the rich legacy that was handed to him to honor. His dedication to that tradition and legacy led some to say, "like father, like son." Dr. David V. Jemison served the Convention with loyalty and true friendship. He supported the previous leadership of the Convention. His administration sought the full cooperation of the constituency of the organization and committed itself to the betterment of the state and condition of all our people. Under his administration, the Convention remained the strong fellowship it was designed to be by such leaders as Dr. E. C. Morris and Dr. L. K. Williams.

Dr. Theodore J. Jemison stated that he sought the presidency of the Convention because of the confidence expressed by so many members. In new and meaningful directions, he expressed the conviction that God brought him to the office through proper methods, and prepared him for his task through dedicated Christian parents and his own day-to-day working relationship with Jesus Christ.

Dr. David V. Jemison   *Dr. Theodore J. Jemison*

The leadership of the Convention pledged its support for Dr. Jemison and his programs which embraced economic participation, improvement, political involvement, educational oppor-

309

tunity and social outreach. In all of these areas, according to Dr. Jemison, it was not a question of what the Convention could afford to do; rather it was a matter of what it could not afford to fail to do. There were those who seriously proclaimed that God brought Dr. Jemison to the leadership of the Convention at a propitious time in the history of the organization, the life of its people and the nation as a whole.

The Foreign Mission Board, along with the total National Baptist Convention, U.S.A., Inc., greeted Dr. Jemison wholeheartedly and pledged to uphold and fully support him as he launched a new era of service.

Immediately after he was elected, Dr. Jemison committed himself to working for unity in our homes, our churches, our denominations, our worldwide Christian family. As a true missionary, he is in our universal family of God's children everywhere.

With less than a year in office, Dr. Jemison made great strides in leading his constituency to unity. On the home front, he spearheaded a nationwide voter registration drive to unite our people in making their voices heard, through their votes, at all levels of government. In our Convention, he urged the membership to raise the levels of their giving so that we might unite in programs and ministries that would take us higher and farther than we had ever gone before.

But perhaps the boldest presidential proclamation came in the realm of missions where he bravely declared, "win three million new souls to Christ!" With such a direct, confident spiritual leader as Dr. Jemison, great progress was quite properly expected.

In one of his first speeches as the newly elected president, Dr. Jemison said, "I believe the time has come for us to make our witness for Christ felt by becoming more supportive of causes through which we believe the work in His Kingdom is being advanced...I intend to work diligently to...lead the Convention to the forefront of the struggle for the liberation of oppressed people.[9]

310

The Reverend Charles Walker Elected Chairman of the Foreign Mission Board

After serving as pastor of the Nineteenth Street Baptist Church since 1972, the Reverend Charles Walker was unanimously elected chairman of the Foreign Mission Board at the 102nd Annual Session of the National Baptist Convention, U.S.A., Inc., held in Miami Beach, September 10, 1982.

Born in Louisiana, Reverend Walker spent his early years in Chicago. As a youth he displayed an unusual talent as a classical pianist and served many churches in Chicago as a pianist, organist and choir director. While a student at DePaul University, Chicago, he studied with the famous Russian composer-pianist Alexander Tcherepnin and his wife, Madam Ming Tcherepnin. He received his bachelor and master degrees from DePaul and continued his studies in Paris, France, at L'ecole Magda Tagliaferro.

He represented the United States in international competitions in Paris and Montreal and participated in the Liszt-Bartok International competition in Budapest, Hungary. He served as artist-in-residence at Southern University and performed with numerous symphony orchestras both here and abroad. While serving as artist-in-residence at Southern University, Reverend Walker accepted the call to the ministry.

He prepared for the ministry at the Colgate Rochester Divinity School, Rochester, New York, and while there composed a work in memory of Dr. Martin Luther King entitled "Requiem to Brother Martin." This work was performed at Carnegie Hall, New York City, by the Charles Walker Chorale, a group organized by Reverend Walker, and the Rochester Philharmonic Orchestra.

In June 1970, Reverend Walker was called to the pastorate of the Nineteenth Street Baptist Church, Philadelphia, Pennsylvania, and assumed leadership of this historic congregation in August 1970. Since assuming this responsibility, the church has experienced phenomenal spiritual and numerical growth and is an outstanding example of youth evangelical participation in church life.

311

Reverend Walker has served on the executive committee of the Foreign Mission Board since 1976 and has travelled to Africa on two occasions as a member of a preaching team. On his second visit to Liberia, he presented a copy of the original manuscript of a symphony written in honor of the Liberian people to (then) President Tolbert. In 1978, he was one of five distinguished pastors to preach in the Soviet Union as a guest of the Russian Baptists.

Reverend Walker served as a member of the Theological Commission of the National Baptist Convention, U.S.A., Inc. He holds membership in the Baptist Ministers Conference, the Missionary Baptist Pastors Conference of Philadelphia and Vicinity, and the W. Russell Johnson Club of the National Association of Negro Musicians.

Reverend Walker brought to the position of chairman a knowledgeable sensitivity to the needs and problems of the mission field and a dedicated loyalty to the National Baptist Convention, U.S.A., Inc., and its national and worldwide objectives.[10]

Response to the Ethiopian Crisis

For many years, the Foreign Mission Board, through the pages of the *Mission Herald*, had called attention to the growing problem of hunger in those African nations bordering on and lying below the Sahara Desert. We were, therefore, saddened but not surprised when the Ethiopian hunger crisis became internationally known and evoked practically a worldwide response.

The Foreign Mission Board and the National Baptist Convention, U.S.A., Inc., were quick to respond to the need that was so urgent in Ethiopia during 1985-1986. This was an extension of the long-established interest of our Convention and our Board in the physical well-being of the people whom we served overseas. The alleviation of hunger has been one of the objectives of the Foreign Mission Board over the years. At the turn of this century, our missionaries began instructing the native peoples in modern methods of agricultural production to increase their food yields. In fact, one of the unique contributions of the National

Baptist Foreign Mission work was the introduction of the idea of "industrial" missions. Our first mission station at Bendoo, Liberia, was named the Bendoo Industrial Mission in 1882. Historically, the idea of ministering to the whole man beyond the establishment of churches did not enter into the Protestant mission programs until the 1920s. Thus, we have been in the forefront of those mission boards seeking to combat the problem of hunger which has haunted millions over the centuries.

When the Ethiopian crisis began, President Jemison immediately initiated the process of soliciting the support of the membership and in encouraging them to respond to this great need. The appeal of the drought-stricken Ethiopia with its accompanying catastrophic hunger did not go unheeded by National Baptists. In 1978 the Foreign Mission Board first called attention to this specific drought which moved across the continent of Africa, beginning in West Africa and travelling east to the Gulf of Aden and the Indian Ocean. The *Mission Herald* carried many articles on the need to give aid to the several countries involved. Some National Baptists responded but, unfortunately, it was not until the white media specifically called attention to Ethiopia that people began an all-out response to the situation.

The response of the Convention to Dr. Jemison's appeal for Ethiopian relief stands as a tribute to the willingness of National Baptists to follow leadership and to evidence compassion for their fellow man in a time of crisis. Our denomination emerged as a living example of Christ's people caring and sharing. Like a sleeping giant awakening from his slumber, so did the National Baptists awake and exhibit the potential power of concerted effort to meet a need. At long last our Convention was motivated to show its strength. The credit for this motivating power belonged to President Jemison who was the catalytic agent whose enthusiasm and faith stirred pastors and laymen alike to realize their potential for greatness as a denomination and as a people.

As of February 5, 1985, contributions for Ethiopia totalled $374,307.72. Before the drive was over, National Baptists raised over $1 million for Ethiopian relief.[11] The size of this contribution is an excellent example of the potential of our people rising to meet a great need.

By the end of the drive, $1,002,633.57 had been raised for Ethiopia alone. The money was used for purchasing medicines, food, farm implements and blankets, and to feed over one million starving people. President Jemison sent a seventeen-member team to negotiate with the Ethiopian Relief and Rehabilitation Commission and to supervise the delivery and distribution of the products sent to the relief camp in Ethiopia. The officials welcomed our delegation. They cut through the red tape that might have arisen on such a project and aided us in obtaining trucks and air freight which were in short supply.[12]

The Foreign Mission Board, while recognizing the tremendous crisis presented by hunger in Ethiopia, reminded its constituency that hunger extended beyond the borders of that drought-stricken country. It was a blessing that Ethiopia benefited from National Baptist gifts, yet other countries faced the same problems. Among these were Chad, Niger, and Mozambique, where thousands were dying due to drought conditions. Thus, even after the Ethiopian crisis was diminished, it was necessary to assist Africans in other countries to meet their problems. There was need for not only food but for well-digging equipment, seed, fertilizer, and farm implements. We gave aid to nations in Africa, whether Christian or non-Christian, as an example of our Christian witness. We aided them in the name of Christ because the love of Christ constrains us to be concerned, to care and to aid them in a practical way to survive.

Vermont Avenue Baptist Church in Zululand

In 1986, the Reverend Christopher Machi assumed the pastorate of the Vermont Avenue Baptist Church in Zululand. He was a native of Durban in Natal City, one of the four states that make up the Republic of South Africa. As a young boy, he was educated at one of our mission schools. For him, our National Baptist Convention was always considered "family" — there when he needed us. We were there when he heard God's call to full time ministry.

314

Through our Foreign Mission Board scholarship aid, he was brought to the United States to study at the American Baptist Seminary in Nashville. After graduation, he went on to further his studies at the California State University. We were very pleased when, upon returning to his native home, he assumed the pastorate of the church named for one of our leading congregations in Washington, D. C.

So alive is the Vermont Avenue Baptist Church of Zululand that new classrooms are being added to serve its growing membership. This is just one of the ninety-four seed churches the Foreign Mission Board has founded in South Africa with the help of US congregations such as the Vermont Avenue Baptist Church in Washington, D. C.

We send out missionaries to spread God's word. A young boy hears and answers the call. Mission giving provides for his education through the scholarship program. A congregation here responds with giving to purchase a church in South Africa, a church now to be served by such a man as the Reverend Machi. As a native pastor, he reaches out to others, thus continuing to expand and draw more people into our circle of God's love.[13]

S. Willie Layton Memorial Hospital for Women, Malawi

The S. Willie Layton Memorial Hospital was named in honor of the first president of the Women's Auxiliary of the National Baptist Convention, U.S.A., Inc., who served in that office from 1900 to 1948. For a number of years Mrs. Layton had envisioned the addition of an up-to-date obstetrical wing with full facilities for maternal care to be added to the original building. It was her feeling that this was necessary to complement the existing facilities at the hospital. The new wing, therefore, represented the realization of the dream for the woman whose name it bears.

In 1972, representatives from the Women's Convention, led by its president, Dr. Mary O. Ross, visited the mission fields of Africa. With Secretary Harvey serving as tour guide, the group of twenty-one sisters were able to witness on a first-hand basis the work

Women's Delegation: *Dr. Mary O. Ross, President; Mrs. Robyn Penn, PA; Miss Edna Cottom, PA; Mary J. Hackney, NY; Susie McClure, TN; Alvana Wilson, MS; Nettie L. Drummer, GA; Joyce Justice, KS; M. L. Sanders, OK; C. M. Pearson, GA; Betty Harvey, PA; Beverly Robinson, LA.*

of the Foreign Mission Board and the missionaries on the field. Of all their experiences, the work in Malawi was the most impressive and as a result, Dr. Ross recommended to the Women's Convention that they construct a wing to the S. Willie Layton Memorial Hospital for Women. Secretary Harvey secured estimates for the proposed construction and, because of topological difficulties regarding obtaining water for the hospital, the decision was made to build a new unit altogether. The Women's Convention donated $65,000 toward the construction and equipment, the cost of which eventually totalled $185,000.

There were many problems that had to be solved prior to construction. A geologist had to be employed to supervise the digging of a bore hole to secure an adequate water supply. The

S. Willie Layton Memorial Hospital

Ministry of Health and the Malawi government had to approve all building plans. A survey of the health facilities in the area had to be made to avoid duplication of obstetrical services in that region. Well over twenty-four months passed before all of this could be achieved and the work started.

With the erection completed and the equipment supplied, the Ministry of Health then, according to their laws, aided in the selection of the professional staff. The Board insisted that the professional staff be Christian and, since housing had to be provided on the mission, that they maintain Christian behavior as residents of the mission.

On March 18, 1984, a delegation of members of the Women's Convention participated in the dedication of the hospital. One of the highlights of the dedication program was the announcement that on the night prior to the dedication, an emergency delivery was made and the mother named the baby girl in honor

317

of Dr. Mary O. Ross. Dr. Ross promised that the Women's Convention would adopt the child and provide for all her needs.

When we consider that the World Health Organization early in the 1980s reported that, in the rural areas of West and East Africa, the mortality rate of pregnant women is 50% and that infant mortality is approximately 60% the need for an obstetrical hospital was readily apparent. The S. Willie Layton Memorial Hospital is the attempt of our Women's Convention to carry out the great commission of our Lord Jesus Christ when He said, "Go unto all the world" and to obey His command to "heal the sick," and thus implement the preaching of the Gospel. The Foreign Mission Board has always been grateful for the cooperation of the Women's Convention in this and other vital projects throughout their history.[14]

75th Anniversary of the Suehn Industrial Mission

Founded in 1912 by Miss Emma B. Delaney, an indomitable woman who literally carved the mission out of the bush country with her bare hands, the growth of the Suehn Industrial Mission was quick and marked by continuous success. At first the native chiefs were hostile and instructed their people to have nothing to do with the "God-talk lady." She was denied the privilege of settling near the Suehn village but, with an undaunted faith, Sister Delaney selected an area that was viewed as taboo because it had been the site of a tribal battleground upon which much blood had been shed and lives lost. It was believed that on this parcel of ground the spirits of the dead still lived. Thus, the chiefs felt that she could build her mission at her own spiritual risk.

Sister Delaney constantly declared that Almighty God, through His Son Jesus Christ, overcame all evil spirits. She began her work by ministering to sick children from this site of her early beginnings. The Suehn Mission took its roots and gradually developed into one of the most influential missions in Liberia.

By 1922 there were three buildings comprising the mission complex: a ten-room house used as a girls' dormitory, a seven-room cottage used as a boys' home and a one-room combination chapel and school.

Suehn is strategically located with superior access to both Monrovia and West Coast shipping. One of the most used native trails in the entire Republic of Liberia cuts directly across the campus.

In 1938 our school there had an unprecedented enrollment of 165 students. The instructors concentrated on a broad spectrum of trades to raise the lifestyles of their pupils.

Primarily a high school for girls and boys, Suehn's academic ratings have been commended by the Liberian government. This, in turn, has helped the Christian-based influence of Suehn to spread. Missionary-led evangelistic teams comprised of native converts have brought many people in the surrounding area into the family of Christ.

One of the most visible rewards of our seventy-five years of witness in Suehn is that today native converts, led by our missionaries, are carrying out their own vigorous programs of evangelism. In 1987 there were fourteen native Baptist churches in the Suehn district. Our missionaries assisted lay leaders to work in these churches, helping them develop such vital programs as Sunday school and Women's Missionaries Societies.

Secretary Harvey travelled to Suehn to participate in the celebration of the Diamond Jubilee of the school. He gave the principal address during which he endeavored to inspire the students to develop into self-sufficient citizens with the determination to overcome all obstacles.

The general chairman of the anniversary celebration was Sister Evangeline D. Varnah. She sent a message to her constituents and her friends and colleagues in which she pointed out certain of the blessings which the mission had received through the grace of God. Among other things she said:

> "God Sent Us Light — God put His light into the heart
> of missionaries to lead the needy and send sick souls
> out of darkness into the marvelous light of Christianity
> in the wilderness of Suehn.

319

"God Sent Us Love and Grace — The missionaries brought us the message of God's love for man...The missionaries rocked the cradles of many motherless babies who are outstanding citizens today in our communities as teachers, lawyers, farmers, preachers, evangelists, doctors, nurses, diplomats and the like.

"God Sent Us Knowledge and Wisdom — The training of the mind was one of the main objectives of the missionaries. They sought to help children in dire need. Most of the children in need were of aboriginal origin whose parents were mostly non-Christian and not educated in Western culture. The first knowledge the children learned was about Jesus mainly from Bible verses and songs during morning and evening devotions...We are happy that the missionaries taught their students to be industrious...The missionaries sacrificed their lives to make us what we are today."[15]

Throughout the history of the Foreign Mission Board, we have made numerous references to the Suehn Industrial Mission. The Foreign Mission Board and all members of the National Baptist Convention, U.S.A., Inc., may very well take pride in the contributions which the Suehn Industrial Mission made during the first seventy-five years of its existence. Certainly it is a monument to the efforts of hundreds of people who invested their material resources, their physical energies and their prayers that the work of this mission should go forward.

Assessment of Progress Since 1962

As we close this chronicle of the development of the Foreign Mission Board, it is proper that we take time to reflect upon the work of the Board between 1962 and 1987. The following represents some of the more personal reflections of the author.

"As I stepped foot on African soil, the Motherland, on my first inspection of Africa, I was unprepared for the sights that would fill my eyes and the emotions they would trigger in my heart. It was 5 a.m. An intrepid sun was just rising, its pale golden rays mixing in the azure blue light before blending to a soft mauve and orange. It was cool, very cool. In the background the tom-tom set my soul singing. Africa! I had landed in Monrovia, Liberia, the country where my missionary activity had begun. As I visited various mission stations throughout that country, it did not take long for me to recognize the need for improvement in our efforts to raise the quality of life for the dedicated missionaries as well as the people to whom they came to bring the message of the saving power of Christ."

In keeping with this insight, we were able to improve the living conditions of the missionaries and to provide them with hospitalization and fringe benefits comparable to those given professionals outside the realm of missionary work. A major benefit was the provision of vehicles which greatly reduced the time our missionaries spent travelling to isolated outposts and villages. Mission nurses, preachers and teachers now found even the most remote potential convert much more accessible. Thus, the sphere of influence and service of each worker was greatly extended.

During the twenty-five year period between 1962-1987, new challenges rose and changes were required with respect to the policies of missionary work as well as the missionary selection process. As the African nations achieved independence, the new governments established increasingly stringent requirements for mission work which extended beyond the teaching of religion to the native peoples. Each missionary was required to teach either at the elementary or secondary level, in vocational training classes, or to provide professional health services. In Liberia, for example, each mission station was required to have a school. Mission schools had to follow the prescribed curriculum of the government. Any missionary whose credentials did not meet governmental standards was not granted a visa or work permit.

This meant that early on the requirements for securing appropriate people to serve had to extend well beyond mere dedication and willingness to go. The world of today demands much more of missionaries than in earlier times. Today our Foreign

321

Mission Board is sending out missionaries who are not only filled with the Holy Spirit but who are also professionals trained to demonstrate God's love through actions and services that really make a difference in the physical as well as spiritual lives of the people they serve.

In 1970, the Foreign Mission Board began work in Swaziland. This date represents the birth of new hope and the opening of new frontiers for Christian work and witness. Although Swaziland nestles in the corner of the Republic of South Africa, it is in direct opposition to the way of life and the policies of apartheid existing in its neighboring Republic. When, in 1970, the Foreign Mission Board purchased land and established a mission station in Swaziland, the sluice gates of heaven were opened to hundreds of persecuted Black Africans seeking refuge from the oppressive laws of the Republic of South Africa. This mission became the headquarters of the National Baptist Convention of Southern Africa and serves as a residence for our southern African supervisors as well as a point of departure for American missionaries in that area.

By grasping hold of the unlimited opportunities offered in Swaziland through the establishment of preschools as well as other schools and programs, it is our hope that we may, in time, begin to penetrate the barriers of apartheid and truly reach millions with Christ's message of love, hope and salvation.

Already we have commented on the important impact made by preaching and work teams to Africa. These have constituted a vital link between the work on the foreign field and the developing sense of responsibility for missions on the part of churches on the home front. As we reflect over the last twenty-five years, no moments stand out more richly than those spent with the various preaching teams we have led. The people, the places, the events, the countless times when hands have clasped hands in friendship and love will never be forgotten. From the jungle outpost of Liberia to the fledgling churches of Sierra Leone, a hospital in Malawi, a school in Lesotho, a village in Ghana and, yes, even in the dark oppression of the Republic of South Africa, we have seen the smile of God on the faces of His people. We have seen His love in the work being carried on. We have seen His promise fulfilled as a better, brighter future has unfolded before our eyes. Each preaching team visit has brought its own moments of joy and thanksgiving. Each has forged a stronger tie between the people in our mission countries and the people who support our work.

"If all of the foregoing represent my spiritual high points, the increase in financial support during the past twenty-five years most certainly marks a new height in praise and thanksgiving. Since I assumed the position of corresponding secretary, the income of the Foreign Mission Board has increased 500%! But this increase and support did not begin at once. During my first year in office we raised only $143,000 — a drop of $100,000 from the previous year. Part of this decrease in support came as the result of the serious division which took place in our denomination in 1962. At the time I took office, the people in our churches were given very little information about our work, progress and needs. Through a rigorous program of providing promotional and educational materials to people in our member congregations, the lines of communication between the mission field and home were opened. People became better informed and, therefore, more concerned about our mission work. There developed a new unity of purpose between "senders" and "sent ones." This resulted in the increased support and success of the work of the Board.

"The history of the past twenty-five years is rich in chronicles of personal experiences and memorable occasions. My commuting weekly between my church in Pittsburgh and the Foreign Mission Board office in Philadelphia during the first five years of my tenure as corresponding secretary represented a personal struggle which was alleviated when I resigned my pastorate and moved my family to Philadelphia. We recalled the satisfaction resulting from our writing the *Missionary Manual*, the only mission manual of its kind written by a Black for the Black church.

"Another of the many personal highs came in 1973 when the Republic of Liberia made me a Knight Grand Band of the Humane

Order of African Redemption. This award, bestowed for "exceptional work in Liberia in the field of Evangelism and Missions," will be forever cherished in my heart. Although presented to me personally, I accepted it as the representative of the National Baptist Convention, U.S.A., Inc., for I sincerely believe that all members share equally in this honor."

Other major developments which have taken place under the twenty-five year period under discussion may be mentioned here. Since 1961, forty-nine missionaries have been sent to the foreign field. (See Appendix F) Their salaries have been raised 650% to bring them up to a level in keeping with their peers in other denominations. They have been covered by health insurance, provided with housing accommodations and have been furnished with vehicles where needed. In addition, the latest in educational material have been supplied to increase their classroom efficiency.

New buildings have been erected at the Suehn and Bendoo Missions in Liberia. Classroom buildings have been erected at Vine Memorial Mission in Sierra Leone. A new seventeen-bed obstetrical hospital, named in honor of S. Willie Layton, late president of the Women's Auxiliary, National Baptist Convention, U.S.A., Inc., has been added to the Board's facilities at the Providence Industrial Mission, Chiradzulu, Malawi. A church and a preschool complex have been added at the National Baptist Mission in Swaziland, new classrooms built at National Baptist Convention missions in Lesotho, Southern Africa, and the classroom building has been constructed in Bluefields, Nicaragua. The Foreign Mission Board now boasts of new churches in Malawi, Swaziland, the Republic of South Africa, Southern Africa, Jamaica and Barbados in the Caribbean.

Secretary Harvey instituted a modern preschool program in Swaziland which uses the world renowned Peabody Method; village schools in Liberia and a School of Domestic Arts at the Providence Industrial Mission in Malawi.

In addition, Secretary Harvey launched an effective child adoption program in Liberia and a seed church program in South Africa. As of March 1987, the Foreign Mission Board is supporting 152 Black churches, two colored churches and ninety-four seed churches in the Bantustands of South Africa. These programs are a part of the Board's financial promotion emphasis. Because of these and other similar efforts, the Board's general income increased thirty-fold in twenty-five years going from $142,000 in 1961-1962 to $3,713,025 in 1986-1987.

Special programs in agriculture have been launched. Mission stations continue to receive the latest and best in Bible and church supplies. Significant emphasis has been placed in audio-visual education including slides accompanying printed commentary and video cassettes. Moreover, Secretary Harvey has promoted and authored many new publications including the *Missionary Workers Manual, Missionary Education for Tomorrow's Leaders, A Century of Mission*, a revised *Mission Herald* magazine and mission education study materials. The Board also publishes a complete set of mission education tracts every three years for use in National Baptist Convention churches.[16]

Many workshops and seminars have been carried out in South Africa, Lesotho and Swaziland. In addition, nine preaching teams were sent out at two-year intervals. These teams, as we have noted, have been the basis of stimulating new interest in and support for the work of the Foreign Mission Board.

In all of these developments, Secretary Harvey has enjoyed the blessing of Almighty God and the ever-growing support of ministers, churches and individuals throughout the constituency of the National Baptist Convention, U.S.A., Inc. Thanks to God for all that He has allowed to be accomplished through us. The Christian religion is indeed a faith which can transform the world providing it is preached to all the world and practiced by those who hear it.

The account of the work of the Foreign Mission Board which we have chronicled in these pages represents one of the great chapters in the history of Christian missions. It is indeed a tribute to the men and women who have volunteered their services, risked their personal safety, and, in many tragic instances, literally given their very lives to the cause. The latter died in service to God as ministers to people with tremendous needs. Their deeds will not be forgotten. All those who have been a part of these efforts have been partners in the building of bridges of faith across the seas. These bridges must continue to be maintained. Our ears must be constantly attuned to hear the Macedonian Call, and the Foreign Mission Board and National Baptist Convention, U.S.A., Inc., will resolutely make certain to respond to that insistent plea with all the resources at their command.

Notes

1. *Mission Herald*, (July-August 1980) pp. 3-8.
2. *Mission Herald*, (January-February 1978) p. 6.
3. *Mission Herald*, (January-February 1980) p. 15.
4. *Mission Herald*, (January-February 1979) pp. 4-5.
5. *Mission Herald*, (September-October 1984) pp. 4-5.
6. *Mission Herald*, (May-June 1980) pp. 5-6.
7. *Mission Herald*, (July-August 1980) pp. 9-10.
8. *Mission Herald*, (May-June 1980) p. 3.
9. *Mission Herald*, (March-April 1983) p. 10.
10. *Mission Herald*, (November-December 1982) p. 11.
11. *Mission Herald*, (January-February 1985) p. 3.
    Mission Herald, (September-October 1985) p. 7.
12. *Mission Herald*, (September-October 1985) pp. 3-7.
13. *Mission Herald*, (March-April 1986) p. 3.
14. *Mission Herald*, (March-April 1984) pp. 6-7.
15. *Mission Herald*, (March-April 1987) p. 11.
16. *Mission Herald* (March-April 1987) p. 6.

Members of the Foreign Mission Board 1987

ALABAMA	Rev. Odie Hoover, Jr.
	Dr. W. Coleman
ARIZONA	Rev. Warren Stewart
ARKANSAS	Rev. A. King
	Rev. C.W. Sims
BAHAMAS	Rev. Charles Smith
CALIFORNIA	Rev. Charles Cook
	Dr. Earl Cotton
DISTRICT OF COLUMBIA	Rev. Andrew Fowler
	Rev. E.V. Cunningham
FLORIDA	Rev. W.C. Edcar
GEORGIA	Mrs. C.M. Pearson
ILLINOIS	Rev. Amos Waller
	Rev. J.N. Lightfoot
IOWA	Rev. David Benton
INDIANA	Rev. Everett Gray
	Dr. Calvin Blanford
KANSAS	
KENTUCKY	Rev. B.S. Ransom
LOUISIANA	Rev. M. Carmbs
	Rev. E.A. Henry
MARYLAND	Rev. Clifford Johnson
MASSACHUSETTS	Rev. Paul A. Fullilove

MICHIGAN	Rev. James L. Newby Dr. Stacy Williams
MISSISSIPPI	Rev. Royal L. Jordan Rev. J. Bailey Rev. Dr. Carl E. Jordan, Sr. Rev. A.D. Lewis
MISSOURI	Rev. George McFoulon
NEBRASKA	Rev. William L. Blake
NEVADA	Rev. Willie Davis
NEW JERSEY	Rev. R.L. Douglas Rev. A. Ovilla Johnson
NEW MEXICO	Rev. J.A. Hopkins
NEW YORK	Dr. Samuel B. Joubert
NO. CAROLINA	Rev. F.O. Bass, Jr.
OHIO	Rev. Curtis A. Brown Rev. Lacy Anderson
OKLAHOMA	Rev. J.D. Phillips
PENNSYLVANIA	Rev. Charles Walker
SO. CAROLINA	Dr. Maxie Gordon
TENNESSEE	Rev. P. Moody
TEXAS	Rev. R.L. Parrish Rev. L.B. Adams Rev. L.V. Wicks
VIRGINIA	Rev. J.A. Braxton
WASHINGTON	Rev. E.H. Hankerson
WEST VIRGINIA	Rev. James Burnett
WISCONSIN	Rev. J.H. Henderson

Our Mission Stations 1963

WEST AFRICA
Rev. John B. Falconer, Supervisor
Monrovia, Liberia, West Africa

SUEHN INDUSTRIAL MISSION
Liberia, West Africa
Mrs. Mattie Mae Davis, Principal
Number of teachers and workers — 23

BIBLE INDUSTRIAL MISSION
Fortsville, Grand Bassa
Liberia, West Africa
Rev. Woodward Gardner in charge
Teachers and workers — 6

BENDOO INDUSTRIAL MISSION
Cape Mount, Liberia, West Africa
Rev. Rufus Prunty, Principal
Teachers and workers — 11

ROOSEVELT SCHOOL
Freetown, Sierre Leone
West Africa
Mrs. Constance Cummings-John, Principal
Workers — 11

KLAY MISSION
Liberia, West Africa
Workers — 2

PILGRIM BAPTIST MISSION
Issele Uke, Nigeria
West Africa
Rev. S. W. Martin, Principal
Teachers and workers — 85

GOLD COAST NATIONAL BAPTIST MISSION
Accra, Ghana, West Africa
S. A. Orukatan, General Secretary
Workers — 10

A NUMBER OF SUB-STATIONS

CENTRAL, EAST, SOUTH, AFRICA
Dr. Daniel S. Malekebu, Supervisor
Chiradzulu, Nyasaland

PROVIDENCE INDUSTRIAL MISSION
Chiradzulu, Nyasaland

BAPTIST MISSION AND SEMINARY
Basutoland
Rev. E. G. Ngubeni in charge

BUCHANNAN MISSION
Middledrift S. A.

BAPTIST MISSION
Harding, Natal S. A.

BAPTIST MISSION
Capetown Providence S. A.

W. W. BROWN MEMORIAL MISSION
Johannesburg, Union of South Africa
Teachers and workers — 47

ASIA

JAPAN CHRISTIAN UNIVERSITY
Cooperative undertaking of 22 Boards,
Division of Foreign Missions
Tokyo, Japan

BAPTIST MISSION STATION
Bangalore, India
Rev. H. Douglas Oliver

WESTERN HEMISPHERE

JORDAN MEMORIAL BAPTIST TRAINING SCHOOL
Nassau, Bahama Islands, B. W. I.
Rev. Thedford Johnson, Supervisor
Rev. T. E. W. Donaldson in charge
Teachers and workers — 17

JORDAN MEMORIAL BAPTIST STATION
Bluefields, Nicaragua
Central America
Rev. F. G. Downs in charge
Number of workers — 4

Hospitals

CARRIE V. DYER MEMORIAL HOSPITAL
Monrovia, Liberia, West Africa

JAMES E. EAST MEMORIAL HOSPITAL
Nyasaland, East Africa

Clinics

BENDOO MISSION

SUEHN MISSION

BASSA MISSION

NIGERIA MATERNITY HOUSE

331

Our Mission Stations
1987

WEST AFRICA, Entered 1882

Sierra Leone
ROOSEVELT-VINE MEMORIAL SECONDARY SCHOOL,
Entered 1950
Miss Elvira Porter, *Principal*
Miss Pauline Holland-Campbell, *Headmistress*
Rev. H. Mano Davis, *Missionary-Chaplain*
Rev. B. A. Taylor, *Chaplain's Assistant*

Liberia
SUEHN INDUSTRIAL MISSION SECONDARY SCHOOL,
Entered 1912
Mr. Ballah Davis, *Principal*
Mr. Henry Askie, Jr., *Registrar*
Rev. Ghessi W. Kemah, Sr., *Chaplain*
Meatta Sorrie, *Dean of Girls*
Mrs. Erma Bailey Etheridge, *Missionary-Matron*
Mrs. Wilma Rose, *Missionary*

BENDOO INDUSTRIAL MISSION PRIMARY SCHOOL,
Entered 1882
Bendoo, Grand Cape Mount County
Rev. V. Alexander Benson, *Principal*
Mrs. Josephine Minter, *Missionary-Nurse*
Rev. & Mrs. Rufus Prunty, *Chaplain & Missionary —
Retired*
Miss Malissa Gray, *Dean of Girls*
Deacon Wesley, *Dean of Boys*
Rev. John Bridges, *Missionary-Teacher*
Mrs. Julia Williams, *Missionary-Teacher*

Medical & Maternity Clinics — 21
Village Extension Schools — 3

BIBLE INDUSTRIAL ACADEMY, Entered 1914
Fortsville, Grand Bassa County
 Rev. Charles Reeves, *Principal*
(in cooperation with the Liberia Baptist Missionary and
Educational Convention)

Ghana, Entered 1958
National Baptist Churches — 3
Accra
 Mr. Frank Akinode-Solomon, *Lay Leader*

CENTRAL AFRICA

Malawi, Entered 1900

PROVIDENCE INDUSTRIAL MISSION, Chiradzulu,
Southern District
 Rev. Macford Chipiliko, *Supervisor*
 Rev. L. C. Muocha, *Supervisor — Retired*
 Rev. Addison Mabuwa, *Missionary*
S. Willie Layton Memorial Hospital for Women
Primary & Secondary School
Domestic Arts School
Churches — 492
Church Extensions in Zambia, Zaire, Tanzania,
Zimbabwe — 27

SOUTH AFRICA, Entered 1894

Rev. Stanley Hlwenga, *Supervisor*
Rev. Elliot G. Ngubeni, *Supervisor — Retired*

Republic of South Africa, Entered 1894
Churches in Republic — 152 African — 2 Colored
Churches in Bantustans — 94

Lesotho, Entered 1961
W. J. HARVEY SEMINARY & SECONDARY SCHOOL
  L. Lechesa, *Headmaster*
  Rev. L. Kehena, *Chaplain*
Churches — 19

Botswana
MAHALAPYA
  Rev. Steven Kgoroeadira, *Pastor*

Swaziland, Entered 1971
NATIONAL BAPTIST PRE-SCHOOL, Woodlands Township
  Mrs. Dudu Little, *Principal*
Churches in Mbabane, Manzini, Lombobo, Shesselman — 9

WESTERN HEMISPHERE

Bahamas, Entered 1946
BAHAMAS OUT-ISLAND MISSIONARY SUPPORT
St. John's Native Baptist Society, Nassau
  Rev. Michael Symonette, *General Superintendent*
Churches — 68

SALEM UNION BAPTIST ASSOCIATION
  Rev. J. D. Cox, *Moderator*
Churches — 28

ZION BAPTIST ASSOCIATION
  Rev. Charles C. Smith, *Moderator*
Churches — 72

L. G. JORDAN — PRINCE WILLIAMS SCHOOL
Bahamas National Baptist Missionary & Educational
Convention
  Dr. Charles Saunders, *President*

Barbados, West Indies, Entered 1976
NATIONAL BAPTIST CONVENTION OF BARBADOS
   Rev. Sinclair Rudder, *President & Supervisor*
Churches — 3

Jamaica, West Indies, Entered 1971
JAMAICA FELLOWSHIP BAPTIST CONVENTION
   Rev. Lester J. Brown, *President*
Churches — 31

CENTRAL AMERICA

Nicaragua, Entered 1958
ZION BAPTIST MISSION, Bluefields
   Rev. Orlando Rigby, *Chaplain — Supervisor*
Baptist Mission Primary School
Churches — 3

APPENDIX C

Statement of Cash Receipts and Disbursements from July 1, 1961 to June 30, 1962

RECEIPTS

Cash Balance July 1, 1961		$ 92,149.99
CONTRIBUTIONS:	$144,607.27	
Less Returned Checks Uncollected	714.17	$143,893.10
OTHER INCOME:		
Herald Subscriptions	42.20	
Book Sales	25.45	
Rents.	907.00	
Income from Investments	175.00	
Pictures Slides — Sales	19.00	1,168.65
Total Receipts		145,061.75
GENERAL:		
Payroll Taxes Withheld	3,789.06	
Refunds.	336.19	
Returned Checks Collected	3,144.35	
Accounts Receivable	450.00	
Special Reserve — Withdrawals	16,673.66	24,393.26
Transfer of Funds — Contra		39,141.24
Total		$300,746.24

DISBURSEMENTS

Administration		$ 33,465.66
Taxes		3,123.44
Building Operation		3,183.31

MISSION EXPENDITURES:

Mission Work	$172,421.06	
Printing Plant	9,324.99	
Mission Herald	1,005.67	182,751.72

GENERAL:

Notes on Equipment	1,652.00	
Returned Checks	3,144.35	
Office Furniture & Equipment	832.56	
Deposit on Booth	500.00	
Accounts Payable	73.31	
Payroll Taxes	3,834.63	
Refunds	1,178.04	
Prepaid Indemnity Insurance	739.98	
Picture Slides — Inventory	399.68	12,354.55

Total Disbursements		$234,878,68
		39,141.24
Transfer of Funds — Contra		26,726.32
Cash Balance June 30, 1962		
Total		$300,746.24

Statement of Cash Receipts and Disbursements from June 30, 1986 to June 30, 1987

Cash Balance June 30, 1986 $324,159.37

RECEIPTS:

Contributions — Missions	$1,286,540.59	
Contributions — Ethiopian Relief	11,217.36	
Mission Herald	2,916.49	
Literature Sales	1,201.88	
Teachers Guides	308.14	
Slides	198.85	
Manuals	5,647.41	
Postage	388.55	
Anniversary Books	60.00	
Refunds	53,076.22	
Redeposits	35,800.00	
Advances (Foreign Transfers)	677,186.52	
Transfers Domestic	600,000.00	
Interest Income	2,674.88	
Exchange Checks	1,675.00	
Contributions Receivable	10,295.28	
Receivables — Other	2,879.39	
Miscellaneous	6,962.86	
Total Receipts		2,699,029.42
Total Funds Available		$3,023,188.79

LESS DISBURSEMENTS:

Salaries — Office (Net)	$ 62,366.15	
Executive Salary (Net)	31,587.93	
Administration	137,785.66	
Building Maintenance	10,046.56	
Mission Herald	97,179.46	
Field Workers	86,108.24	
Domestic Travel	37,424.68	
Taxes Paid	55,728.74	
Advances (Foreign)	677,186.52	
Mission Maintenance	786,545.80	
Transfers	600,000.00	
Foreign Travel	66,940.46	
Miscellaneous	3,240.45	
Exchange Checks	1,500.00	
Total Disbursements		2,653,640.65
Cash Balance June 30, 1987		$ 369,548.14

Mission Herald, Vol. 87, No. 4 (July-August 1987)

APPENDIX D

Missionary Societies and their Foreign Fields

The Foreign Mission Board of the National Baptist Convention, U.S.A., Inc., is among the largest of the agencies engaged in the work of carrying the gospel to foreign lands. The list of such Boards engaged in foreign mission work as of 1968 is as follows:

American Baptist Foreign Mission Societies: Congo, Hong Kong, India, Japan, Malaysia-Singapore, Okinawa, Philippines, Switzerland (residence of A.B.F.M.S. European representative), Thailand.

American Baptist Home Mission Societies (Foreign Work): El Salvador, Haiti, Mexico, Nicaragua, Puerto Rico.

Association of Baptists for World Evangelism (U.S.A.): Brazil, Chile, Colombia, Hong Kong, Japan, Pakistan, Peru, Philippines.

Australian Baptist Missionary Society: India, New Guinea, Pakistan.

Baptist General Conference, Board of Foreign Missions (U.S.A.): Argentina, Brazil, Ethiopia, India, Japan, Philippines.

Baptist Mid-Missions (U.S.A.): Austria, Bahama Islands, Brazil, Canada, Central African Republic, Chad, Congo, Dominican Republic, France, Germany, Ghana, Guyana, Haiti, Honduras, Hong Kong, India, Italy, Jamaica, Japan, Korea, Liberia, Mexico, Netherlands, Peru, Puerto Rico, Venezuela, West Indies.

Baptist Missionary Society (Britain): Angola, Brazil, Ceylon, Congo, Hong Kong, India, Jamaica, Nepal, Pakistan, Trinidad.

Baptist Union of Sweden (Foreign Work): Congo, India, Japan.

Brazilian Baptist Convention, Foreign Mission Board: Bolivia, Paraguay, Portugal.

Canadian Baptist Foreign Mission Board: Bolivia, Congo, India.

339

Conservative Baptist Foreign Mission Society (U.S.A.): Argentina, Brazil, Congo, France, Hong Kong, India, Indonesia, Italy, Ivory Coast, Japan, Jordan, Madagascar, Pakistan, Philippines, Portugal, Senegal, Taiwan, Uganda.

Danish Baptist Union, Foreign Mission Board: Burundi, Rwanda.

European Baptist Mission Society: Cameroon, Sierra Leone.

German Union of Evangelical-Free Churches, Foreign Mission: Alaska, Argentina, Cameroon, Chad, Ethiopia, India, Indonesia, Japan, Jordan, Kenya, Mexico, Nepal, New Guinea, Nigeria, Pakistan, Paraguay, Philippines, Tanzania, Thailand.

Irish Baptist Foreign Missions: Peru.

Japan Baptist Convention, Foreign Mission Committee: Brazil, Okinawa.

Lott Carey Baptist Foreign Mission Convention (U.S.A.): Haiti, India, Liberia, Nigeria.

National Association of Free Will Baptists, Board of Foreign Missions (U.S.A.): Brazil, Ecuador, France, India, Ivory Coast, Japan, Panama, Uruguay.

National Baptist Convention of America, Foreign Mission Board (U.S.A.): Bahama Islands, Jamaica, Liberia, Kenya.

National Baptist Convention, U.S.A., Inc. Foreign Mission Board (U.S.A.): Bahama Islands, Ghana, India, Lesotho, Liberia, Nicaragua, Malawi, Sierra Leone, South Africa, Rhodesia.

The Netherlands Baptist Union, Mission Committee: Congo, Cameroon.

New Zealand Baptist Missionary Society: India, Pakistan.

Nigerian Baptist Home and Foreign Mission Board (Foreign Work): Sierra Leone.

North American Baptist Association: Australia, Bolivia, Brazil, Cape Verde Islands, Costa Rica, France, Guatemala, Italy, Japan, Mexico, Nicaragua, Portugal, Taiwan.

The North American Baptist General Missionary Society: Cameroon, Japan, Brazil.

Norwegian Baptist Union, Congo Mission: Congo.

Orebo Mission Society (Sweden): Brazil, Central African Republic, Congo, India, Japan, Nepal, Pakistan.

Polish Evangelical Missionary Association, Inc. (U.S.A.): Poland.

Portuguese Baptist Convention, Mission Committee: Angola, Mozambique, Africa, Zambia.

Seventh Day Baptist Missionary Society (U.S.A.): Guyana, Jamaica, Malawi.

South African Baptist Missionary Society: Zambia.

Southern Baptist Convention Foreign Mission Board (U.S.A.): Argentina, Austria, Bahama Islands, Bermuda, Botswana, Brazil, Chile, Colombia, Costa Rica, Dominican Republic, Ecuador, Ethiopia, France, French West Indies, Gaza, Germany, Ghana, Guam, Guatemala, Guyana, Honduras, Hong Kong, Iceland, India, Indonesia, Israel, Italy, Ivory Coast, Jamaica, Japan, Jordan, Kenya, Korea, Lebanon, Liberia, Libya, Luxembourg, Macao, Malawi, Malaysia, Mexico, Morocco, Nigeria, Okinawa, Pakistan, Paraguay, Peru, Philippines, Portugal, Rhodesia, Singapore, Spain, Switzerland, Taiwan, Tanzania, Thailand, Togo, Trinidad, Turkey, Uganda, Uruguay, Venezuela, Vietnam, Yemen, Zambia.

Southern Baptist Convention, Home Mission Board (Foreign Work): Cuba, Panama, Puerto Rico.

Strict Baptist Mission (Britain): India.

Taiwan Baptist Convention, Foreign Mission Committee: Korea, Malaysia.

Mission Herald, (January-February, 1968) pp. 4-5.

PREACHING TEAMS

Team 1-1967
Dr. William J. Harvey, III
Rev. Alfred Waller, OH
Rev. William Haney*, MI
Rev. Ivor Moore*, NY
Rev. Roosevelt Williams*, MI
Rev. I. T. Bradley, OH

Team 2-1971
Dr. William J. Harvey, III
Rev. Leon Whitney, MI
Rev. Leslie Wainwright*, NY
Rev. W. W. Weatherspool, GA
Rev. Earl Bartley, PA
Rev. William R. Harris, PA

Team 3-1973
Dr. William J. Harvey, III
Rev. Samuel Austin, NY
Rev. Grant Coleman, KY
Rev. William T. Crutcher, TN
Rev. John D. Hearn, MI
Rev. Willard Lamb, PA
Rev. George C. McCutcheon, OK
Rev. James Newby, MI
Rev. Frederick Sampson, MI
Rev. Charles Walker, PA
Rev. John R. Wheeler, DC
Rev. Lawrence Wicks, TX
Rev. J. Van Alfred Winsett, PA
Rev. William R. Harris, PA

Team 4-1975
Dr. William J. Harvey, III
Rev. John R. Wheeler, DC
Rev. James F. Scott, PA
Rev. Neal Haynes, MO
Rev. F. B. Jackson, IN
Rev. Henry Lyons, FL
Rev. Charles Smith,
   Nassau, Bahamas
Rev. Billy Bissic, LA
Rev. Lawrence Wicks, TX

Team 5-1977
Dr. William J. Harvey, III
Rev. William R. Harris, PA
Rev. Lawrence Wicks, TX
Rev. John R. Wheeler, DC
Rev. Robert Lovett, PA
Rev. Charles Walker, PA
Rev. Pontius Todd*, PA
Rev. Robert Davis, OH

Team 6-1979
Dr. William J. Harvey, III
Rev. Ed N. Henry, OH
Rev. Clifford Johnson, MD
Rev. W. J. Mason*, DC
Rev. D. R. Paige, PA
Rev. A. R. Awkard, KY
Rev. Billy Bissic, LA
Rev. J. H. Corbitt, SC

*Deceased

Rev. Roscoe Cooper, VA
Rev. Dwight Jones, VA
Rev. John R. Wheeler, DC
Rev. Donald Walton, CA
Rev. Lawrence Wicks, TX
Rev. Edgar Williams, DC
Rev. A. B. Patterson, AK
Rev. Robert Porter, MN
Rev. Robert Rasberry, NY
Rev. W. Franklyn Richardson, NY
Rev. William R. Harris, PA

Team 7-1983
Dr. William J. Harvey, III
Rev. Charles Walker, PA
Rev. William R. Harris, PA
Rev. John R. Wheeler, DC
Rev. John McGruder, IL
Rev. W. B. McMahand, SC
Rev. Morris Shearin, NC
Rev. Odel D. Brown*, VA

Team 8-1985
Dr. William J. Harvey, III
Rev. Carl Jordan, MS
Rev. W. T. Alford*, AL
Rev. Colvin Blanford, IN
Rev. Henry Bridges, MI
Rev. Emmet Buford, MI
Rev. Daryl Rollins, Va

*Deceased

Rev. John R. Wheeler, DC
Rev. Warren H. Stewart, Sr., AZ
Rev. William R. Harris, PA
Rev. R. Davis, OH

Team 9-1987
Dr. William J. Harvey, III
Rev. Marshall Griffin, Sr., PA
Rev. Elijah Bennett, NY
Rev. Allan P. Weaver, NY
Rev. L. L. Kirby, WI
Rev. Rafe Taylor, DC
Rev. J. Albert Bush, NY
Rev. Colvin Blanford, IN
Rev. Dennis Meredith, CA
Rev. Granville Smith, MI
Rev. R. B. Lewis, VA

Team 10-1989
Rev. Willard Ashley, NJ
Rev. Ronald Bobo, MD
Rev. Timothy L. Careathers, NY
Rev. Ronald Packnett, MO
Rev. Allen Stanley, NY
Rev. J. C. Wade, IN
Rev. Charles Walker, PA
Rev. Keith L. Whitney, MI
Rev. David E. Goatley, KY
Rev. William Harris, PA

Missionaries Serving Under Secretary Harvey, 1961-1989

Ms. Virginia Antrom	Philadelphia, PA
Rev. Enoch Backford	Nassau, Bahamas
Dr. C. N. Bennett	Manassas, VA
Mrs. M. W. Bennett	Manassas, VA
Rev. V. A. Benson	Liberia, West Africa
Rev. Gilbert Bent	Bluefields, Nicaragua
Mrs. Harry Bonner	Ann Arbor, MI
Mr. Harry Bonner	Ann Arbor, MI
Rev. John Bridges	Flint, MI
Rev. Lester Brown	Jamaica
Rev. J. Chinyama	South Africa
Rev. Mackford Chipuliko	Malawi
Mrs. Sarah Williamson Coleman	Washington, DC
Rev. John D. Cox	Nassau, Bahamas
Mrs. Sarah Cyrus	Philadelphia, PA
Mr. Ballah Davis	Monrovia, Liberia
Rev. H. M. Davis	Freetown, Sierra Leone
Mrs. Mattie Mae Davis	High Point, NC
Rev. T. E. W. Donaldson	Nassau, Bahamas
Mrs. F. G. Downs	Bluefields, Nicaragua
Rev. F. G. Downs	Bluefields, Nicaragua
Mrs. Christine Drew	Camden, NJ
Ms. Gladys East	Philadelphia, PA
Mrs. Erma Etheridge	Brandywine, MD
Rev. John Falconer	Shibuta, MS
Ms. Verlene Farmer	Oklahoma City, OK
Rev. Reginald Hlongwane	South Africa
Rev. John Hlope	Swaziland
Mrs. Roberta Jackson	Philadelphia, PA
Mr. Jerry Jones	MS

Mrs. Charlotte Levi	Muncy, IN
Mrs. Duduizle Minisi Little	Swaziland
Ms. Annie P. Littlejohn	Gafney, SC
Rev. Addison Mabuwa	Malawi
Rev. Christopher Machi	South Africa
Dr. Daniel Malekebu	Malawi
Mrs. Flora Malekebu	Malawi
Dr. Samuel Martin	Issele Uku, Nigeria
Mr. Cleo McConnell	Pacoima, CA
Mrs. Cleo McConnell	Pacoima, CA
Ms. Sandi McFadden	Philadelphia, PA
Ms. Della McGrew	Oklahoma City, OK
Mrs. Josephine Minter	Topeka, KS
Rev. P. Morgan	Nicaragua
Rev. L. C. Muocha	Malawi
Rev. Arthur Myers	Philadelphia, PA
Mrs. Barbara Myers	Philadelphia, PA
Rev. H. Douglas Oliver	Indianapolis, IN
Rev. S. A. Oruktan	Ghana

Foreign Mission Field Workers 1961-1989

Rev. H. S. Bailey
Rev. Calvin Blanford, NJ
Rev. M. D. Bobbitt, NJ
Mrs. Oneida Branch, CA
Rev. E. S. Brazill, WA
Rev. Louis Butcher*, PA
Rev. T. R. Carter, DE
Rev. T. Caviness, OH
Rev. Willie S. Chambers, MD
Rev. C. H. Churn*, MD
Rev. Charlie Cook, CA
Rev. Earl C. Cotton, CA
Rev. J. O. Crittenden, PA
Rev. E. V. Cunningham, DC
Rev. C. C. Cyphers*, TX
Rev. F. M. Dews, TX
Rev. W. C. Edcar, FL
Rev. S. L. Foote, NJ
Rev. A. P. Fowler, DC
Rev. Paul A. Fullilove, MA
Dr. Primrose Funches, IL
Rev. I. G. Gooden*, SC
Dr. Maxie S. Gordon, SC
Rev. Elijah Hankerson, WA
Rev. Neal J. Haynes, MO
Rev. E. A. Henry, LA
Rev. A. P. Hines*, OH
Rev. Odie Hoover, AL
Rev. Brannon Hopson*, PA
Rev. J. D. Jackson, NY
Rev. Hylton L. James*,NY

Mrs. Edith Jamison, PA
Rev. J. T. Jennings*, DC
Mrs. Bernice D. Johnson*, GA
Rev. Clifford Johnson, MD
Rev. Robert Johnson, AL
Rev. Theodore Johnson, FL
Rev. Robert Jones*, MS
Rev. Samuel Joubert, NY
Rev. A. M. Lampkin, KY
Rev. A. B. Lee*, TX
Rev. A. D. Lewis, MS
Rev. Wendell Liggins, CO
Rev. J. N. Lightfoot, IL
Rev. Ronnie Linden, TX
Mrs. Bernice Love*, OH
Rev. C. L. Marks, NJ
Rev. Obie Matthews, MI
Rev. George McFoulon, MO
Rev. L. M. McNeal, TN
Rev. James Melton, PA
Mrs. A. C. Mitchell, IL
Rev. T. C. Morris, OH
Mrs. Corine Moses, PA
Rev. Matthew Neil, NJ
Rev. James Newby, MI
Rev. R. L. Parrish, TX
Mrs. C. M. Pearson, GA
Rev. I. C. Peay, MO
Rev. Collins Pettaway, AL
Rev. J. D. Phillips, OK
Rev. J. L. Roberts*, KY

Mrs. Leola Stephens, PA

Dr. Warren H. Stewart, Sr., AZ

Rev. S. S. Swinson*, MD

Rev. W. H. Thomas, IN

Rev. Jessie White, IN

Rev. W. W. Williams, MI

Rev. Etheridge Williamson*, NJ

Rev. A. P. Young*, VA

*Deceased

Staff Members 1961-1987

Mrs. Florence Broaddus
Rev. William R. Harris
Rev. Willard M. Lamb
Rev. Charles S. Lee*
Rev. James F. Scott
Mrs. Leola H. Stephens*

*Deceased

Corresponding Secretaries 1880-1989

1880-1883	Rev. W. W. Colley
1883-1893	Professor Joseph E. Jones
1893-1893	Rev. J. J. Coles
1893-1895	Mrs. Lucy A. Coles
1895-1895	Rev. Lucius M. Luke
1896-1921	Rev. Lewis G. Jordan
1921-1934	Rev. James E. East
1934-1941	Dr. Joseph H. Jackson
1941-1961	Dr. C. C. Adams
1961-Present	Dr. William J. Harvey, III

The Office Staff of The Foreign Mission Board 1961-1989

Andrea Battle . . . . Bookkeeper
Malissa Batten . . . . Secretary
Barbara Buxton . . . . Secretary
Edward Corbin . . . . Mailroom and Custodian
Juanita Davis . . . . Secretary
Cornelius H. Garlick . . . . Bookkeeper (deceased)
Anna Goodnight . . . . Secretary
Mary Ann Craig . . . . Secretary
Hawa Gray . . . . Secretary
Willa Harris . . . . Secretary
Betty Harvey . . . . Office Manager
Janice Harvey . . . . Secretary
Irene Huirt Johnson . . . . Secretary
Louis Johnson . . . . Tax Consultant (deceased)
Gladys Massaquoi . . . . Secretary
Manuel Miller . . . . Tax Consultant
Pauline Montague . . . . Bookkeeper (deceased)
Javon McBurrows . . . . Mailroom
Flora Parker . . . . Secretary
Mary Nutt . . . . Secretary
Marcella O'Neal . . . . Secretary
Ida Swann . . . . Public Relations
Gwendolyn Traore . . . . Secretary
Sybil McIver Williams . . . . Secretary

The Executive Committee
Of The Foreign Mission Board
1961-1989

Rev. A.R. Adkins*

Rev. Alpheus Bright

Rev. Albert F. Campbell

Rev. Leonard G. Carr*

Rev. Harold O. Davis*

Rev. Allen Dixon*

*Deceased

351

The Executive Committee
Of The Foreign Mission Board 1961-1989

Rev. Perry E. Evans

Rev. M.L. Gayton

Rev. V.S. Griggs*

Rev. William R. Harris

Rev. William J. Harvey, III

Rev. D.W. Hoggard*

Rev. J.W. Jackson*

Rev. Hylton L. James*

Rev. Austin Jefferson

*Deceased

The Executive Committee
Of The Foreign Mission Board 1961-1989

Rev. Roland Jones

Rev. J. Luke Jones*

Rev. Samuel Jordan

Rev. Samuel Joubert

Rev. George Kenner

Rev. R.C. Lamb*

Rev. Willard M. Lamb
*Deceased

Rev. Charles S. Lee*

Rev. Robert J. Lovett

The Executive Committee
Of The Foreign Mission Board 1961-1989

Rev. Randall McCaskill

Rev. G.C. McCoy*

Rev. James F. Scott

Rev. C.M. Smith*

Rev. R.D. Smith*

Mrs. Leola H. Stephens*

Rev. Silas Thomas
*Deceased

Rev. R.L. Thomas*

354

Rev. Frank Tucker

The Executive Committee
Of The Foreign Mission Board 1961-1989

Rev. Charles Walker

Rev. J.B. Waller*

Rev. W.H. Waller*

Rev. John R. Wheeler

Rev. Ethridge Williamson*

*Deceased

355

BIBLIOGRAPHY

Main Sources

Afro-American Mission Herald, published by the Foreign Mission Board, National Baptist Convention, 1897-1901.

Mission Herald, published by the Foreign Mission Board, National Baptist Convention, U.S.A., Inc., 1902-1987.

Minutes of the National Baptist Convention, 1896-1987.

Other Sources

Adams, C. C., and Marshall A. Talley. *Negro Baptists and Foreign Missions.* Philadelphia: The Foreign Mission Board of the National Baptist Convention, U.S.A., Inc., 1944.

Aptheker, Herbert. *American Negro Slave Revolts.* New York: International Publishers, 1969.

Ashley, Willie Mae. *Far From Home.* The Foreign Mission Board of the National Baptist Convention, U.S.A., Inc., 1944.

Bell, Howard H. *A Survey of the Negro Convention Movement, 1830-1861.* New York: The Arno Press and the New York Times, 1969.

Biographical sketch of Miss Emma B. Delaney. Typescript 1978.

Brooks, W. H. "The Priority of the Silver Bluff Church." *Journal of Negro History,"* Vol. 2, (April 1922).

Cook, Richard B. *The Story of the Baptists in All Ages and Countries.* Baltimore: R. H. Woodward and Co., 1889.

Curtain, Philip D. *The African Slave Trade: A Census,* 1969; *The Atlantic Slave Trade,* 1969; *Economic Change in Precolonial Africa,* 1975, University of Wisconsin Press.

Davison, Basil, *Africa in History.* New York: Macmillan, 1968.

DuBois, W.E.B. *Black Reconstruction in America.* Cleveland: World Publishing Co., 1967. *The Philadelphia Negro.* New York: Schocken Books, 1967.

Duff, John B., and Mitchell, Peter M., eds. *The Nat Turner Rebellion: The Historical Event and the Modern Controversy,* (a pamphlet). New York, 1971.

Fitts, Leroy. *Lott Carey: First Missionary to Africa.* Valley Forge: Judson Press, 1978.

Franklin, John Hope. *From Slavery to Freedom.* New York: Knopf, 1967.

Frazier, E. Franklin. *The Negro in the United States.* New York: Macmillan Company, 1949.

Frobenius, Leo. *The Voice of Africa,* Vol. I and II. London: Hutchinson & Co., 1913.

Guild, June Purcell. *Black Laws of Virginia.* Richmond: Whittet and Shepperson, 1936.

Herskovitz, Melville J. *The Myth of the Negro Past.* Boston: Beacon Press, 1958.

Hodges, S. S., (a tract). Home Mission Board of the Southern Baptist Convention, 1974.

Jones, C. C. *The Religious Instruction of Negroes in the United States.* Savannah: T. Purse, 1842.

Jordan, L. G. *Up the Ladder in Foreign Missions.* Nashville: National Baptist Publishing Board, 1901.

Klein, Herbert S. *The Middle Passage: Comparative Studies in the African Slave Trade.* Princeton, 1978.

357

McKinney, George P., and Richard I. *History of the Black Baptists of Florida, 1850-1985.* Miami: Florida Memorial College Press, 1987.

Nashville, Baptist Sunday School Publishing Board, 1901.

Pachai B. *The Early History of Malawi.* Evanston: Northwestern University Press, 1972.

Pius, N. H. *An Outline of Baptist History.* Nashville: National Baptist Publishing Board, 1911.

Trowbridge, M. E. D. *History of Baptists in Michigan.* Published under the auspices of the Michigan Baptist Convention, 1909.

Vansina, Jon. *Oral Tradition.* Chicago: Aldine Publishing Co., 1965.

Walshe, Peter. *The Rise of African Nationalism in South Africa.* University of California Press, 1971.

Williams, Edwin L. "Negro Slavery in Florida." *Florida Historical Quarterly,* Vol. 28, No. 2, 1949.

Williams, Eric. "Journal of Negro History". Vol. 25. *"The Golden Age of the Slave System in Britain,"* 1940.

Woodson, Carter G. *History of the Negro Church.* Washington: Associated Publishers, 1921.

Publications of the Foreign Mission Board

Mission Herald (Published six issues per year)

Sacrifice and Dedication in a Century of Mission

Missionary Workers Manual (10th Printing)

Mission Study Guide

Mission Education for Tomorrow's Leaders

INDEX